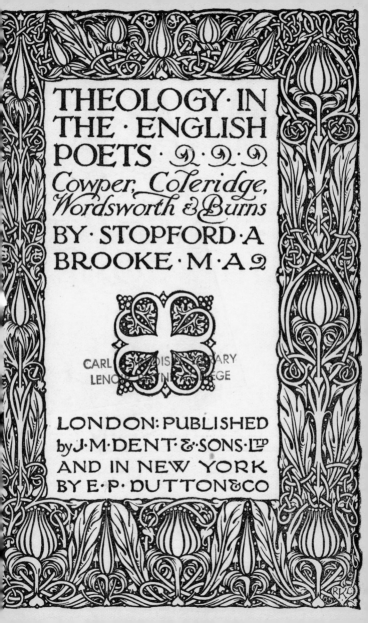

# THEOLOGY · IN THE · ENGLISH POETS · 𝒟 𝒟 𝒟

*Cowper, Coleridge, Wordsworth & Burns*

## BY · STOPFORD · A BROOKE · M · A 𝒟

LONDON: PUBLISHED
by J · M · DENT · & · SONS · Lᵗᴰ
AND IN NEW YORK
BY E · P · DUTTON & CO

# EDITOR'S NOTE

In giving his consent to the reprinting of the present volume, Mr. Stopford Brooke has preferred that the lectures should still retain their original form, and not be in any way altered or modified. This decision will without doubt gratify all those who first learnt to know the book in previous editions, and who would as certainly resent any change in it, seeing that a specific part of its charm consists in its use of the wisdom and knowledge of criticism, applied with the discursive art of the lecturer, and with a spontaneity which any after-thought might spoil. There is no need now to point out how much of that criticism and how many of its lucid terms and sympathetic distinctions have entered into the very currency of our time. The account it gives of the evolution in the English poets of a new idea of Nature is of a part with its author's abiding faith and philosophy expressed in divers ways and books, and both in prose and verse. A nobler appreciation of Wordsworth is not to be found anywhere, not even in Coleridge, than we have in the lectures here devoted to him. At the heart of it lies the thought which may be found concentrated in one of its author's own poems—

> " Impose your moods on Nature, and the moods
> Alone return to you. Her joyful ways
> Where great and solitary Beauty broods,
> And makes the world—are hidden from your gaze.
>
> But love her for herself, unfold your breast
> To hear her music, and receive her fire—
> You shall have joy, and beauty, and the rest
> Of self-forgetfulness and dead desire."

There is the whole law of the Nature-worshipper expressed in eight lines; and in true accordance with its principle, these spiritual portraits treat of the essential religion of the inspired men they describe—"theology in the rough," as it is expressively termed in the opening lecture.

E. R.

# BIBLIOGRAPHY

Freedom in the Church of England, 1871; Theology in the English Poets: Cowper, Coleridge, Wordsworth, Burns, 1874; Primer of English Literature, 1876, and several later editions; Milton: An account of his Life and Works, 1879; Riquet of the Tuft, a Love Drama, 1880; Spirit of the Christian Life, 1881; Notes on the Liber Studiorum, 1882, and later editions; Future Probation (Nisbet's Theological Library), 1886; Inaugural Address, Shelley Society, 1886; Poems, 1888; Dove Cottage, Wordsworth's Home from 1800-8, 1890; Reasons for Secession from the Church of England, 1891; Christian Hymns, 1891, 1893; History of Early English Literature—English Poetry from its Beginnings to the Accession of King Alfred, 1892; The Development of Theology as Illustrated in English Poetry from 1780-1830, 1893; The Need and Use of getting Irish Literature into the English Tongue: An Address, 1893; Jesus and Modern Thought, Discourses, etc., 1894; Tennyson, his Art in relation to Modern Life, 1894, 1900; The Ship of the Soul, and other Papers (Small Books on Great Subjects), 1898; The Gospel of Joy, 1898; English Literature from the Beginnings to the Norman Conquest, 1898; A Treasury of Irish Poetry in the English Tongue (with T. W. Rolleston), 1900; Religion in Literature and Religion in Life, 1900; King Alfred, as Educator of his People and Man of Letters, etc., 1901; English Literature . . . with Chapters of English Literature, 1832-92, and on American Literature, by G. R. Carpenter, 1901; The Poetry of Browning, 1902, 1905; On Ten Plays of Shakespeare, 1905; The Life Superlative, 1906; Christianity and Social Problems, 1906; Studies in Poetry, 1907; The Sea-charm of Venice, 1907; Four Poets: A Study of Clough, Arnold, Rossetti, and Morris, with Introduction on the Course of Poetry from 1822-52, 1908.

Further works were several volumes of Sermons, Introductions to Shelley's Epipsychidion (Shelley Society), 1887, to Poems Dedicated to National Independence, 1897; to With the Wild Geese, verses by E. Lawless, 1902; and to Treasury of English Literature, by K. Warren, 1906. The author was also Editor of Life and Letters of F. W. Robertson, 1865, and later editions; Lectures, Addresses, and other Literary Remains of F. W. Robertson, 1876; of Poems from Shelley, 1880; Golden Book of Coleridge, 1895, in *Everyman's Library*, 1906; and Selections from Wordsworth, 1907.

# CONTENTS

# INTRODUCTION

THE Lectures contained in this volume were delivered on Sunday afternoons in St. James's Chapel, during the season of 1872. Others, on Blake, Shelley, Keats, and Byron, delivered in 1873, will be published, I hope, before the close of this year. The thing was an experiment. I began it in May 1871, when I asked the Rev. J. M. Capes to deliver a course of lectures for me, which should not take the form of sermons, but, on the contrary, should avoid it. He chose as his subject the "Inner Life of the Romish Church," and afterwards the "Relation of Music to Religion." When he had finished his lectures on these subjects, which were as well attended as they eminently deserved to be, I began another course on "Theology in the English Poets," which I have continued to the present time. Since I began to carry out the experiment in 1871, the lectures on week-days in St. Paul's have been established, and in St. James's Church, Piccadilly, discourses have been preached on a few Sunday afternoons on such subjects as the Drama and the Press, by eminent clergymen. I believe if a similar effort could be made in many of the London churches in the Sunday afternoons, that much good might be done. It would give variety to clerical work on Sunday, and much knowledge that now remains only as latent force among the clergy might be made dynamic, if I may borrow a term from science. If rectors of large churches would ask clergymen who know any subject of the day well to lecture on its religious aspect in the afternoon, and give them half the offertory, if needful, for their trouble, they would please themselves, enlighten their congregations, and fill their churches. And they would assist the cause of religion among that large number of persons who do not go to church, and who think that

Christianity has nothing to do with Politics, Art, Literature, or Science.

When I made this experiment, I had long desired to bring the pulpit on Sunday to bear on subjects other than those commonly called religious, and to rub out the sharp lines drawn by that false distinction of sacred and profane. If what I believed were true, and God in Christ had sanctified all human life; if every sphere of Man's thought and action was in idea, and ought to be in fact, a channel through which God thought and God acted—then there was no subject which did not in the end run up into Theology, which might not in the end be made religious. I wished then to claim as belonging to the province of the Christian ministry, political, historical, scientific, and artistic work, in their connection with Theology; and to an extent greater than I had hoped for, the effort, so far as I have carried it, has succeeded. The blame of many accustomed to hear nothing but sermons from the pulpit has been wholly outweighed in my mind by the fact of the attendance of many persons who were before uninterested in religious subjects at all. And then, neither the blame nor the praise of the present is any proof of the goodness or badness of a thing.

The Poets themselves formed the only text book I have used, but in the two first lectures, when treating of the growth of the Poetry of Man and of Nature, I have had much help from an admirable Essay of Mr. F. Palgrave's, which appeared in the *Quarterly Review* of July 1862.

STOPFORD A. BROOKE.

MANCHESTER SQUARE,
     LONDON, *April*, 1874.

# THEOLOGY
# IN THE ENGLISH POETS

## LECTURE I

### FROM POPE TO COWPER

THE Lectures which I begin to-day, and which I hope
to be able to carry on Sunday after Sunday in the after-
noons, are on the Theology which may be found in the
English Poets. Spoken from this place, they will not
enter into poetical criticism, or attempt to estimate the
poet; for that would carry me too far from the main
subject, within the limits of which I shall endeavour
always to remain. The subject is delightful, and it is
not difficult to define its special interest.

The poets of England ever since Cowper have been
more and more theological, till we reach such men as
Tennyson or Browning, whose poetry is overcrowded with
theology. But the theology of the poets is different from
that of churches and sects, in this especially, that it is
not formulated into propositions, but is the natural growth
of their own hearts. They are, by their very nature,
strongly individual; they grow more by their own special
genius than by the influence of the life of the world
around them, and they are, therefore, sure to have a
theology—that is, a Doctrine of God in his relation to
Man, Nature, and their own soul—which will be inde-
pendent of conventional religious thought. They will
be, as poets, free from those claims of dogma which
influence ordinary men from their youth up, and from
the religious tendencies of surrounding opinion. Their
theology will therefore want the logical order which pre-

vails in confessions and articles: and as each will give expression to it in vivid accordance with his natural character, it will be a different thing in each.

The great interest, then, of looking into this subject lies in the freedom and individuality of the thoughts on a subject in which men are so seldom free or individual. We see theology, as it were, in the rough; as, at its beginnings, it must have grown up in the minds of earnest and imaginative men around certain revealed or intuitive truths, such as the Being of God, or the need of redemption.

At the same time I shall confine the inquiry to their poetry. I shall not seek in their letters or in their every-day talk for their theology. For in their ordinary intercourse with men they were subject to the same influences as other men, and if religious, held a distinct creed or conformed to a special sect; and if irreligious, expressed the strongest denial of theological opinions. It is plain that in ordinary life their intellect would work consciously on the subject, and their prejudices come into play. But in their poetry, their imagination worked unconsciously on the subject. Their theology was not produced as a matter of intellectual co-ordination of truths, but as a matter of truths which were true because they were felt; and the fact is, that in this realm of emotion where prejudice dies, the thoughts and feelings of their poetry on the subject of God and Man are often wholly different from those expressed in their everyday life. Cowper's theology in his poetry soars beyond the narrow sect to which he belonged into an infinitely wider universe. Shelley, when the fire of emotion or imagination was burning in him, is very different from the violent denier of God and of Christianity whom we meet in his daily intercourse with men. He does carry his atheism and hatred of religion into his verse, but these are the least unconscious portions of his poetry. When he is floating on his wings, he knows not whither, his atheism becomes pantheism, and his hatred of Christianity is lost in enthusiastic but unconscious statement of Christian conceptions.

Therefore I put aside the letters and conversations of

the poets as sources for these lectures, except so far as they illustrate the treatment of theological subjects in their poetry.

The theological element in English poetry becomes strong in Cowper; but before lecturing on its development in him, it will be necessary to trace its growth up to his time, along the lines on which English poetry mainly ran. This will be the work of the first two lectures, and in carrying it out I shall lay down the mode in which the main subject will be treated.

The devotional element in our English poetry which belonged to Donne, Herbert, Vaughan, and some of the Puritan poets, died away in the critical school which began with Dryden and ended with Pope. The *Religio Laici* of Dryden is partly a reproduction of the scholastic theology, partly an attack on the Deists, and it does not contain one single touch of personal feeling towards God. The *Essay on Man* is the preservation in exquisite steel-work of the speculations of Leibnitz and Bolingbroke. It is true the devoutness which belonged to Pope's nature modified the coldness of his philosophy, and there are lines in the *Essay on Man* which in their temperate but lofty speech concerning charity, are healthier than the whole of Cowper's hymns, while the *Universal Prayer* is of that noble tolerance and personal humility which, whether it be called deistical or not, belongs to the best religion all over the world.

It has not been sufficiently said that Pope was sincerely devout in heart, just as it has been ignorantly assumed by many that the century in which he lived was irreligious. His age may seem so in contrast with the two centuries that preceded it, in which religious subjects took so overdue a part, and theological feeling ran into bitter uncharitableness. But it was most useful for the whole future of English religion and theology, that with the newly-awakened interest in science, philosophic inquiry, and commerce, religion also should learn to extend its influence over other realms; and, in the reaction from intolerance which a wider intellectual life taught it, learn to do more justice to all opinions, and to

teach and practise a wider charity. We have not so
learned Christ as to call that irreligious. The work of the
Latitudinarian School was distinctly a work of charity,
and they and the scholars of the age of evidences are not
to be accused of want of religious feeling, because it seemed
to them that to submit their faith to the challenge of free
inquiry, and to establish a kindly tolerance for the sake of
more united work for God, was better and more needful
for the time than the zeal for doctrine which condemns
one's neighbour, or the passionate expression of devotional
feeling which tends to isolate oneself from one's neighbour.
It is still more absurd to call the century irreligious, when
we remember that in its very midst—not so much in
opposition to this sober religion as in reaction from its
lower tone in the less educated clergymen, and in the
indignant desire to make a religion for the common people,
who were certainly neglected—the revived religious life
of the personal soul took its rise with the preaching of
Wesley.

With this movement, however, the critical school of
poets had nothing to do. They had written much before
it arose; they belonged not to the country and the people,
but to the city and the cultivated classes, nor did they,
any more than the theologians, speak much of their
religious feeling, or indeed possess much. But it is a very
different thing to say that they had no devotion, and
the change, of which I shall speak, does not assume that
there was no personal religion, but that there was no
predominance of it, and that therefore it was not ex-
pressed. Now and then, to our surprise, it breaks out,
and it does so in the *Universal Prayer*. Beginning with
the ordinary and systematic view of God as universal
Ruler, but graced with the wider charity of a poet, it
passes in the end into personal devotion. No one can
read the following lines without hearing in them some-
thing of the same melody which afterwards was varied
through every key by Cowper.

> If I am right, Thy grace impart
> Still in the right to stay;

If I am wrong, oh teach my heart
  To find that better way.
Save me alike from foolish Pride,
  Or impious discontent
At aught Thy Wisdom has denied,
  Or aught Thy goodness lent.
Teach me to feel another's woe,
  To hide the fault I see;
That mercy I to others show,
  That mercy show to me.
Mean though I am, not wholly so,
  Since quickened by Thy Breath;
Oh lead me wheresoe'er I go,
  Through this day's life and death.

Nevertheless, this devoutness is of a wholly different quality from that which we find in Cowper. It is man bending before an infinite God whom he cannot understand; it is not man rejoicing in being redeemed and living with God as a child with its father. It is without deep emotion, without that sense of personal union or personal absence from God which comes of a vivid realisation of Christ as the master and redeemer of the soul. It is a religion which the absence of Christ made cold, and it so little tinges the poetry that one can scarcely say that the poetry was religious at all.

At the same time we must not imagine with those who lay down the rule that the poets always represent their age, that there was little or no personal feeling of devotion at this time in England, because its poetry was not in that way devout. That poetry was of the city, representing the disputes of the sharp wits who argued on theology as they argued on Whig or Tory politics: but outside the city, where intellectual life was not vivid and discussion scarcely known, there was a world of quaint and homely piety of which we get no inkling in the poets. Many a grave Puritan household, hidden in its orchards, handed down the tradition of the deep devotion of their forefathers; many a quiet parsonage held in it men who had succeeded to the spirit of Herbert, who ministered to English homes where dwelt, behind the village green and among their clipt yews and grassy plots, women who devoted their lives to God, and men who prayed with all the spirit of Wilson.

It was this religious life in the country which in the growth of the religious element in our poetry first took form in verse.   But how did it happen that English poetry got face to face with this devouter tone, with this simpler religion?   One reason may be that the deistical struggle, having reached its height for a time, began to need some repose before its new outbreak.   Both sides had, in fact, exhausted all they had then to say on the subject, and men, wearied with looking after God through the laby- rinth of the intellect, now turned to see if they had any chance of finding Him in their hearts, and in that region naturally passed from an intellectual to an emotional religion which at once sought relief in poetry.   Another reason was that a slow change had begun to work in our poetry even before the death of Pope, and the change may be described as a migration from the town to the country.   Poets began to look at Nature, not as it was around the villa at Twickenham, but as it was in its own solitudes.   Thomson took men to the moors and placed them in the woods; Gray went to the country church- yard, Collins to the hilltop in the evening, Goldsmith to the village and its rustic life.   At last we reach Cowper, in whose verse the town is as wholly disliked as the country was by Pope, and Crabbe, in whom the whole interest centres round the morals and manners and annals of the agricultural poor.

In this wonderful passage of change, poetry found religion in the country and took it up into itself.   That devotional element entered our poetry which in one form rose to its height in Cowper; but which, in different forms, each created by the individuality of the poets, has continued with a few exceptions to influence it to the present day.

Green, in his *Spleen*, 1737, a gay little poem too much neglected, marks a transitional period in this change.   He retires to the country to seek contentment and quietude, but the influence of the city lingers round him, and he takes his trip to town to amuse his life, to purchase books, and hear the news,—

> To see old friends, brush off the clown,
> And quicken taste at coming down.

He is tired of the theological contests between Non-conformists and the Church, between the opinions of the enthusiast and those of the cooler inquirer; and he resolves, in the peace of his retirement, to win his own way to a religion of his own. It is almost the first touch we get at this time of that individual work on theological subjects which we find so strongly developed in the poets of our century. He is largely influenced by Pope and the prevailing Deism, but he works out his own belief, and makes his own speculations; and though he is not Christian, he expresses his belief in a personal relation between himself and God. It is more personal than Pope would have made it, it is infinitely less than Cowper would have made it, and the absence of Christ makes it of an altogether different quality. But the transitional element in it makes it interesting enough to quote. After saying that his verse cannot dare to try and express God, nor paint His features, " veiled by light," he goes on—

> My soul the vain attempt forego:
> Thyself, the fitter subject, know.
> He wisely shuns the bold extreme,
> Who soon lays by the unequal theme,
> Nor runs, with wisdom's sirens caught,
> On quicksands swallowing shipwrecked thought:
> But, conscious of his distance, gives
> Mute praise, and humble negatives.
> In One, no object of our sight,
> Immutable and infinite,
> Who can't be cruel or unjust,
> Calm and resigned, I fix my trust:
> To him my past and present state
> I owe, and must my future fate.
> A stranger, into life I'm come,
> Dying may be our going home;
> Transported here by angry fate,
> The convicts of a prior state.

Hence I no anxious thoughts bestow
On matters I can never know;
Through life's foul way, like vagrant, passed,
He'll grant a settlement at last,
And with sweet ease the wearied crown,
By leave to lay his being down.

. . . . . .

He for His creatures must decree
More happiness than misery,
Or be supposed to create,
Curious to try, what 'tis to hate:
And do an act which rage infers,
'Cause lameness halts, or blindness errs.

There is more of the speculative audacity of the century in that than there is of piety; there is a fine moral certainty that God, however unknown, must be just and loving, but the point in it on which I dwell is its individuality. It is not a systematic philosophy of religion like Pope's, it is a personally wrought out religion, and it owed that to his country life. For in such a life, men, removed from the conventional thought of the literary circles in London, had room for individual development, if they had received some previous culture. This was especially true of religious feeling, and a little before the *Essay on Man* was written, a true devotional element entered into our poetry in the hymns of Watts, and entered it outside of the town. Watts lived an easy retired life, in a great country house, from 1712 to 1748. There is in his hymns that pleasant devotion to God which arises from piety and comfort, from placid enjoyment of the beauty of the world, from a distant contemplation of the sufferings of the poor beyond the gates of the park and from the gratitude to God which both these enjoyments are likely to create. Many of them strike a note of very fine praise, others of a didactic charity; and some are touched with a quaint and simple joy. Few hymns are better and brighter than that which begins—

I sing the Almighty Power of God,
That made the mountains rise;
That spread abroad the flowing seas,
And built the lofty skies.

But still, we have in them no special tendency in doctrine, and no passionate or personal feeling of devotion.

It is the quiet, sober, moral religion of England on which we touch; but even so, it is a wholly different atmosphere from that which Pope breathed, and I doubt if he could have drawn a single breath in it. It is impossible to fancy Pope " abroad in the meadows to see the young lambs," still less to fancy him linking religious feeling to such a sight. The kind of devotion, and the scenery that stirred it, were both out of his sphere. Half a century passes by and the change has deepened; the seed Watts sowed has sprung into a mighty tree; the quiet and sober religion of his hymns has become the impassioned and storm-tossed religion of the hymns of Cowper. The praise which filled the heart of Watts when he looked abroad on Nature has become the agonised prayer of Cowper as he looked into the depths of his own soul.

What was the cause of this change, what new influence from without had come upon English poetry? It was the great religious movement, led by the Wesleys, joined afterwards by the fiery force of Whitfield, which descended through Newton to the hymns and poetry of Cowper. It was a preaching which, beginning in the year 1739, seven years after the first books of the *Essay on Man* appeared, woke up, and into fierce extremes, the religious heart of England. The vast crowds which on moor or hillside, in the deserted quarries of Devon and Cornwall, listened to Wesley, excited by their own numbers, almost maddened by his passionate preaching and prayer, lifted into Heaven and shaken over Hell in turns as the sermon went on, crying aloud, writhing on the ground, tears streaming down their cheeks, could not find in the hymns of Watts or the metrical Psalms any expression of their wild experience; and the inexpressible emotion of their hearts demanded voice for itself in poetry and in music, the two languages of emotion. Both the Wesleys, but chiefly Charles, had already, in 1738, seen and prepared for the want, and a new class of devotional poetry arose. It was impassioned, personal, and doctrinal; it was impassioned, for its subject was the history of the heart in its long struggle with sin, in its wrestling with God, in the horror of its absence from Him, in the unspeakable joy of its presence with Him, in its degradation, its redemption, and its glory, above all in its personal relation to Christ, and the world of feelings which arose from that relation; nor was there a single chord of religious feeling left unsounded, nor any that was not strung to tension. It was also made especially personal. The first person was continually used, so that each who sung or read the hymn spoke of himself and felt Christ in contact with himself. And it was doctrinal, for whether it sprang from the party of Wesley or that of Whitfield, or from their subdivisions, it was built on clear lines of theological thought; and the opposition between the parties, who knew well the power of verse as a teacher and fixer of doctrine, caused the lines to be drawn with studious clearness.

Three things then belonged to it—passion, the personal element, and expression of doctrine. Neither of the first two were by their nature apart from poetry, and the fact is that so much are they of the essence of poetry, that most of these hymns are by force of them, poetical. Passion had been long asleep in English poetry, ever since the time of Elizabeth, and though I do not say that this religious movement made the passion of the coming poetry, yet it was one of its elements; and it is quite plain that its emotional element was not out of harmony with a school which in a few years, in Wordsworth, Shelley, Byron, and Keats, was destined to express almost every phase of emotion. Neither was its insistence on personal feeling out of tune with the work of a class of men like the poets who "in themselves possess their own desire." In fact both these elements are characteristic of the poetry which was now about to arise in England. They both took root in Cowper, but they were sown and watered by religion. He struck the first note of the passionate poetry, but the passion in him was in connection with religion. He struck the first note of that personal poetry which was afterwards carried so far in the *Prelude* of Wordsworth, the *Alastor* of Shelley, the *Childe Harold* of Byron, but he struck it in connection with religion. Other poets led their passions and their personal history into other realms, but Cowper kept them within the sphere of his relation to God. Other poets derived their passion from different sources—from Nature, from Beauty, from the ideas of political rights and freedom, but Cowper derived it from the daily wrestling of his soul with God. And both the passionate and the personal element came down to Cowper from without, from the great Methodist movement. For the friend of Cowper was Newton, and Newton was the child of Whitfield.

Both these elements run through the whole of Newton's well-known book, the *Cardiphonia*, and (expanded over the whole range of the relations of the soul to Christ constitute what was then called experimental religion. As such they appear in the *Olney Hymns*, written jointly by Newton and Cowper. Of Newton's share in them, with the exception of the beautiful hymn—" How sweet the name of Jesus sounds," I know nothing; but if they are anything like the *Cardiphonia*, they must be characterised by a robust and insensitive piety, and an ardent display, somewhat too public, both of his own sinfulness and of his love of Christ. Those which are written by Cowper are passionate indeed, but it is passion modified by the poet's tender and reserved individuality; are personal indeed, but it is egotism decently veiled, and where it is outspoken it is so sudden, so spontaneous— the hymn seeming to burst out of his heart with a cry— that it is redeemed from the charge of deliberate exposure of the sanctuary of the soul. Nothing can be finer, for example, than the swift rush, as if feeling could no longer be repressed, with which this hymn begins—

> Hark, my soul! it is the Lord;
> 'Tis thy Saviour, hear His word;
> Jesus speaks, and speaks to thee:
> " Say, poor sinner, lov'st thou me? "

The same elements in connection with religion run through the whole of his poetry, and they deepen into tragedy at the last. But on that I will not touch at present. I only ask you now (for I am but sketching the growth of the religious element in our poetry, not as yet distinctly touching on Cowper) to think of the new world into which we have entered. Compare the *Universal Prayer*—

> Father of all, in every age,
> In every clime adored,
> By saint, by savage, or by sage,
> Jehovah, Jove, or Lord.

with " O, for a closer walk with God," or with " There is a fountain fill'd with blood," and it is not that they are different, it is that owing to the overmastering presence of Christ, as the Saviour of the personal soul, there is scarcely any point of comparison. Compare the two following quotations, the first from the *Essay on Man*, the second from the *Task*—the lines of Pope, impersonal, apart, touched with scorn, thinking of God as Creator alone—with the lines of Cowper, so personal, so self-compassionate, so intense in their realisation of Christ, that though no devotion is expressed, they yet thrill with devotion. We step from the one to the other as from a frozen to a tropic isle of religion.

> Placed on this isthmus of a middle state,
> A Being darkly wise, and rudely great:
> With too much knowledge for the sceptic side,
> With too much weakness for the Stoic's pride,
> He hangs between; in doubt to act, or rest;
> In doubt to deem himself a God, or beast;
> In doubt his mind or body to prefer;
> Born but to die, and reas'ning but to err;
> Alike in ignorance, his reason such,
> Whether he thinks too little or too much:
> Chaos of Thought and Passion, all confused;
> Still by himself abused, or disabused;
> Created half to rise, and half to fall;
> Great lord of all things, yet a prey to all:
> Sole judge of truth, in endless error hurl'd;
> The glory, jest, and riddle of the world.

There is no passion and there is no personal feeling. Now listen to this in which both these elements are intense:—

> I was a stricken deer that left the herd
> Long since; with many an arrow deep infixed
> My panting side was charged, when I withdrew
> To seek a tranquil death in distant shades.
> There was I found by one who had Himself
> Been hurt by the archers.  In His side He bore,
> And in His hands and feet, the cruel scars.
> With gentle force soliciting the darts
> He drew them forth and healed, and bade me live.

The other element which came from the Methodist movement to Cowper was the doctrinal, and coming to him early in life it was afterwards beaten into his heart by Newton. It took with him the special form of Calvinism, and we shall see what a terrible power it had over him.  But at present, we ask what there could be in Calvinism, whether derived from Whitfield or from the Puritans, which could find a home in poetry?  Its mere doctrinal scheme, set out with logical severity, its debtor and creditor account, its hard outlines supplied little food to the imagination.  But there was one doctrine among others which did supply food, and that of a terrible kind, to the imagination.  It was the doctrine that God had created some men for destruction, that they were born into the world the victims of a stupendous fate. They might struggle, they might desire to love God, they might cry passionately for redemption, but there was no hope.  Over them always hung the thundercloud, and out of it, sooner or later, would issue the lightning of their eternal doom.  This mastery of some by a divine and unpitying fate, and their long struggle against it is distinctly poetic; and wherever it has taken form and in whatever manner, it has created poetry.  The same sort of idea, only in a less revolting form, was at the root of Greek Tragedy, which represented the freedom of Man struggling with destiny, but preserving or attaining to moral force through the struggle.  And the tragic element was deepened when, in spite of the moral victory, the victor yet received the blow of Fate.  Something of the same element we find in the dramas of Shakespeare, as, for example, *Romeo and Juliet*, where, from the very beginning of the play, we feel that all the passionate force of young love is doomed to be broken by the iron hand of irresistible circumstance.   But the religious form it took in Calvinism did not enter our poetry as a personal element till the time of Cowper and Burns.   It has deeply influenced it ever since.   And the manner in which it worked was twofold.   One was when the poet accepted it and gave tragic importance to his life by it, either by yielding to it in heartbroken humility, as Cowper; or by yielding to it in pride, since it marked him from mankind, as Byron did.   And in both these men the emotions it roused were creative of poetry.

The other mode in which it bore upon the poetic power in men was in the hot hatred, the fierce emotion of anger, which it stirred in hearts full of love to men, either in those who, like Burns, disbelieved in it as having anything to do with Christianity, or in those who, like Shelley, believed that it was Christianity, and poured out all the passion of their heart against it.   Introduced by Cowper as a personal question into our later poetry, no one can doubt the influence it has had; in fact, its introduction into it has led to the whole question of the relation of the soul to God becoming a distinct element in English poetry up to the present day.

Again I ask you, on this doctrinal side of the question, to look back to the critical school and to compare its theological poetry with that of Cowper.   In the fourth act of Dryden's *State of Innocence*, Gabriel and Raphael and Adam discuss all the arguments which can be urged on the subject of Fate and Freewill with the greatest precision and clearness.   But the matter is treated wholly from the outside, as an abstract question which interested the poet intellectually.   To Cowper the question was one which tortured his heart; it was a personal matter on which hung his whole life; and it made all the difference to him between reason or madness. In this matter also the whole poetic atmosphere is changed, we are again in a different world.

I have now traced, and in brief outline only, the growth of the devotional element in our poetry from Dryden to Cowper. With it statements about the theological element have necessarily been mingled, but in accordance with the plan of my lectures, and indeed in accordance with the actual facts, I have spoken of the theological element as it appeared when modified by the distinct personality of the poet. That is one of the lines on which these lectures are to run; the theology of each poet as created by his special individuality.

There were two other lines of thought on which I resolved to place these lectures; the theology imported by each poet into the poetry of Man, and the poetry of Nature. For a poetry which had to do with all the questions which belong to man as a whole, and to the growth, origin, and destiny of the individual man:—and a poetry which had to do especially and separately with Nature, with the whole of the outward world and all its parts, with the emotions it stirred and the thoughts that we gave to it, took clear form for the first time towards the close of the eighteenth century, and has never ceased to grow and to add branch to branch, up to the present time. It may be truly said to date from the publication of the *Task* of Cowper in 1785, of the *Village* of Crabbe in 1783, of the first poems of Burns in 1786. But nothing is born all in a moment in this world, and the poetry which dealt specially with Man, as well as that which dealt specially with Nature, though they first became clearly defined in Cowper, had been slowly growing into form before him. The different stages of the growth of each I must be permitted to sketch with as much conciseness as possible. I will do that for the poetry of Man to-day, in the rest of this lecture. In the following I shall do the same work for the poetry of Nature, and then take up the poets themselves, and show how in each the poetry of Man, the poetry of Nature, as well as their personal poetry, became tinged by theology. In each poet, then, we shall trace the theology in his human, natural, and personal poetry.

Our object now is to trace the growth of the poetry of

Man up to the time of Cowper, when theology distinctly entered into it.

In Dryden, Pope, Swift, Prior, Roscommon, and the rest, we find the searching and critical spirit of the eighteenth century looking on Man as an intellectual and social being, and their poetry reflects with clearness the leading thoughts about Man of that masculine and vigorous time. They seek from the intellectual point of view for an explanation of the problems which beset us; they go on to ask how such circumstances as riches and poverty, the follies of society and its oddities of taste, bear upon his life; they describe the variety of characters in men and women. Even the new scientific discoveries of the time, its credulity and scepticism are touched on in this poetry, and an attempt is made in the *Essay on Man* to reduce to a system the dim questionings with regard to the spiritual nature which science and scepticism had awakened.

Pope said that the proper study of mankind was Man. But he approached that study from the side of the intellect alone. It was by the criticism of the understanding, not by the emotion of the heart, that he worked on his subject. The result was cold speculation and brilliant satire, and in neither of those tempers is any one fit to write fairly or nobly about the whole of human nature; though he is fitted to write about that which Man does, or Man has, up to a certain point. The surface of the "study of mankind" is touched, it may be, in all its points, but the writer does not penetrate into its depths. It is just the difference between Ben Jonson and Shakespeare: the one not seriously caring for his characters, but only how he may develop them; the other loving, pitying, being personally indignant with his characters: so that in the one we study not men but the humours of men; in the other we study men, nay mankind. The one creates images of men, and dresses them and makes them play their part by strings upon his stage: the other creates living men, and bids them act, and sits by watching them with passion. There is the same kind of difference between Pope's study of Man and that study of him to which Wordsworth, Shelley, and Byron have accustomed us.

Again, we find no large study of mankind as a whole in Pope. It is classes of men whom we meet, not the conception of the race. The idea of the Universal Man, of one common mankind, rising above all distinctions of clan, caste, race, and nation, did not exist in Pope's time; we owe it to the Revolution. There were dreams of it, suggestions, hints, but of the clear, concise, world-subduing conception there is little or no trace; no real poetry of Man in the true sense of the word existed. Whereas since Wordsworth's time it breathes in every English poem. In both the particular and universal view the change is immense.

The same kind of study of Man lasted during Pope's life, and after his death in 1744. It lives in Johnson's *London*, 1738, and in his *Vanity of Human Wishes*, 1749, as observant and indignant satire; it lives in that poem of Akenside's which continued the speculations of Hutcheson and Shaftesbury. It was the spirit of Pope enduring after Pope was gone, and even less than Pope did Akenside bestow human emotion on his speculations. But even before the death of Pope a change had begun. Pope's study of Man did not carry him beyond the city; he has no interest in the rustic, in the uneducated, in the relation of Man to Nature apart from society, in the past history of Man, even of Englishmen. But, in 1726, Thomson makes us touch the farmhouse and the labourer, the traveller lost in the snow, the far-off lives of men of other nations where winter rules over half the year. We have got out of England, as we have in Dyer's *Ruins of Rome* in 1740. In Warton's poems, though his own personality overshadows everything, we again find ourselves among country people, the milkmaid singing and the woodman at his work. In the exquisitely pencilled *Elegy* of Gray we are brought face to face with the ploughman, the rude forefathers of the hamlet, the village of Hampden, the solitary who, far from cities and society—

Along the cool sequestered vale of life
Has kept the noiseless tenor of his way.

B

Again, the speculative study of Man, his origin, duties, and destiny, from the point of view of the inquiring intellect, has now passed away, and there is a tender, but somewhat sentimental treatment of Man, as the subject of the musing moralist, as the victim of the passions and changes and ills of life, and as listening to the soothing or warning voice with which Nature speaks to him in his enjoyment or his pain.

There is also a distinct delight shown in the history of Man in the Past, a thing almost impossible to the previous school in which the Present was so powerful that it filled all the view. Both the *Bard* and the *Progress of Poesy* illustrate this new element. The poetry of the two Wartons, about the same date, continually goes over the past glories of the English nation, and Thomas Warton's *History of English Poetry* was but the beginning of that vivid delight in what our forefathers did, to which Chatterton afterwards gave a fresher life, and which runs through all the minor poets of the time. This new interest in the men of the past—though it is necessary to observe that it did not travel beyond the men of our country, so as to become an interest in mankind—was afterwards stimulated by the influence of the elder Pitt, whose whole life and work exalted England in her own eyes.

The interest in Man was defective then in that it did not embrace mankind. It had also lost, in losing Pope's interest in social life, and in the intellectual and speculative side of human questions, and in its transference from the town to the country, elements which were afterwards to be revived. But though it lost something for the time, it gained new elements, and in a few years after the death of Pope we have seen that we are in a new poetic world upon the subject. Still the interest even in Man in the country, in a simpler, kinder, more rugged, human life, was not the living, close, direct thing it afterwards became. It is the distant, rather dainty, interest nursed by college life, which scholars, like Warton, or like Gray, looking out on the world from the window of Peterhouse, would be likely to take—a quiet contemplative interest such as

he describes in lines, which, written in 1742, embody the
spirit in which he looked on Man,—

> Where'er the oak's thick branches stretch
>   A broader, browner shade,
> Where'er the rude and moss-grown beech
>   O'ercanopies the glade,
> Beside some water's rushy brink
> With me the Muse shall sit and think
>   (At ease reclined in rustic state)
> How vain the ardour of the Crowd,
> How low, how little are the Proud,
>   How indigent the Great!
> Still is the toiling hand of Care:
>   The panting herds repose;
> Yet hark! how through the peopled air
>   The busy murmur glows!
> The insect youth are on the wing,
> Eager to taste the honied spring
>   And float amid the liquid noon;
> Some lightly o'er the current skim,
> Some show their gaily-gilded trim
>   Quick-glancing to the sun.
> To Contemplation's sober eye
>   Such is the race of Man:
> And they that creep, and they that fly
>   Shall end where they began.
> Alike the Busy and the Gay
> But flutter through Life's little day,
>   In Fortune's varying colours drest:
> Brushed by the hand of rough Mischance,
> Or chilled by Age, their airy dance
>   They leave, in dust to rest.

Changed as that is from the spirit of Pope, it is a still
greater change to turn from its spirit to the stern severity
of Crabbe's painting of the human life of the country in
the *Parish Register*.

If we pass on from Gray a little further to Goldsmith's
*Traveller* in 1764, and to his *Village* in 1770, we find that
the village life is more homely, more truly sketched, but
that its ruder realities are hidden. It is the same sort
of interest which Gainsborough took in his rustic children
and his cottages, the interest of the artist more than of

the man.  But in the *Traveller* a new element is added to
the poetry of Man—interest in other peoples than the
English people; the horizon of mankind has widened,
and this enlargement of our poetic interest in Man beyond
the bounds of England which began in Goldsmith, rapidly
developed in Cowper, and in the next age grew so intense
in Wordsworth that in order to save a great idea neces-
sary as he thought for the progress of the race, he wished
in lines which thrill with excitement, that the fleets and
armies of England might be beaten by the foreigner.  It
is perhaps needless to say here that one of the causes of
this wider sympathy with man was the growth of prosperity
and wealth under the peaceful administration of Walpole.
Men had money to travel, and peace and new openings
for commerce made it easier to see the world.

In the meantime, the interest in the poor deepened.
Adam Smith, 1776, and afterwards others, set on foot a
series of inquiries which forced men to look sharply into
the relations of capital to labour, of landowners to tenants,
of the poor to the rich; and these, combining with the
sentiment which had been growing up for country life and
its indwellers, entered as a power into men's hearts, and
naturally struck with emotional force upon the poets; and
a few minor poems of the day served as heralds to the
intimate treatment of the life of the poor by Crabbe and
Cowper.  Along with these, as a continuous subject, and
indeed always a poetic subject in England, were poems
that touched on or glorified Liberty.  The change of which
I speak enters into them in the way they altered from
vague declamations about English liberty to deliberate
attacks, for the sake of human liberty, on slavery and
oppression—either imposed by England on subject races,
or by nations beyond our doors on their own subjects.
We shall find this element in the change fully set forth by
Cowper.

We have now arrived at Cowper.  After 1770, a pause
in poetic production took place, and not till more than
twenty years afterwards did the new school spring to
light along with the dawn of freedom.  The interval
is filled with Cowper and Crabbe and Burns.  Burns,

who stands somewhat apart from the influences of the day, belongs to so different a poetic descent from that of the English poets that I shall leave him aside for separate consideration; but on Cowper and Crabbe the influences which led men to investigate the wrongs and pains of the poor, to extend their human sympathies, to be indignant with oppression, to see the Man in every one, however miserable like the cottager, however degraded like the slave — fell with immense force, and became creative of a new poetry of Man. The poetry of Man in relation to intellect and fine society, the poetry of satire and speculation, the sentimental poetry of Man, the light and graceful treatment of the subject of the pastoral man by Goldsmith—all have vanished; and in Crabbe, in his *Village*, 1783, and in the *Parish Register*, 1807, we are brought face to face with the sternest portraiture of the crimes, the miseries, the starvation of the labourer. We see the same passions moving him as moved the fine gentlemen of Pope, and the scholars who exchanged letters with Gray, and the wits who met Goldsmith at Johnson's club; only the passions are coarser and the sorrows uglier. We find in his tales, not only the darker but the nobler side of this humble life, its sacrifices, its struggles, its purity in temptation; and the effect of it all in deepening and widening human sympathy cannot be overestimated. We are shown the cottages of the poor, the life of the ploughman, the bargeman, and the fisher; they are sketched, filled in with an unrelenting hand. We are led into the dreadful prisons which disgraced that time, but which Howard had bettered already. We are brought over the wretched hospitals, and find ourselves in the poorhouse, where the neglected, the vain, and the extravagant were rudely housed till death. Nothing is omitted, and as we turn back fifty years, and read the *Essay on Man*, we rub our eyes and ask, In what new world are we?

This is the history of the change in the poetry of Man from 1730 to 1790; and its literary and historical interest is considerable. Enough has been said, for our purpose, about this human element in Crabbe. It needs but a slight touch, for it was not tinged in him by any special religious colour. His theology was not individual but conventional, though it was profoundly felt. But when the new poetry of Man was directly connected with the individual emotions of a religious mind like Cowper's on the subjects of theology — and doctrinal as he was, his heart ran continually beyond doctrine — it becomes of special interest to us, and of still more special interest when we find that his religion was one of the causes of its much wider development. When, therefore, I have sketched in my next lecture the growth of the poetry of Nature to the same point as I have brought to-day the poetry of Man, I shall begin the lectures on the separate poets with Cowper.

# LECTURE II

THE Poetry of Nature which I have already defined, and which is a distinct thing in our poetry after 1790, did not come into being without previous warning, and the object of this lecture is to sketch its growth from the time of Pope to the time of Wordsworth. In the previous lecture I sketched the growth of the poetry of Man, and of the doctrinal and theological elements in our poetry, and sketched them separately for the sake of greater clearness; but in this lecture I shall throw the theological and poetical subjects together, and while I trace the growth of the poetry of Nature, trace along with it, step by step, the theology that accompanied it, or the elements in it which resisted the presence of a theology.

The poetry which speaks directly of Nature for its own sake is not to be found in England till the time of Cowper, when it distinctly began, is not developed till Wordsworth, when it rapidly reached its full growth. Chaucer's landscape is for the most part conventional, though what there is of it is touched with the dewy brightness and affection of the poet. But he saw but little, and nothing solely for its own sake. The Elizabethan poets introduce bits of landscape, but these are chiefly as a background for the setting off of their own feelings or for the display of their characters; and though the natural poetry of Shakespeare has his quality of perfectness, it has little personal love of Nature. It is not till we get to Milton, to the *Allegro* and *Penseroso*, that we find any pure natural description, any deliberate choice of natural beauty as a thing to be studied for its own sake. When we arrive at the Critical School, Nature is wholly put out of the field. It is looked at, when it is at all touched, from the windows of the suburbs; the country is despised,

23

and life in it considered inconceivably dull. Pope con-
doles with those who are driven from the city, who
dream in the rural shade of triumphs in the town and
wake to find the vision fled, left in "lone woods or
empty walls." The descriptions in his pastorals have
no resemblance to Nature, and when he steps aside to
praise natural beauty, it is when it has been subjected to
the critical hand of Art. It was characteristic of the
time that Nature had to undergo the same sort of polish
as verse. Wild Nature was as bad as wild poetry, and
the art of the landscape gardener must be employed to
check her extravagance and lessen her horrors. We will
try Pope, however, when he describes a piece of pure land-
scape that he had seen,—Windsor Forest, in the pastorals:

> There, interspers'd in lawns and op'ning glades,
> Thin trees arise that shun each other's shades.
> Here in full light the russet plains extend:
> There wrapt in clouds the bluish hills ascend.
> Ev'n the wild heath displays her purple dyes,
> And midst the desert fruitful hills arise,
> That crowned with tufted trees and springing corn,
> Like verdant isles the sable waste adorn.

That is concoction, not composition; it is full of stock
phrases, and it is plain that Pope made it up in his study
with no recollected pleasure of the scene, with even a
recollected distress at the distance he was then from town,
which expresses itself in such absurd terms as the desert
and the sable waste. Indeed, one can scarcely imagine
the physical discomfort, the confusion of mind, the bore-
dom which Pope, and Belinda and her court, would have
suffered if they had been placed side by side with Words-
worth,—

> when from the naked top
> Of some bold headland, he beheld the sun
> Rise up and bathe the world in light!

or asked, with Byron—

> Where mortal foot hath ne'er or rarely been,
> To climb the trackless mountain all unseen,
> With the wild flock that never seek a fold.
> Alone o'er steeps and foaming falls to lean.

But if we can imagine it for a moment, we have some idea of the change in the temper of society with regard to Nature, some cause for wonder at the new world into which, since the days when Pope wrote, we have been brought by the poets.

The Nature, then, of which Pope thought was a wholly different thing from that which we conceive; and the theology which he connected with it was just as different. The Nature of which Wordsworth conceived, the living things of earth, and air, and water, that spoke to him like friends, and moved by their " own sweet will," was separate from Man, and God spoke through it to Man. In Pope's idea it was mingled up as a part of the system of the universe with Man, and both had the same kind of life from the immanent presence of God. In fact, the Nature of which Pope spoke was nothing more than that order of the universe which the recent scientific activity had begun to impress on cultivated men; and in that order, and not in the disorder of revealed religions with their supernatural interferences, God, the Great Unknown, so far as Man could presume to scan Him, was most clearly to be seen. Here is his view in well-known lines, which seem, but are not, pantheistic, for Pope, as in the line, " The workman from his work distinct was known," takes care always to separate the first cause from the things caused.

> All are but parts of one stupendous whole,
> Whose body Nature is and God the soul;
> That changed through all, and yet in all the same;
> Great in the earth, as in th' ethereal frame;
> Warms in the sun, refreshes in the breeze,
> Glows in the stars, and blossoms in the trees,
> Lives through all life, extends through all extent,
> Spreads undivided, operates unspent;
> Breathes in our soul, informs our mortal part;
> As full, as perfect, in a hair as heart;
> As full, as perfect in vile man that mourns
> As the rapt seraph, that adores and burns:
> To him no high, no low, no great, no small—
> He fills, he bounds, connects and equals all.

That is not the Nature we love or we know; we give a

wholly different meaning to the term; and we approach Nature in a different way. Pope, looking on it as a great system, considered it from his study with all the means of the observing and inquiring intellect, and never thought of its beauty as a source of pleasure. We look on it as the storehouse of some of our deepest pleasures; we consider it with a love which may be called passionate, and we study it by all the means with which emotion furnishes us. Owing to this—and especially to its being seen as separate from us—we are forced, when we come to think of God in connection with it, to have a theology of Nature wholly distinct from this of Pope's, and we shall see how in Wordsworth the whole of the natural theology of the eighteenth century disappears. It is this change we shall trace to-day.

It was during the life-time of Pope that the change began; it was when the English heart had been almost exiled from the woods and hills, that the door into the Paradise in which we have wandered with Coleridge, Wordsworth, Shelley, and Keats, and a hundred other lovers of the wild world of earth and air and sea, was opened for our entrance. In 1726, nearly twenty years before the death of Pope, James Thomson published his *Winter*, and in 1730 the whole of the *Seasons* was given to the world. The greater part of it must have been, so far as its feeling went, incomprehensible to Pope. That " recollected love," which Thomson said he embodied in his descriptions of Nature, could never have been felt by a single one of the followers of the Critical School.

It is true that the taint of the artificial spirit lingered in his poetry, but for all that it was a new world to the English people. The woods, the rivers, the moors, the cornfields, the mountain floods, the summer skies, the tempests, all the broad aspects of Nature were seen and detailed with some real care and affection. One sees that he is often painting directly from the scene; that sometimes his monotonous and turgid style is forgotten, that the beauty and peace of the outward world bring him so much emotion that his verse becomes spontaneous and tender. But for the most part he wants the simplicity of description which passionate love of Nature produces, and, above all, the sweetness and pathetic truth that comes of self-consciousness being lost in the life of Nature. We stand only on the threshold of the new world when we read Thomson. He has none of that solitary emotion for Nature herself which complains and creates and trembles with its own excitement in Shelley; none of that intense quiet of enjoyment which broods like sunlight over Wordsworth's soul when he steps into a nook in the woods, and treads lightly lest he should disturb its living spirit.

For there is as much difference between the feeling of Thomson about Nature and the conventional coldness of his descriptions, and the feeling of a poet like Shelley, as there was between Thomson and Pope. It is worth while to compare them at the same work. Here is Thomson treating an autumn noon,—

> For now the day
> O'er heaven and earth diffused, grows warm and high,
> Infinite splendour! wide investing all.
> How still the breeze! save what the filmy threads
> Of dew evaporate brushes from the plain.
> How clear the cloudless sky, how deeply tinged
> With a peculiar blue! The ethereal arch
> How swelled immense, amid whose azure throned
> The radiant sun how gay—how calm below
> The gilded earth!

Contrast the note of that—how heavy, elaborate, and yet how true in parts, how unemotional—with this, and think how wonderful the change,—

> Noon descends around me now:
> 'Tis the noon of Autumn's glow,
> When a soft and purple mist
> Like a vaporous amethyst,
> Or an air-dissolvéd star
> Mingling light and fragrance, far
> From the curved horizon's bound
> To the point of heaven's profound
> Fills the overflowing sky:
> And the plains that silent lie

Underneath; the leaves unsodden
Where the infant Frost has trodden
With his morning-wingéd feet
Whose bright print is gleaming yet;
And the red and golden vines
Piercing with their trellised lines
The rough, dark-skirted wilderness;
The dun and bladed grass no less
Pointing from this hoary tower
In the windless air; the flower
Glimmering at my feet; the line
Of the olive-sandalled Apennine
In the south dimly islanded;
And the Alps, whose snows are spread
High between the clouds and sun;
And of living things each one;
And my spirit, which so long
Darkened this swift stream of song,—
Interpenetrated lie
By the glory of the sky;
Be it love, light, harmony,
Odour, or the soul of all
Which from heaven like dew doth fall,
Or the mind which feeds this verse
Peopling the lone universe.

It is not a development of the former, it is a different thing altogether. In Thomson, the poet stands apart and apostrophises Nature; in Shelley, the poet is absorbed into Nature, and his voice is the voice of Nature herself. Whatever theology Shelley had about Nature would naturally, owing to this interpenetration of himself and her, become pantheistic; or would be content, since delight was so great, not to know and not to care whether it were love from without, or his own mind from within, that made or peopled the universe; but Thomson's theology of Nature, because he was not interpenetrated by her, would recognise a separate First Cause. His nearness to Pope would also lead him to share in the systematic view of the universe, but this would be deeply modified in him by his close study of natural beauty. He sees the world no longer only as a great order under a great Governor. He sees it as full of varied landscapes of infinite beauty, and each of these as the work of God—as revelations of His character. He hovers round, though he does not clearly touch, the thought of Nature as a living personal image of God. He has begun that separation of Nature from Man which led afterwards to the half pantheistic theology of Nature that Wordsworth worked out, to the wholly pantheistic theology of Shelley.

The impulse given by Thomson to the study of Nature went on increasing. That migration of the poets from the town to the country of which I spoke, began: men visited the more accessible parts of England and recorded their impressions; Dyer's *Grongar Hill* is the record of a landscape in South Wales; his *Fleece* and Somerville's *Chase* are both descriptive poems, but they are too slight to contain any theology of Nature. Foreign travel next enlarged the sphere of love of Nature. Every one knows the letters of Gray, and remembers the lucid simplicity and directness, mingled with the fastidious sentiment of a scholar, of his description of such scenes as the Chartreuse. That is a well-known description, but those in his journal of a *Tour in the North* have been neglected, and they are especially interesting since they go over much of the country in which Wordsworth dwelt, and of which he wrote. They are also the first conscious effort—and in this he is a worthy forerunner of Wordsworth—to describe natural scenery with the writer's eye upon the scene described, and to describe it in simple and direct phrase, in distinction to the fine writing that was then practised. And Gray did this intentionally in the light prose journal he kept, and threw by for a time the refined carefulness and the insistence on human emotion which he thought necessary in poetic description of Nature. In his prose, then, though not in his poetry, we have Nature loved for her own sake.[1]

---

[1] I insert here two of these descriptions; they may perhaps induce some to read Gray's letters, and few letters in the English language are so good:—" I walked out under the conduct of my landlord to Borrodale. The grass was covered with a hoar frost, which soon melted and exhaled in a thin bluish smoke. Crossed the meadows obliquely, catching a diversity of views among the hills over the lake and islands, and changing prospect at every ten paces; left

It was different, as I say, in his poetry. The exquisite choice and studious simplicity of the natural description in such poems as the *Elegy* and the *Ode to Eton College* is the result of art more than of the pure imagination; and Gray weighed every word, especially every adjective, till he reached what I suppose to be his ideal—that every line was to suggest a sentiment and a landscape. We feel, then, too much the art and too little the emotion

Cockshut and Castlehill (which we formerly mounted) behind me, and drew near the foot of Walla-crag, whose bare and rocky brow cut perpendicularly down above 400 feet, as I guess, awfully over-looks the way; our path here tends to the left, and the ground gently rising, and covered with a glade of scattering trees and bushes on the very margin of the water, opens both ways the most delicious view that my eyes ever beheld. Behind you are the magnificent heights of Walla-crag; opposite lie the thick hanging woods of Lord Egremont, and Newland valley, with green and smiling fields embosomed in the dark cliffs; to the left, the jaws of Borrodale, with that turbulent chaos of mountain behind mountain, rolled in confusion; beneath you, and stretching far away to the right, the shining purity of the lake, just ruffled by the breeze enough to show it is alive, reflecting woods, rocks, fields, and inverted tops of mountains, with the white buildings of Keswick, Crosthwaite Church, and Skiddaw for a back-ground at a distance."

" Mr. Gray to Dr. Wharton.

" Past by the little chapel of Wiborn, out of which the Sunday congregation were then issuing. Past a beck near Dunmailrouse, and entered Westmoreland a second time, now begin to see Helm-crag, distinguished from its rugged neighbours, not so much by its height, as by the strange, broken outline of its top, like some gigantic building demolished, and the stones that composed it flung across each other in wild confusion. Just beyond it opens one of the sweetest landscapes that art ever attempted to imitate. The bosom of the mountains spreading here into a broad basin, discovers in the midst Grassmere-Water; its margin is hollowed into small bays with bold eminences, some of them rocks, some of soft turf, that half conceal and vary the figure of the little lake they command. From the shore a low promontory pushes itself far into the water, and on it stands a white village with the parish church rising in the midst of it; hanging enclosures, corn-fields, and meadows green as an emerald, with their trees, hedges, and cattle, fill up the whole space from the edge of the water. Just opposite to you is a large farm-house at the bottom of a steep, smooth lawn, embosomed in old woods, which climb half-way up the mountain side, and discover above them a broken line of crags, that crown the scene. Not a single red tile, no flaring gentleman's house or garden walls, break in upon the repose of this little unsuspected paradise; but all is peace, rusticity, and happy poverty in its neatest and most becoming attire."

in his work; but then work like this introduced an ideal of style and expression into our poetical language about Nature — a demand for perfection — which it has never since lost, but which it never, except in Milton, possessed before. After lines like these, for example, in which every word tells,—

> There pipes the woodlark, and the songthrush there
> Scatters his loose notes in the waste of air,

it was quite impossible to go back wilfully to the careless profusion of epithets, and the hazarded meanings of the Elizabethan writers. Gray established a standard of careful accuracy in natural description which has never left our poetry, and in the great writers of our century nothing is more delightful than the mingling of imagination and emotion with a close and minute truthfulness in their work on Nature.

We find the same exquisite choice and care in Collins. His *Ode to Evening* is as finished and concise in description as it is finished and subtle in sentiment. The key of feeling in which it is written is not for one moment transposed. The landscape and the emotion of the poet interpenetrate one another, so that a pleasure made up of both blended into one impression is given to the reader. Evening, "maid composed," is to teach him some softened strain,—

> Whose numbers, stealing through thy darkening vale,
> May not unseemly with its stillness suit.

Every epithet is chosen and weighed by an art which, first submitting itself to the work of observation, and then letting emotion work on the materials, at last creates such a distant landscape as this,—

> Or if chill, blustering winds or driving rain
> Prevent my willing feet, be mine the hut
> > That from the mountain's side
> > Views wilds and swelling floods,
> And hamlets brown, and dim-discovered spires;
> And hears their simple bell; and marks o'er all
> > Thy dewy fingers draw
> > The gradual dusky veil.

But in neither Gray nor Collins is Nature, I do not say first, but on an equality with Man, in interest. Nothing is distinctly written for her and her alone. On the contrary, Man is always the centre, the landscape clusters round him; it is used as a means of pleasure for him, or as echoing his feelings, or as an illustration of moral lessons useful to him. It is never the first thing in the poetry. And Gray put it himself in this position. For, in writing to Beattie about the Minstrel, he says, " As to description, I have always thought that it made the most graceful ornament of poetry, but never ought to make the subject." I need scarcely say how different it is in the poetry of Wordsworth, in which man and his emotions are frequently left out altogether. And yet it is worth saying, for it was this predominance of man in the poetry of which we speak, that prevented in it any distinct theology of Nature. We know that both Gray and Collins were religious men, but there is not a trace in their poetry of any religious feeling connected with Nature.

The next step in this poetry of Nature is a curious one. Both Gray and Collins in the midst of natural scenery speak of Man, and not of themselves. But the Wartons and Logan, and others of that time, when they retire to the woods or hills, speak of themselves alone. They see only their own feelings in Nature, and use her as the mirror to reflect their melancholy and morbid moods. They are without any joy or gratitude for her brightness and life. Seeking only sympathy for their spleen, they prefer darksome shades, and gloomy valleys, and autumn in its decay, and, above all, night. Nor can they bear company; they fly from the face of man to the solitudes of Nature, and find there not misery, as Pope would have found, or rapture, as Wordsworth would have found, but a sentimental and faded pleasure.

" Oh tell," cries Warton,—

> How rapturous the joy, to melt
> To melody's assuasive voice; to bend
> The uncertain step along the midnight mead
> And pour your sorrows to the pitying moon;

By many a slow trill from the bird of woe
Oft interrupted; in embowering woods,
By darksome brook to muse, and there forget
The solemn dulness of the tedious world.

How remote from Pope! but in the following description of the delights of the woodman's life, note the genuine enthusiasm for beauty and the fresher feeling which, with all their sentiment, these poets did not want.

When morning's twilight-tinctured beam
Strikes their low thatch with slanting gleam,
They rove abroad in ether blue
To dip the scythe in fragrant dew;
The sheaf to bind, the beech to fell
That nodding shades a craggy dell.
Midst gloomy glades in warbles clear
Wild Nature's sweetest notes they hear;
Or green untrodden banks they view
The hyacinth's neglected hue;
Each native charm their steps explore
Of Solitude's sequestered store.

We find, then, the poets bringing to Nature that personal element which we traced in the devotional poetry: and though they only saw themselves in Nature, a kind of personal affection for her could not but begin to grow in poetry. They were led to look more directly at Nature, though it was only to find additional food for their own pensiveness; they were led to look at the smaller beauties of Nature, to count the primroses on a woodland bank, to mark the changing lights on a mountain pool. And for the first time the pleasure of being alone with Nature in her solitudes now became a distinct element in modern poetry. It was freed from its sentimentality by Wordsworth and others; it was freed also from its habit of self-consciousness. The new poets felt the frank joy of Nature, and could not burden it with faded sentiment; they felt ravished by her beauty and could not think of themselves. Logan or Warton walking by a brook would have compared it with the sorrows and solitude of their hearts: Wordsworth writes as if from another world than theirs—hearing no echo of himself or of human pain in

the rapture of life that he feels around him by the brook-
side,—

> The spirit of enjoyment and desire
> And hopes and wishes, from all living things
> Went circling, like a multitude of sounds—
> .    .    .    .    .    .
>                          up the brook
> I roamed, in the confusion of my heart,
> Alive to all things, and forgetting all.

Lost, you see, in the gaiety and life of Nature!

It is no wonder where self intruded so much into
natural contemplation as with these poets, that one finds
no religion linked to their love of Nature. It is no
wonder that, when self, as in Wordsworth, is lost, one
finds religion.

The next step, in the order of growth in the poetry of
Nature, is made by Goldsmith. We possess from him
clear descriptions of natural scenery, uninfluenced by
human feeling, untroubled by moralising thought. The
landscapes in the *Traveller* are pure pictures; but they
are wholly uncoloured with emotion. Not for a moment
does he feel such love to a place for its own sake as
Wordsworth expresses forty years after the *Traveller*
was published, about a glade of water and one green
field,—

> And if a man should plant his cottage near,
> Should sleep beneath the shelter of its trees,
> And blend its waters with his daily meal,
> He would so love it, that in his death hour
> Its image would survive among his thoughts.

Nor is another touch in the same poem—

> This spot was made by Nature for herself—

less remarkable as a proof of the great change of thought
and feeling about Nature between Goldsmith and Words-
worth. Goldsmith coldly delineates the landscape, and
never dreams that it may have a life of its own, or share
in the life of a spirit. Wordsworth thinks of the whole
of Nature as a living person, and of a landscape as dwelt

in, even chosen as a special retreat, by Nature, through a special love of it. It is all the distance between a dead and a living universe, and with the conception of a living universe our true poetic theology of Nature begins. But we could not get to that theology till we had conceived Nature as having a life distinct from ours, and Goldsmith made one step forward to that when he freed the landscape in his descriptions from the burden of human feeling which Gray, Collins, Beattie, and Warton had imposed on it.

The next step, and an immense one, was made by Burns, Crabbe, and Cowper.

Leaving Burns aside for separate treatment, I pass on to the two others in whose work we have for the first time Nature distinctly studied and loved for her own sake. The moralising of Gray on the landscape, the transference of emotion to it by Burns, the sentimental note of Warton, have passed away, and we see Nature as a whole, and separated from Man.

Crabbe's poetry of Nature is as direct in description as his poetry of Man. He was a botanist and mineralogist, and his close study of flowers and stones made him look accurately into all things. He paints the very blades of grass on the common, and the trail of the shell-fish on the sand. It is the introduction into our poetry of that minute observation, and delight in minute things in Nature, which is so remarkable in the subsequent poets, which led Coleridge to paint in words the dancing of the sand at the bottom of a tiny spring, and Wordsworth the daisy's shadow on the naked stone, and Shelley the almost invisible globes of vapour which the sun sucks from a forest pool. The difference is that Crabbe writes without the imagination which confers life on the things seen, while the later poets, believing that all Nature was alive, conceived a living spirit in the sand, the daisy, and the vapour. And this distinction, as we shall see, has its force in relation to the poetical theology of Nature.

Cowper's natural painting is not like Crabbe's, pre-Raphaelite. He paints broad landscapes, and his range is as extensive as the scenery he lived among, and often goes beyond it, neither does he disdain minuteness. He also loved Nature for her own sake, and if Crabbe rode, as we are told, sixty miles in twenty-four hours for the sake of catching one glimpse of the sea, Cowper speaks of the love of Nature as an inextinguishable thirst in Man, and bringing his religion to bear on it, declares that this love was infused by God into Man at the creation.

Therefore now, for the first time in English poetry, we have got three things—Nature studied as a whole, Nature loved for her own sake, and therefore Nature conceived as a distinct subject for poetical treatment.

And when this was done, a distinct theology of Nature, in our sense of the word, became for the first time possible. Pope had, as we have seen, his own natural theology. It was of God's relation to the great whole conceived of as a system which appealed to the intellect and its admiration: and this great whole involved Man and Nature together. When the poets who came after him little by little divided Nature from Man for separate consideration, and described and dwelt on separate portions of her beauty, they lost the idea of Nature as a whole, and that had to be recovered before a theology of Nature was possible. When it was recovered, as it was by Wordsworth, it was a different conception from that of Pope. Man had been taken out of it. It is plain that as long as Nature was only loved for the feelings it awoke in Man, or for the lessons it gave him, he could not help mingling it up with himself, and there could be no theology of it which was not also a theology of Man. But when it began to be loved for its own sake as separate from us, the poets began to ask, how is God related to it? what is it in Nature which we love? what is the One Spirit in this mighty whole which speaks to us in another voice than that which we hear in our heart?

Again, as long as isolated landscapes and things in Nature were alone described, no conception of the whole was formed. When it was, the poet naturally asked, what is the source of this Oneness of life, in whom is this whole contained? And out of the effort to reply to these

questions the distinct theology of Nature in our poetry
took its rise.

Moreover, the new attitude of man towards the whole
of Nature tended in the poets to make the new theo-
logy religious. It was not the attitude of those who
reasoned, like Pope, on what they saw, it was the attitude
of those who loved, and were content alone to love. And
the love ended in worship. Some, like Shelley, not
believing in revealed religion, not even being Deists,
created an all-pervading Spirit in the world, and would
not call it God, nor give it personality, but called it Love
and Life, and in the love and worship that they gave it
found their religion, and had the emotions of religion. It
was not the great Order of Pope which awoke their intel-
lectual admiration, it was the animating Love in Nature
which stirred their heart. Others, like Wordsworth,
believing in God, saw Him in the loveliness and tender-
ness and quiet that they loved, and worshipped not the
author of a great system whom they dared not scan, but
a Divine Spirit in the Universe—not necessarily personal
there, though personal in them—and said, " This Presence
which disturbs me with the joy of elevated thoughts, this
Wisdom and Beauty, is revealing itself to me. I can
listen, I can understand its voice. It is in Nature the
same voice, though in a different language, which belongs
to God my Father in my heart, and the work it is doing
on me is a work of education. Not by reason but by
feeling, not by admiration but by love, I make its lessons
mine. Therefore I shall give myself wholly, when I am
with Nature, to absolute self-forgetful love of her." In
that way the theology of Nature became religious, and
that reacted in turn on the poetical contemplation of
Nature, and made it more loving and more intense.

We shall find all this in Wordsworth, but we only find
its beginning in Crabbe and Cowper. They had lost, in
dividing Man from Nature, Pope's thought of a life
immanent in the whole order of things. And in their
theology of Nature they were driven to think of it as only
" dull matter " in Cowper's phrase, but matter subject to
laws which God had ordained. When they looked then at

natural things from the poet's point of feeling, they saw
their beauty as the result of this order, and referred the
whole to God who directed it from without.  Nature was
a machine which God had set in motion, but it moved
without any living consciousness of its own motion.

The last step, therefore, in the poetic theology of
Nature had not then been made.  The poets had not
reached the stage in which they were forced, not only by
their own feelings, but also by the needs of their art, to
conceive of the universe beyond themselves as living.
Crabbe made no advance towards it; his was the
mechanical theory alone of God and the universe.  But
Cowper, though he held the same theory for the most part,
made one step towards the higher view, and he made it
through his religion.  His intense personality forced him,
when under poetic emotion, to lay aside the mechanical
theory, and we find passages where he ceases to inter-
pose laws between Nature and God.  He transferred from
his theological creed the doctrine of the personal super-
intendence of God over every human life to the realm
of Nature, and bringing God directly into contact with
it, declared that He maintained its course by an unre-
mitting act.  How else could matter seem as if it were
alive,—

> unless impelled
> To ceaseless service by a ceaseless force,
> And under pressure of some conscious cause.
> The Lord of all, Himself through all diffused,
> Sustains and is the Life of all that lives.
> Nature is but the name of an effect
> Whose cause is God.

But his special personal theology which abode in worship
of Christ, carried him still further; and he makes Christ
Himself as the Eternal Word, as the acting Thought of
God—the ruler of the universe, and the author of its
forms.

> One spirit, His
> Who wore the plaited thorns with bleeding brows,
> Rules universal Nature.   Not a flower
> But shows some touch in freckle, streak, or stain,

Of His unrivalled pencil.  He inspires
Their balmy odours, and imparts their hues,
And bathes their eyes with nectar, and includes
In grains as countless as the seaside sands
The forms with which he sprinkles all the earth.

We have now made, you observe, a step further.  Nature,
it is true, is not yet alive, but a spirit of life is now in it,
separate from it, but working in it.  So near, in fact,
have we got to the conception of Nature as alive, that
Cowper is betrayed unconsciously into phrases which
mingle God up with the universe and make it living.
The lines above, which speak of the diffusion of God
through all, are repeated in idea in this other phrase:

There lives and works
A soul in all things, and that soul is God.

This is a contradiction of his position of a God wholly
distinct from the universe, but it marks the transition
to the last step in the poetic idea of Nature.  It is
the conception of Nature as a living Being to whom
affection was due, who could of herself awake feeling and
thought in Man, whom we could love as we love our
fellow-men, who lived her own life and had conscious
pleasure in it—it is this conception which unconsciously
in Cowper began to tremble into being.  It sprang into
full being in Wordsworth, and then, when Nature was
conceived of as alive, its theology took a new form, or
rather several forms — each modified by the personal
theology of philosophy of the poet — in the poetry of
England.

I shall trace that through Wordsworth and Shelley;
we shall see how it influenced or did not influence the
poetry of Byron and Keats; I shall mark the transitional
position of Coleridge with regard to it; but before I
enter upon it, I must discuss, not only how far Cowper
carried the poetry of Man and how he made it theo-
logical, but also how far his theology influenced his
personal poetry.  That will form the subject of my next
lecture.

# LECTURE III

## COWPER

I TRACED in my first lecture the growth of the poetry of Man from the Critical School to Cowper. In Cowper's hands, it took a much wider development. I only laid down the larger lines of its growth, omitting for the sake of clearness a number of branch lines, such as that of the new interest taken in the romantic past, which, touched by Macpherson in his *Ossian*, and by Chatterton in his forgeries, was afterwards fully worked out in narrative poetry by Sir Walter Scott: such as the ballad, which chose a short narrative of human passion and related it with simplicity and intensity—or the shorter lyric, which in its treatment of a passing phase of meditative or violent passion of the heart, and in its strict limitation of itself within that phase, so as to preserve what is called lyrical unity, is strictly analogous to the hymn in its treatment of a sudden and transient phase of the life of spiritual feeling.

These and others I pass by — though one sees how largely they entered the work of the poets on Man— because theology of any kind would not be likely to intrude into them.

I remain close then to the large lines I have spoken of; and my object in the first part of this lecture is, to show how largely Cowper extended the poetry of Man, and how it was influenced, and in him indeed drenched with theology.

I approach the subject by asking where we find him writing, and the question has its meaning. We find him retired in the heart of a very quiet country. The slow eddying Ouse flowed close to his dwelling through its willow-haunted meadows; it accompanied his walks, and its quiet movement seems to flow through his poetry.

Day after day, Yardley Wood and the park of the Throck-
mortons saw the silent poet-face moving amidst their
trees. But little society disturbed that sequestered life;
few were the men and fewer the women whom he met;
he companied with sheep and birds, with his hares and
his spaniel, till he grew to know them as his friends;
and one would say that in such a life the poetry of
Man was not likely to flourish, nor was a wide view of
mankind possible. Was it probable that this lawyer's
clerk, who had made a hopeless failure of his public life,
should say more of human nature and strike deeper into
the world of men than the brilliant Londoner, Pope, or
the courtly scholar, Gray—that the voice which spoke of
Man from the solitude of the country should say more
than the voice which spoke of him from the crowded
society of the city?

In one point certainly this rural retirement spoiled the
largeness of Cowper's view. He saw cities and their evils
through the exaggeration of distance, and in that glare of
morality in which sin is so magnified that the good which
balances it is lost. His doctrinal views had also power
over him, and he saw the curse which rested on man and
nothing else, when he looked upon the city. It was
different when he turned his eyes upon the village and the
country poor. Seeing clearly their evil he also saw their
good, and it is with some naïveté that he imputes more
than half the evil in the country to the influence of those
who drift thither from the town. But whether in the
country or the town, Cowper's religion led him to trace
all moral guilt and folly to the world's rejection of Christ.

But the point I wish to draw your attention to is, that
unlike the town poet of the past to whom the dwellers in
the country are nothing, we have now the country poet
deeply interested in the life of towns as well as in the life
around him. It is no longer classes of men which awake
sympathy, nor special societies; it is no longer the
passionate or the moral or the intellectual side of human
nature, each alone, on which the poet dwells—it is the
whole of mankind, it is the whole of human nature.

The truth is, the first swell of the great wave which put

Man in the foremost place and interest, Man independent
of rank and caste and convention and education, Man in
his simple elements, was now flowing over Europe.   Poets
are quick to feel, and it reached the quiet Cowper in his
hermitage, as it reached the lowland lad who,

> in his glory and his joy,
> Followed his plough along the mountain side,

and for the first time, as one smells the brine before one
sees the ocean, we scent in English poetry, too distinctly
to be explained away, the air of those ideas of which the
French Revolution was the most local and the most
violent outburst.   For the first time an attempt is made
in poetry to cover the whole range of Man, to think of
Man as one people; to spread poetical interest over all
who wear a human face.   And it was done, as is a
commonly the case when the impulse is received from an
idea which has not yet taken any political form, quite un-
consciously.   Cowper talked as naturally of *all men* as
Pope did of one of two classes of men:  he asks how he
and any man that lives could be strangers to each other;
he conceives of his poetic work as for the service of man-
kind; and such an aim was now for the first time possible.
A universal idea of Man had passed from political philo-
sophers to the people, and the undefined emotion it stirred
in the people was felt and thrown into form by the poets.

But the revolutionary idea of the unity of Man was in
Cowper's mind grounded on a theological one, on God as
the common Maker of Man.   He speaks of " the link of
brotherhood, by which one common Maker bound him to
the Kind."   And his work for men was to make them out
of sin and death into life with God, for they are

> Bone of my bone, and kindred souls to mine.

To this religious element of a universal brotherhood in
God is to be traced the large range of his human view.   He
looked abroad and saw all men related to God, it mattered
not of what nation, caste, or colour.   As such they had
equal rights and equal duties in a spiritual country of
which all were citizens; for, as he writes, the limiting power

of his doctrinal theology departs and the individual theo-
logy of the poet who sympathises with all men, takes the
upper hand. East, west, north, and south, his interest
flew. In his satires he touches, not with savage bitterness,
but with a gentleness which healed while it lashed, on
nearly every phase of human life in England; on the
universities and the schools, the hospitals and the prisons;
on cities and villages; on the statesman, the clergyman,
the lawyer, the soldier, the man of science, the critic,
the writer for the press, the pleasure-seeker, the hunter,
the musician, the epicure, the card-player, the plough-
man, the cottager, and fifty others. Their good side,
their follies, their vices, are sketched and ridiculed and
praised. The range of his interest was as wide as human
life, and as he sketched, he saw as the one ideal and the
one remedy for all—the Cross of Christ. Whatever we
may think of his religion or the manner of it, there is
no doubt but that it indefinitely extended his poetic
sympathy, and that in this extension of sympathy we
find ourselves in another world altogether than that of
Dryden, Pope, or Gray. It is no longer intellectual
interest in man, or sentimental interest; it is vivid,
personal, passionate.

It went beyond classes of men, it was an interest in his
nation; but he derived his patriotism and drew the
passion with which he informed it from the connection of
his country with God. It was God who was the King of
England, and was educating the nation; and this concep-
tion bound all citizens together into mutual love of one
another and the whole. On this ground he made his
impassioned appeal to his countrymen to throw off their
vices and follies and to be worthy of their high vocation;
would they not, he asked, be true to Him who had
wrought so gloriously among them? This is the note
of many a passage in the *Task*, of the whole of his poem
of *Expostulation;* and it is not a note of merely lyric
interest in England's glory on the seas, like Thomson's
*Rule Britannia,* nor one of intellectual passion, like the
references to her noble periods of history in the *Bard*—
it is a note that thrills with emotion for England as

God's nation, and having a work to do for Man. We already breathe the air of the patriotic poetry of Wordsworth.

Nor does this interest in Man remain fixed in England. God had children, bone of the poet's bone, and flesh of his flesh, in other lands. From the banks of the Ouse his heart carried him to Greenland, to Italy, to France, to the islands of the Pacific, to the shores of Africa and South America. In these distant lands were his brothers, and he transferred the inalienable rights of Man from the free and civilised European to the slave and the savage; there was no man, he thought, who ought not to feel himself allied to all the race.

The noblest right of Man was liberty, and this in Cowper's thought was the gift of God to Man. Whoever took it away did the most accursed of all sins. His poetical theology saw God as the deliverer and avenger of the oppressed. He traces the ruin of Spain to the wrath of God for its crimes against its subject races. He places the cause of the slave in the hands of God.

In Cowper the poetry of human wrong begins, that long, long cry against oppression and evil done by man to man, against the political, moral, or priestly tyrant, which rings louder and louder through Burns, Coleridge, Wordsworth, Shelley, and Byron, ever impassioned, ever longing, ever prophetic — never, in the darkest time, quite despairing.

The wide range given to it by Cowper, the personal passion in it, the glance it took forward to a brighter time, its theological element of God as the source of freedom and the avenger of tyranny, are all elements distinctly new to our poetry, above all new in their tremendous power of awakening and maintaining the humane emotions which must create a human poetry. Cowper carried this poetry of human wrong into the prisons with Howard, and into the cottages and lives of the poor; he denounced the landowners who abandoned them, and the merchants who " built factories with blood." Passing on, inspired by this cause, he poured out his indignation and his scorn on kings and nobles who used the common-weal for their own purposes. " Patience itself," he cries, " is meanness in a slave." That there should be men base enough to bear the caprice of despots, and to have freedom only on sufferance was the very folly of infamy in his mind. Then he turns to sketch the English King, and his sketch makes the preceding still more forcible.

> We love
> The King who loves the law, respects his bounds,
> And reigns content within them: him we serve
> Freely and with delight, who leaves us free:
> But recollecting still that he is man,
> We trust him not too far. King though he be,
> And King in England too, he may be weak
> And vain enough to be ambitious still,
> May exercise amiss his proper powers,
> Or covet more than freemen choose to grant:
> Beyond that mark is treason.

We may hear in all this nothing more than the old Whig doctrines in which the Cowpers had been brought up; but there is a newer element in it which insensibly entered into Cowper, the cry of the coming revolution. We feel that plainly when he suddenly places us in front of the Bastile,—

> Ye horrid towers, the abode of broken hearts,
> Ye dungeons and ye caverns of despair,
> That monarchs have supplied from age to age
> With music such as suits their sovereign ears,
> The sighs and groans of miserable men!
> There's not an English heart that would not leap
> To hear that ye were fallen at last.

And high an English heart did leap when, a few years afterwards, Wordsworth heard that they were fallen, and recorded his triumphant joy by the voice of the Solitary in the *Excursion*. Nor is it less new in English poetry to find a poet putting aside blind patriotism and rejoicing

> to know
> That even our enemies, so oft employed
> In forging chains for us, themselves were free.

For he who loves freedom does not limit his zeal for it to his own country—its cause, he says, is the cause of Man, for it is the cause of God.

But here Cowper could not stop. He saw a higher liberty than any on earth, a liberty without which political liberty was in vain, with which even the slave felt free, the liberty of heart derived from Heaven:

> Bought with His blood who gave it to mankind.

The whole passage is a noble one, and as emotional as that which precedes it: in both together, the passion of religion and the passion of political freedom are fused into one, and they run up into the highest expression then given in the English language of the poetry of human liberty. It had been touched before: Glover, in his *Leonidas ;* Akenside, in a now forgotten poem; Burke, in prose which we may almost call poetic, and which itself went forth to influence the poets; Darwin, in *The Botanic Garden,* had condemned slavery on the ground more or less of the unity of Man; but by none was so bold, so impassioned, so complete an expression given of the rights of Man as Man as by the retired lawyer's-clerk at Olney. He struck the first note of the revolutionary poetry. He struck it in connection with God, and with us it has never lost that connection.

But even further Cowper carried the poetry of Man. International union rose before him like a dream; he thought of a higher earth in which wars and hatreds should cease and each nation enjoy the other's good. It was a dream, partly caused by the results of the peaceful and commercial administration of Walpole, but it was like many other dreams, in the air. Cowper grounded it on the natural bond of brotherhood among men, a bond which their common fellowship in sorrow ought to draw closer. Social intercourse, " benevolence and peace and mutual aid," commerce and art were designed, he thought, " To associate all the branches of mankind."

Nor did Cowper forget the work of the natural philosopher, and though driven by his notion of the evil of pride of intellect he set philosophy too much in opposition to

religion, yet even here his predominant idea of the union
of all men into one mankind comes in to unite the work
of science with that of art and commerce. "He too,"
speaking of the natural philosopher,

> has a connecting power, and draws
> Man to the centre of the common cause.

All these passages of which I speak were written in 1782,
and no one can deny the novelty of their idea in English
poetry nor the great expansion which that idea gave to
its subjects. For, treated from Cowper's point of view,
from the emotional conception of Man as a great whole,
this thought of an international union, and of its means,
free trade and the rest, becomes a subject capable of
poetical treatment, and it remains such to the present day.
Wordsworth took it up, Shelley idealised it in his aerial
sketches of a world of Love; and Tennyson in well-known
lines embodies the same idea.

Then comes to close this long poetry of Man, Cowper's
vision of the restoration of all things, in which he brings
for the last time God into Man, not now as the Judge,
but as the Redeemer of the race, "to visit earth in
mercy, to descend, propitious in his chariot paved with
love." All climes are made beautiful in an eternal spring,
"all creatures worship man, and all mankind one Lord,
one Father." Error has no place, nor evil; "all is
harmony and love; for heavenward all things tend;"
and all nations bound together have their centre in Zion
where God reigns.

It was a vision which now for the first time came into
English poetry. Here and there it may be found before
this time, but it was limited by the want of a universal
idea of Man. But, now, when the great conception of
mankind as One, one in rights and powers and destiny—
of mankind as one universal brotherhood, was to be
proclaimed in the political and social realms, and to
bring with it the slow overthrow of all exclusive systems
of society — the idea of a universal regeneration of the
race became for the first time possible. In Cowper's mind
it was limited by his exclusive theology, but that does

not appear in this poetical passage where he rises on the wings of emotion above his theology. In the after poets it becomes a noble element in their song. For whenever it arose, the poet, filled with faith and hope in the fortunes of mankind, rushed into noble verse. We see how it told upon our poetry and told religiously, in the finest expression of it, in the *Prometheus Unbound* of Shelley: but the note here struck by Cowper in connection with the idea of a universal mankind has never ceased to echo in our poetry.

I turn, in conclusion, to that personal element in Cowper's poetry, in which theology plays so sad a part. But first let me say two things. In connection with the poetry of Man as seen from the personal point of view, no English poet has ever excelled Cowper when he writes of the daily human affections. In him, one might almost say, began in English poetry that direct, close, impassioned representation, in the least sensational manner, of such common relations as motherhood, filial piety, friendship, married love, the relation of man to animals —and in him they are made religious. There is nothing more pathetic yet more simple in English poetry than the lines on his mother's picture, or the sonnet and lines addressed to Mary Unwin. In the lines on the picture and in the sonnet, the natural piety of the relations of a son to a mother, and of a friend to a friend, are bound up with religion; and the infinite pitifulness of both are somewhat relieved by hope in God. In the later lines to Mrs. Unwin, when she was nearly as insane as he, there is no religion. It is " passionless despair, but the despair which loves to the last."

The second thing I remark leads me to the personal poetry of Cowper in its theological aspect. Much of it is a terrible record, stained with insanity, wretched with horror and despair. It has also, as we have seen, its gentler, sweeter, nobler aspect when he was happy with God; but even here it is often morbid with overwrought feeling. But we must not think that this personal misery or the morbid element in his religion extended over his whole moral life, so as to make him or his poetry unmanly. He was partly saved from that by his humour—humour which is the guard of intellectual and moral sanity. But however saved, Cowper's treatment of all moral subjects is distinguished from his treatment of his personal religion by an essential manliness of tone. Nowhere in our poetry is there heard a finer scorn of vanity, ambition, meanness; nowhere is truth more nobly exalted, or justice more sternly glorified. And his tenderness for the weak and poor and wronged is as sweet as his hatred of oppression is strong. We breathe throughout an invigorating air.

It is different when we return to his relation to God. That is almost darkness throughout. His Calvinism, which he seems to have had before meeting with Newton, combined with the tendency to madness in him, had produced a religious insanity, which, occurring at intervals through his life, finally fixed its talons on his heart, and never let him go, even in the hour of death. He believed himself irrevocably doomed by God. We can trace the first hints of it in some of his earlier poems. At last an outward event hurried the evil to a head, and he attempted suicide. During the madness which followed we have one poem written which is almost too terrible to read, lit with a lurid light and full of ghastly power.

> Hatred and vengeance—my eternal portion
> Scarce can endure delay of execution—
> Wait with impatient readiness to seize my
>         Soul in a moment.
>
> Damned below Judas; more abhorred than he was,
> Who for a few pence sold his holy Master!
> Twice-betrayed Jesus me, the last delinquent,
>         Deems the profanest.
>
> Man disavows, and Diety disowns me,
> Hell might afford my miseries a shelter;
> Therefore, Hell keeps her ever-hungry mouths all
>         Bolted against me.
>
> Hard lot! encompassed with a thousand dangers;
> Weary, faint, trembling with a thousand terrors,
> I'm called, if vanquished! to receive a sentence
>         Worse than Abiram's.

D

> Him the vindictive rod of angry Justice
> Sent quick and howling to the centre headlong;
> I, fed with judgment, in a fleshly tomb, am
>       Buried above ground.

Whether his madness would have passed away under the influence of a higher theology than that which Newton presented to him, it is fruitless to inquire. Again and again it settled down on his life in profound gloom; it always threatened him, and days when he was happiest and best were often followed, even interspersed, by hours of misery. It is a dreadful thing to have the spirit mad and the intellect sound, and this was not rarely the case of Cowper. Some of his finest work was done when his soul trembled with the horror of coming hell, and it is possible here and there, in the midst of poems which breathe peace and simple gladness, to catch far off the note of that terror and pity which gives to the sequestered life of this lawyer's clerk the interest and power of tragedy. No pity is more touching than that he bestows on suffering, none more childlike and pathetic than that which he lavishes upon himself. He speaks of his fate as if it belonged to another man, caressing, as the case is with many of the insane, his own misery with the gentlest words. I have quoted the passage before, but in a different connection:—

> I was a stricken deer that left the herd
> Long since; with many an arrow deep infixed
> My panting side was charged, when I withdrew
> To seek a tranquil death in distant shades.
> There was I found by one who had Himself
> Been hurt by the archers. In His side he bore,
> And in His hands and feet, the cruel scars.

What an infinite, long-continued self-compassion in the words! The note heard in them is low and sorrowful, and does not rise into passion; but the whole passage is exalted not into, but towards the region of great poetry, partly by its pictorial quality, but chiefly by the sudden yet natural introduction of Christ coming through the woods to heal him, and the association of his fate with that of the

Saviour. In the " Lines on receipt of my Mother's Picture,"
where he uses one of his favourite sea similes, the same
self-pity takes to itself the element of passion, but it
does not touch its deepest depth, for a shadow of hope
remains.

> But me scarce hoping to attain that rest,
> Always from port withheld, always distressed—
> Me howling blasts drive devious, tempest tost,
> Sails ripped, seams opening wide, and compass lost,
> And day by day some current's thwarting force
> Sets me more distant from a prosperous course.
> Yet oh! the thought that thou art safe—and he!
> That thought is joy, arrive what may to me.

One sees that most of the intensity in that arises from the
conviction that there is an irreversible fate against him.
Continually, by hard striving, bringing himself near to
port, continually driven away by a superior power; con-
tending, weak as he was, with destiny till the last, yet
knowing the contest to be in vain; he has unconsciously
put himself into the position in which Greek Tragedy placed
its heroes, but in the midst of an unheroic time and
scenery, and with a heart not fitted to wage the battle
of Œdipus; so that, though the mental position is tragic,
the poetry wants the sublimity and the force of tragedy.
Still there is profound passion in it, working especially in
the complete transference of himself into the soul of the
tormented ship, and in the splendid use of the word
" devious " in the third line. Unpretentious as the verses
are, the stamp of passion is far deeper set upon them than
in similar lines in Byron, where even his colossal power
could not overcome the unreality of his self-pity.

But it is in the last poem which Cowper wrote, in the
midst of the three last years of his madness and his life,
that this self-compassion does reach the centre of in-
tensity. In the *Castaway*, a poem in its sphere of the
very highest class, where simplicity of pitiful narration
is set in melodious verse by an art which had now
become Nature—Cowper mingles up his fate with that
of the drowned sailor of Anson's ship. He cannot help

beginning in the first person; realising the terrible night and the swift ruin as his own. He makes himself the sailor:—

> Obscurest night involved the sky,
>     The Atlantic billows roared,
> When such a destined wretch as I,
>     Washed headlong from on board,
> Of friends, of hope, of all bereft,
> His floating home for ever left.

He changes then to description in the third person, but we feel as we read of the long struggle of the swimmer, " supported by despair of life; " as he describes the pitiless blast which forbade his friends to rescue him, the useless succour of the cask and cord which served only to prolong his agony, the bitter thought that they were right to leave him—that we are looking into the heart of Cowper's life. With what exquisite simplicity of words, and yet with what a grasp of misery, is the next verse conceived—

> He long survives, who lives an hour
>     In Ocean, self-upheld;
> And so long he, with unspent power,
>     His destiny repelled;
> And ever as the minutes flew
> Entreated help, or cried Adieu.

We are now relieved by a change from the doom of the sailor to the grief of Anson for his fate, and then, in a sudden rushing of misery, in which the impassioned imagination rises almost into a wild cry, and the verse in the last two lines becomes abrupt, and the voice choked, he again dashes himself into the fate of the sailor, and both perish in the seas:—

> No voice divine the storm allayed,
>     No light propitious shone,
> When, snatched from all effectual aid,
>     We perished, each alone;
> But I beneath a rougher sea,
> And whelmed in deeper gulfs than he.

The poetic life of Cowper lies between this poem at the
end, and those terrible Sapphics at the beginning. He
entered it in despair, he left it in despair. For a time,
during which he wrote most of the *Olney Hymns,* he
enjoyed the sense of that " assurance " of salvation on
which his friend Newton dwelt so much, and the humble
ecstasy of some of the hymns is wonderfully touching.
But the lines which have found a place in every hymn
book—

> " God moves in a mysterious way,
> His wonders to perform," etc.

mark the close of this period, and prophesy the relapse
which followed. When the attack was over, he never
recovered his sense of acceptance with God. He even
learned to acquiesce, at times, in God's condemnation of
him to eternal misery. But the weight of this dreadful
belief did not always oppress him. It came and went like
dark clouds upon an April day of sunshine, and till the
last three years, his life had many intervals of happiness.
Many lovely landscapes lay between these three valleys of
the Shadow of Death, where he rested and was at peace;
sweet idleness and fruitful contemplation—tender friend-
ships and simple pleasures—hours where charming humour
and simple pathos ran through one another, and inter-
changed their essence like the colours on a sunset sea—
days of sweet fidelity to Nature in her quietest and most
restoring moods—times when the peace that passeth all
understanding made him as a child with God; but in the
end the darkness settled down, deep and impenetrable:
and the poet, who, of all English artists, has written, to
my mind, the noblest hymns for depth of religious feeling
and for loveliness of quiet style; whose life was blameless
as the water-lilies which he loved, and the way of life of
which on silent streams he made his own; whose heart
breathed the sweetest air of natural piety, and yet could
sympathise with the supersensuous world in which Guyon
lived — died in ghastly hopelessness, refusing comfort

to the last. On the physician asking how he felt, he answered, " I feel unutterable despair."—It is a strange commentary on the demand which the school of his friend Newton make, that on the death-bed there should be, or else one may scarcely dare to hope, a triumphant confession of faith.

# LECTURE IV

## COLERIDGE

COLERIDGE has not written much poetry, but he has written a great deal of theology. We know him as a theologian and his views, and the difficulty, of course, in such a lecture as this, which keeps strictly to the theology in his poetry, is to prevent oneself from slipping into discussion of his philosophic prose, and to think and speak of him only as a poet. I shall try to get what I have to say about his poetic view of Nature, Man, and God, into one lecture.

First, he, too, with the rest of the God-fearing English poets, saw in the proclamation of the revolutionary ideas the revelation of God; saw that the truth of universal brotherhood, and of the right of the meanest man to equal liberty, followed on and ought to be founded on the truth of God's universal Fatherhood. And when the first bright outburst of the Revolution took place, Coleridge was the poet who sang it with the stormiest glee and passion; something of the "storm and stress" (*Sturm und Drang*) period in Germany marks his verses, a violence of words and ideas, as if the more noise the more expression. Such lines as these show what I mean,—

> Thus to sad sympathies I soothed my breast,
> Calm as the rainbow in the weeping West:
> When slumbering Freedom roused by high Disdain
> With giant fury burst her triple chain!
> Fierce on her front the blasting Dog-star glowed;
> Her banners, like a midnight meteor, flowed;
> Amid the yelling of the storm-rent skies
> She came, and scattered battles from her eyes!

They are poor, but still they have a certain strength which will mellow—it is a shout of triumph, it is not the sensational shriek which exhausts itself. And they had a real enthusiasm at their root, that enthusiasm which delights to challenge established beliefs, as when Coleridge claimed heaven as the right of Chatterton the suicide; which is full of wild projects, as when, with Southey and some others, he planned their communistic expedition, and society on the banks of the Susquehanna, where he hoped to realise his new dreams of human peace and equality,—

> O'er the ocean swell
> Sublime of Hope I seek the cottage dell,
> Where Virtue calm with careless step may stray;
> And dancing to the moonlight roundelay,
> The wizard Passions weave a holy spell.
> O, Chatterton, that thou wert yet alive
> Sure thou would'st spread the canvas to the gale
> And love with us the tinkling team to drive,
> O'er peaceful Freedom's undivided dale.

And it was an enthusiasm which, taking fire from the fire of the world, made him think, in the hope and joy which filled his heart, that all things were possible to faith so strong, and aspiration so intense; but which failed in expressing itself, at least at first, with any of the poetic force that is the child of temperance.

Later on, in 1796, when the early excitement had lessened, and he had had time to learn his art, Coleridge put into two odes his past and present feelings about the Revolution. They form the transition between his first wild hopes and his later conservative despair.

The *Ode to the Departing Year* is the first of these, and it has its historical interest as well as its theological. It begins with the statement of his belief in God who regulates into one vast harmony all the events of time, however calamitous some of them may seem. It calls on God by the voice of the *Spirit of the Earth* to avenge the wrongs of the poor and the slave, to speak in thunder to England who has been the oppressor, and who now seeks to league herself against liberty. And its revolutionary character is strongly marked in this, that it dissolves the tie of patriotism in behalf of the interests of mankind. It makes the nations rise to curse England, abandoned of heaven, standing aloof at cowardly distance from the interest of mankind.

Nor is the same character less forcibly seen in the *Ode to France*, where he looks back in 1797 on what he had felt some years before.

> When France in wrath her giant limbs upreared,
>     And with that oath, which smote air, earth, and sea,
>     Stamped her strong foot and said she would be free,
> Bear witness for me, how I hoped and feared!
>     With what a joy my lofty gratulation
> Unawed I sang, amid a slavish band:
>     And when to whelm the disenchanted nation,
> Like fiends embattled by a wizard's wand,
>     The monarchs marched in evil day,
>     And Britain joined the dire array;
> Though dear her shores and circling ocean,
>     Though many friendships, many youthful loves
> Had swoll'n the patriot emotion,
>     And flung a magic light o'er all her hills and groves;
> Yet still my voice unaltered sang defeat
>     To all that braved the tyrant-quelling lance,
> And shame too long delayed and vain retreat!
>     For ne'er, O Liberty! with partial aim
>     I dimmed thy light or damped thy holy flame;
> But blessed the pæans of delivered France,
>     And hung my head and wept at Britain's name.

Like Wordsworth, he divided himself, for the sake of Man, from an attack on liberty, even when made by his own country, for it was an attack on God; and unpartaking of the evil thing, bewailed the vileness of his nation; nor did he remain in solitude, pampering his heart with feelings about human wrongs and liberty too delicate for use, but, made active by his fervour, went among men, doing what practical work he could. Nor, at first, did the blasphemy, and Terror, and blood of the Revolution in Paris daunt his hopes any more than they did Wordsworth's. These evils, he thought, could not be helped; they were the necessary storms that precede the fulfilment of a vast change for the better in human things, and behind them, though they hid its light, the sun was rising.

And soon, when France had quelled domestic treason, and
the terror ceased, and her armies went forth, " insupport-
ably advancing " to overthrow the enemies of freedom,
his heart recovered, his hopes seemed fulfilled.

> And soon, I said, shall Wisdom teach her love
> In the low huts of them that toil and groan!
> And conquering by her happiness alone,
> Shall France compel the nations to be free,
> Till love and joy look round, and call the earth their own.

It was not, then, the horrors of the Revolution that
shook his faith in it.   But it was this—it was the attack
of France, the champion of freedom, upon the freest spot
in Europe, upon the " stormy wilds " of Switzerland and
on her bloodless liberty.   It was when she " mixed with
kings in the low lust of sway," and insulted

> the shrine of liberty with spoils
> From freemen torn,

that Coleridge fell back in hopelessness of the world, in
hatred of the Revolution, upon the sense of Liberty in his
own heart, and taking refuge in the solitudes of nature,
declared, with a certain impatient petulance, that he could
only truly feel the spirit of freedom when he sent his being
out of himself through earth and sea and air, and possessed

> All things with intensest love.

And the reaction was deepened when England herself
was threatened with invasion, and when France that
threatened her was no longer the apostle of liberty but
the apostle of despotism.   It seemed a duty then to lay
aside wild hopes of universal love of Man, and to fall
back on the old idea of patriotism; and doing so, the last
large idea of the Revolution passed away from men like
Coleridge.

They might have been able to be true to their first
love, even when England was menaced, if France had
been without Napoleon.   But the Empire was more than
human nature could bear.   The hope had been so high,
and the disappointment so deep, that it produced anger

towards the ideas that had given birth to the hope, and
men felt towards them as one does to a treacherous friend
whose love has promised much and ended in deceit.
Mingled with this was anger at the attack on England, a
natural feeling, and now justified as against a tyrant who,
under the name of liberty, was enslaving Europe; and
both these, combined with a backward look to the horrors
of the Terror for which there seemed now no excuse, forced
these men back at last, step by step, into a blank con-
servatism for which they have been bitterly blamed as
traitors to the cause of liberty.   But they had something
to say for themselves.   After all, they said, England has
been bad and is bad enough.   But she is better than this;
in her we find the bulwark of freedom, the true defence
against the despot.   We will, then, support her institu-
tions through thick and thin, give up hysterical efforts
after liberty and put them down.   We have dreamt a
dream; but we have awaked and will keep ourselves awake
by keeping things as they are.   And now, we turn and
look at our own dear land, and all our patriotism returns;
of all our fears and abuse of her we are ashamed.   With
her, and round her altars and homes, we are content to
live and die.

"O, native Britain," cries Coleridge,

> O, my mother Isle,
> How should'st thou prove aught else but dear and holy
> To me, who, from thy lakes and mountain hills,
> Thy clouds, thy quiet dales, thy rocks and seas,
> Have drunk in all my intellectual life,
> All sweet sensations, all ennobling thoughts,
> All adoration of the God in Nature,
> All lovely and all honourable things,
> Whatever makes this mortal spirit feel
> The joy and greatness of its future being?
> There lives nor form nor feeling in my soul
> Unborrowed from my country.

This, taken with the rest, is the poetical cry of an
approaching conservatism, but of one which in men who
had once held a higher view than that of mere patriotism,
who had loved Man more than England, was likely as they

grew older to sink into a blind opposition to a ll change
a blind hatred of all new ideas as dangerous. Neither
in Wordsworth nor Coleridge did it quite become that.
Coleridge was saved by his philosophy, Wordsworth by
his poetry, and both by their Christianity, but still in
both the change was great and sad. Yet we should be
merciful when we speak of it. We should remember
the bitterness of the disappointment, the heart-crushing
sorrow that went with it, and not join in the outcry of
Shelley and others, who, born later, had never been raised
so high in hope and never experienced so fatal a reaction.

It was a rapid change, however, in the case of Coleridge,
much more rapid than Wordsworth's. For Coleridge had
been less firm, less quiet, less resolute, less clear-sighted,
less temperate than Wordsworth. His hopes and their
expression were like those of a wild boy; and their strength
was the strength of violence. And when the shock came,
he chilled quicklier, his force was quicklier drained. For
Coleridge wanted will, and with will, perseverance and
continuance. Nothing gave his will force but high-
pitched enthusiasm, and with its death within him, with
the perishing of his youthful dream, the enduring energy
of life visited him no more. And this is specially true
of him as poet. Almost all his best poetic work is co-
incident with the Revolution; afterwards everything
is incomplete. The weakness of will was doubled by
disease, and trebled by opium, and his poetic life, even his
philosophic work, was splendid failure. That which, in
self-reproachful pity, he says of one of his unfinished
poems was true of his whole life, and it has its deep pathos,
" To-morrow I will sing the rest of this song, but the
to-morrow has yet to come." Slowly, surely, premature
age crept upon him, the light faded, and the only fine
thing of his manhood's time is the *Ode to Dejection*, one
verse of which too well represents the ruin of his life.

> There was a time when, though my path was rough,
>     This joy within me dallied with distress,
> And all misfortunes were but as the stuff
>     Whence Fancy made me dreams of happiness:
> For Hope grew round me, like the twining vine,

And fruits, and foliage, not mine own, seemed mine.
But now afflictions bow me down to earth:
Nor care I that they rob me of my mirth.
  But, oh! each visitation,
Suspends what Nature gave me at my birth,
  My shaping spirit of Imagination.
For not to think of what I needs must feel,
  But to be still and patient all I can;
And haply by abstruse research to steal
  From my own nature all the natural man—
  This was my sole resource, my only plan:
Till that which suits a part infects the whole,
And now is almost grown the habit of my soul.

And the only beautiful thing of his later years is the
deep regret which is sung in *Youth and Age*.

Still more pitiful is the poem addressed to Wordsworth
on reading the *Prelude*. He reads this "orphic song,"
chanted to its own passionate music, and he is moved to
the depth of his heart; his youthful passion comes again:
but he has no strength, he falls back, bleeding and worn;
and his misery is deepened when he contrasts his now
broken work with the finished flower of Wordsworth's
mind.

Ah! as I listened with a heart forlorn,
The pulses of my being beat anew:
And even as life returns upon the drowned,
Life's joy rekindling roused a throng of pains—
Keen pangs of Love, awakening as a babe
Turbulent, with an outcry in the heart;
And fears self-willed, that shunned the eye of hope;
And hope that scarce would know itself from fear;
Sense of past youth, and manhood come in vain,
And genius given, and knowledge won in vain;
And all which I had culled in woodwalks wild,
And all which patient toil had reared, and all,
Commune with thee had opened out—but flowers
Strewed on my corse, and borne upon my bier,
In the same coffin, for the selfsame grave!

No dirge can be sadder than these lines; they are the
cry of one who once had a mighty idea, and who, in the
shock of its overthrow, was struck with paralysis. He

sees that Wordsworth after the same shock remained calm and sure, and saw beyond the lost idea a nobler vision that his very loss had led him to; but it was not for him—nothing remained for him but prayer. The poetry-creating thought of a universal mankind, and of God as its king and guide, the theological idea of the poetry of Man had died in him; and with its death his true life as poet ceased. It is a woeful thing to have known a high conception and to fall short of it. It is still more woeful when we have linked it to God and love it, for with its loss our idea of God is lowered from that it might have been. There is no lesson so solemn in the whole range of modern poetry as that given by Coleridge's poetry—genius without will—religion without strength—hope without perseverance—art without the power of finish. What he did well was unique, but it was very little; and the volume we have from him influences us with all the sadness that a garden does in which two or three beautiful flowers rise and flower perfectly, but in which the rest are choked with weeds or run to seed. And to those who can compare the things of Art with the things of the soul and heart, the analogy has its own profound moral lesson.

And now I turn to him as the poet of Nature. What was his poetic conception of the relation of Nature to God and Man? His theology in Nature went through two phases. The first, in his wild young period, is very fantastic. There were multitudes of spirits, he conceived, belonging to the service of God; some contemplating spirits who gazed for ever on the fount of Deity; some in whose hands lay the guidance and the fate of nations, but others who were the forming spirits of creation, by whose operation all nature grew, and made itself, and died, and was born again.

> Ye of plastic power, that interfused
> Roll through the grosser and material mass
> In organising surge—Holies of God!

He conceives, that is, that the one all-conscious Spirit

has within Himself, and sends forth from Himself, infinite
myriads of self-conscious minds; some to weave the fates
of Man and live in Man, others to live in and inform all
the organic and inorganic forms of Nature. All these
God informs

> With absolute ubiquity of thought
> (His one eternal self-affirming act).

So that the whole universe—through God's thought being
always affirmed in all these spirits who make all things
live—is always in God at every moment, and consists by
Him. Nature, therefore, in all its myriad forms is ever
alive in God; and each form, nevertheless, having a
distinct spirit connected with it, seems to have its own
peculiar life, and a self-centred end. Some, he says,
speaking of those monads,

> Some nurse the infant diamond in the mine,
> Some roll the genial juices through the oak,
> Some drive the mutinous clouds to clash in air.

The theory has some relation to Shelley's, only that
Shelley makes Nature self-existent, Coleridge an effluence
from God.

" Glory to Thee," he cries,

> Father of Earth and Heaven,
> All-conscious Presence of the Universe,
> Nature's vast ever-acting energy,
> In Will, in Deed, impulse of All in All.

This is Coleridge's first idea.

He changes afterwards to the idea that it is the Thought
of God in us which makes Nature to us. The existence of
the outward world is only phenomenal, not actual. We
have given us the forms of things in thought; and thinking
these — we see, hear, and feel them, and build up the
world of Nature from ourselves. Thus that which we
call Nature only lives in us, it is we who make it; it can
only be called alive because we are alive, and when we
receive from it impressions, we receive, not something
distinct from us, but our own thoughts. So that when
we think and feel—Nature is.

In a remarkable poem, the *Æolian Harp*, we have the
first touch of this theory. The music of the wind-lute
makes him think, as the wind touches it, of the whole
of Nature breaking into harmony under the Thought of
Man.

> O, the one life within us and abroad,
> Which meets all motion, and becomes its soul,
> A light in sound, a sound-like power in light,
> Rhythm in all thought, and joyance everywhere.

And carried further, he states the same idea more dis-
tinctly—

> And what if all of animated nature
> Be but organic harps diversely framed,
> That tremble into thought, as o'er them sweeps,
> Plastic and vast, one intellectual breeze,
> At once the Soul of each, and God of all.

In the last two lines the idea is made distinctly theo-
logical. We, each in our thinking, make the outward
world for ourselves; but our thinking in this sphere is in
its source the one Thought of God in which, infinitely
varied through a myriad secondary forms of thought, the
universe consists.

In this poem the thought is philosophically stated;
afterwards, in a poem of human feeling, the *Ode to Dejec-
tion*, the same theory is stated from the side of melancholy
sentiment. They are lines which every one has read:

> O Lady! we receive but what we give,
> And in our life alone does Nature live;
> Ours is her wedding garment, ours her shroud!
> And would we aught behold, of higher worth,
> Than that inanimate cold world allowed
> To the poor, loveless, ever-anxious crowd—
> > Ah! from the soul itself must issue forth,
> > A light, a glory, a fair luminous cloud
> > Enveloping the earth—
> And from the soul itself there must be sent
> A sweet and potent voice, of its own birth,
> Of all sweet sounds the life and element!

There may be matter, that is, but matter only lives

when we think it and feel it. But our thinking and feeling of it are God's thinking and feeling of it through us. When we think, then, those thoughts of God that projected from us make the universe, we are thinking so much of God. Whosoever, then, thinks of the universe thinks of it as divine life: whosoever knows this as the truth rejoices in it, and from him goes forth over the whole appearance which the world takes to him, " a light, a glory, a fair luminous cloud," that makes glorious all things,—a sweet and potent voice, the echo of God in his own soul that turns the universe into music. Hence, when we have given life to Nature from ourselves—its " life the eddying of our living soul "—and our life is itself one that feels its source in God, and has conscious communion with Him—then there is nothing in Nature which to our thoughts is not God's life, which to our senses does not seem to speak or sing of Him. And we, finding Him everywhere, transfer our own feeling of thanksgiving and delight in His beauty and power to the world itself, and say, with the Psalmist, " That the Heavens declare His glory and the firmament sheweth His handi-work," that all things praise and bless Him. And Coleridge has written one noble psalm of Nature in his hymn at sunrise in the Valley of Chamouni, in which ice plains, and meadow streams, and pine groves, and flowers, and snow, " utter forth God and fill the hills with praise; " in which, with an image almost too daring, he pictures the great mountain rising and ever rising, like a cloud of incense from the earth, and telling to all the stars and to the rising sun that

> Earth, with her thousand voices, praises God.

Secondly. The question arises, How, if Nature live only in our life, can she be said to have any influence over us? and yet it is plain that she does affect us. Coleridge, as a poet, replies in this way. The worldly man, who has lost his true self in devotion to the transient and the visible, does not of course recognise that Nature is the God within him speaking. It seems to him to be wholly different from himself or anything in himself. But being conceived of as different, he flies to it when wearied of self-seeking and of the busy human heart whose passions and follies have exhausted him; and he hears in it a voice strange to him, but beautiful, but which ought not to be so strange. For it is in truth the voice of God in his own soul that he hears; it is, in truth, his diviner self he hears, only he does not know that. But when heard, it recalls him to himself; it puts him in mind of higher things, and without his will he worships. At first it only seems to him that there is a spirit of unconscious life in trees and wild flowers, in which life he longs to share:

> To be something that he knows not of,
> In winds or waters or among the rocks,—

for in such sharing he will lose something of the importunate, craving, lower self in another life than his own. But as this longing passes into a real communion with Nature, and he forgets his lower being, new hopes, new pleasures come upon him, thoughts sublime, dreams in which his soul forsakes itself, tearful raptures, boyish mirth,

> Silent adorations making
> A blessed shadow of this earth;

and at last—though at first, as I said, he knows not what it is that has lifted him above himself—a light breaks upon him, he recognises that it is God within him who has spoken through Nature's images of beauty or peace or sublimity;[1] that the real lesson he has received did

---

[1] As illustrating all that is said here, I quote a passage from one of the few poems that rise above third-rate importance. It is from *Frost at Midnight* :

> For I was reared
> In the great city, pent mid cloisters dim,
> And saw nought lovely but the sky and stars.
> But thou, my babe, shalt wander like a breeze
> By lakes and sandy shores; beneath the crags
> Of ancient mountains, and beneath the clouds,
> Which image in their bulk both lakes and shores
> And mountain crags: So shalt thou see and hear
> The lovely shapes and sounds intelligible
> Of that eternal language, which thy God
> Utters, who from eternity doth teach
> Himself in all, and all things in himself.

not come to him from a dead Nature, but from his own awakening soul, using the apparent world as the means of teaching him that which his true self is. And when he has once learnt that lesson, then—this is the peculiarity of his relation towards apparent Nature—ever afterwards the impressions made on his senses by any beautiful object, or landscape, do not remain as sense-impressions. The image of the thing begins to be supplanted by the thoughts it awakens, and of which it is in reality the appearance; and ever growing less and less real, as it is replaced by the growing thoughts, becomes at last a vision in the mind, into which the whole soul for the time dilates, and in which if the soul be religious, it is swept upwards towards God, in whom thought and image had their source. For example, he is thinking of Mont Blanc, and says

> O dread and silent Mount! I gazed upon thee
> Till thou, still present to my bodily sense,
> Didst vanish from my thought: entranced in prayer
> I worshipped the Invisible alone.
> Yet, like some sweet beguiling melody,
> So sweet, we know not we are listening to it,
> Thou, the meanwhile, wast blending with my thought,
> Yea, with my life and life's own secret joy:
> Till the dilating soul, enrapt, transfused
> Into the mighty vision passing—there
> As in her natural form, swelled vast to Heaven.

Or at other times, when the image seen is more homely, instead of a lofty mountain, a pastoral valley, or a pleasant glade where the thoughts and associations stirred are human; the visible image is gradually replaced by thoughts of real human love and joy and sorrow, by the vision of friendships gone and living, by hopes for man, by faith in his lofty destiny, by love of the whole race.

In both cases, we lose the sensuous impressions through the thoughts they awaken, and these thoughts are themselves the causes of the sensuous impressions, though that is at first unknown to us.

Our best enjoyment of Nature, then (if we take both

these cases as those which include the greater number of smaller impressions and thoughts within them), is bound up with two things, with the ineffable, invisible life of God, and with the image of a perfect human society.   So that we shall, first, gazing round

> On the wide landscape, gaze till all doth seem
> Less gross than bodily;  and of such hues
> As veil the Almighty Spirit, when yet he makes
> Spirits perceive His presence.

So that, secondly, life with Nature will seem like conversation with noble men and women, and we receive from her human impulse and blessing, tenderer and kinder feelings,

> A livelier impulse and a dance of thought,

" grateful," as Coleridge says:

> That by Nature's quietness,
> And solitary musings, all my heart
> Is softened, and made worthy to indulge
> Love, and the thoughts that yearn for human kind.

But the whole of this view, which makes Nature the reflex of Man, has two special evils.   Its first evil is that it fixes the mind when among natural beauty on self, till even in its highest expression, when it tells of joy and life, the poet closes by saying, that all the rapture we have in Nature is but this:

> We in ourselves rejoice.

Nothing can be further than that from Wordsworth's healthier view, which is the direct opposite.

Its second evil is, that always troubled with self-thought in the midst of Nature, philosophising about himself and her, moving off to visit other things than her, the poet can never see Nature exactly as she is, and consequently never describes accurately, or vividly, or closely.   Wordsworth, on the contrary, gave himself up to what Nature was saying to him, and rarely thought of what he had to say about himself in connection with her till he had received all the impressions she chose to

give him.   He could look at a tree, a cloud, a flower, and
see each as they were, unmixed with human feeling.
Therefore we have from him close, direct description.

There are few passages in Coleridge of direct descrip-
tion; one, however, of special excellence, shows how he
could have described if he could have got rid of the worry
of self-thought, if he could have said, " I receive from
Nature what I do not give; she has her own life, and that
is *not* mine! "   It is this description of the wayside spring
that reads as if the mantle of Wordsworth had fallen on
him as he wrote it:

> This sycamore, oft musical with bees,—
> Such tents the Patriarchs loved!   O long unharmed
> May all its aged boughs o'ercanopy
> The small round basin, which this jutting stone
> Keeps pure from fallen leaves.   Long may the Spring
> Quietly, as a sleeping infant's breath,
> Send up cold waters to the traveller
> With soft and even pulse!   Nor ever cease
> Yon tiny cone of sand its soundless dance,
> Which at the bottom, like a Fairy's page
> As merry, and no taller, dances still
> Nor wrinkles the smooth surface of the fount.

Now and then even he seems to feel that the true poetic
position towards Nature was that which Wordsworth
took up—that of one spirit, looking at and listening to
another different from himself—and he expresses this in
a few lines in his poem of the *Nightingale,* when he
speaks of the poet, who, echoing the thought of the sorrow-
stricken man, calls the nightingale a melancholy bird.
He is one

> Who hath been building up the rhyme
> When he had better far have stretched his limbs
> Beside a brook in mossy forest dell;
> By sun or moonlight to the influxes
> Of shapes and sounds and shifting elements
> Surrendering his whole spirit, of his song
> And of his fame forgetful!  so his fame
> Should share in Nature's immortality,
> A venerable thing;  and so his song
> Should make all Nature lovelier, and itself
> Be loved like Nature.

It is curious that the poem in which Coleridge is truest
to Nature is the *Ancient Mariner*, written directly under
Wordsworth's influence. It, too, shows us how much
might have been done had he worked on a right path,
had he not been led away by a philosophy which mingled
up Man and Nature, not to look at Nature but at himself.
Let me recall to you, in conclusion, the natural descrip-
tion of that poem, and mark how it is at once accurate,
imaginative, and of wide range.

Its range extends from the quiet scenery of a country
wood to the fierce scenery of the tropics, and to that of the
polar zone. Few poems embrace so much, and the work
is all of the best class. There are just incidentally touched,
but touched with perfect pictorial skill and truth, at least
a dozen aspects of the sea: the ship scudding before the
stormy wind towards the south, with sloping masts and
dipping prow; the iceberg-covered sea; the great snow
fog over the sea, dark by day, glimmering white by night
in the moonshine; the belt of calms, with its dreadful
rolling swell and water " that like a witch's oils, burnt
green, and blue, and white; " the sea in the tornado; the
gentle weather of the temperate seas and the quiet
English harbour. Looking at the shortness of the poem,
the range is very great; while its accuracy of description
—not the dull accuracy of mere portraiture, but poetical
accuracy, the thing itself described but lit up with a glory
of feeling or of association with other things—is very
remarkable.

I read this description of the ship in moonlight at sea,
in a tropic calm. The beauty of the illustration of the
frost is equalled by its truth, the motion of the moon is
almost heard in the verse, and yet the whole is a finished
picture:

> The moving moon went up the sky,
> And nowhere did abide:
> Softly she was going up,
> And a star or two beside—
> Her beams bemocked the sultry main,
> Like April hoar-frost spread;
> But where the ship's huge shadow lay,
> The charmèd water burnt alway
> A still and awful red.

But Coleridge is uncontent to leave the description of the sky without throwing round it the light of the higher imagination, and it is characteristic of the quaint phantasy which belonged to his nature that he puts the thoughts which lift the whole scene into the realm of the imagination into the prose gloss at the side—and it is perhaps the loveliest little thought in all his writings:

" In his loneliness and fixedness he yearneth toward the journeying moon, and the stars that still sojourn yet still move onward; and everywhere the blue sky belongs to them, and is their appointed rest, and their native country and their own natural homes, which they enter unannounced, as lords that are certainly expected, and yet there is a silent joy at their arrival."

Nor in contrast with this tropic scene and the fierce character of its landscape is the quiet harbour in the temperate zone less truly felt or less clearly expressed. Though some of the lines are weak, the whole impression is vivid:

> The harbour-bay was clear as glass
> So smoothly it was strewn!
> And on the bay the moonlight lay
> And the shadow of the moon.
> The rock shone bright, the kirk no less
> That stands above the rock:
> The moonlight steeped in silentness
> The steady weather-cock.

Then there are two other descriptions, one of the ship in a swift tropical squall in which the smallest details are true to fact, the other of the ship sailing quietly, which I throw together:

> And the coming wind did roar more loud,
> And the sails did sigh like sedge,
> And the rain poured down from one black cloud,
> The moon was at its edge.
> The thick black cloud was cleft, and still
> The moon was at its side,
> Like waters shot from some high crag
> The lightning fell with never a jag,
> A river steep and wide.

And the other:

> It ceased; yet still the sails made on
>     A pleasant noise till noon,
> A noise like of a hidden brook
>     In the leafy month of June,
> That to the sleeping woods all night
>     Singeth a quiet tune.

In both these descriptions, one of the terror, the other of the softness, of Nature, a certain charm, of the source of which we are not at once conscious, is given by the introduction into the lonely sea of images borrowed from the land, but which exactly fit the sounds to be described at sea; such as the noise of the brook and the sighing of the sedge. We are brought into closer sympathy with the mariner by this subtle suggestion of his longing for the land and its peace. And we ourselves enjoy the travel of thought, swept to and fro without any shock—on account of the fitness of illustration and thing—from sea to land, from land to sea.

Much more might be said on this, but it tells its own tale. The poem illustrates still further—and this gives it its special interest to us—the personal, simple religion of Coleridge. We see in it how childlike the philosophic man could be in his faith, how little was enough for him. Its religion is all contained in the phrase—

> He prayeth well who loveth well
> Both man and bird and beast.

On this the changes are rung throughout; the motiveless slaughter of the bird is a crime; the other mariners who justify the killing of the bird because of the good it seems to bring them are even worse sinners than the Ancient Mariner. He did the ill deed on a hasty impulse; they deliberately agree to it for selfish reasons. They sin a second time against love by throwing the whole guilt on him, and again for selfish reasons. They are fatally punished, he lives to feel and expiate his wrong. And the turning point of his repentance is in the re-awakening of love, and is clearly marked. Left all alone on the sea, " he despiseth the creatures of the calm, and envieth that so many should live and so many lie dead," and in that temper of contempt and envy Coleridge suggests that no prayer can live.   But when seven days had passed, he looked again on God's creatures of the great calm, and seeing their beauty and their happiness, forgot his own misery, and the curse, and himself in them, and blessed and loved them; and in that temper of spirit prayer became possible:

> O happy living things! no tongue
> Their beauty might declare:
> A spring of love gushed in my heart
> And I blessed them unaware.
> The self-same moment I could pray.

The main thought and its details have their own beauty, and they illustrate the new love of animals in English poetry, but there is an often-noticed absurdity which injures the sense of art in the mass of machinery which is used to impress so simple a thought.   It is like making use of a calculating machine to add two and two together.

I have closed this lecture with the Ancient Mariner, for in some sort he resembles his creator.   Like him, Coleridge's soul had been

> Alone on a wide wide sea,
> So lone it was, that God himself
> Scarce seemed there to be.

Like him, though not as poet, Coleridge might say now:

> I pass, like night, from land to land;
> I have strange power of speech;
> That moment that his face I see
> I know the man that must hear me,
> To him my tale I teach.

And like him, finally, the much adventuring man, the poet who had adventured so far into wild seas of mental and religious thought, came home at last and found peace in simple faith in God, in childlike humility, in

mercy and love of man, and in reverence for all
things:

> O sweeter than the marriage feast
> 'Tis sweeter far to me
> To walk together to the kirk
> With a goodly company!
> To walk together to the kirk
> And all together pray,
> While each to his great Father bends,
> Old men and babes and loving friends,
> And youths and maidens gay.
> He prayeth best who loveth best
> All things both great and small,
> For the dear God who loveth us
> He made and loveth all.

It would be no unpleasant thought to compare that close
with that of Tennyson's *Two Voices*.

# LECTURE V

In speaking of the poetry of Nature, we have at length arrived at Wordsworth, and in coming to him we come to the greatest of the English poets of this century; greatest not only as a poet, but as a philosopher. It is the mingling of profound thought, and of ordered thought, with poetic sensibility and power (the power always the master of the sensibility), which places him in this high position. He does possess a philosophy, and its range is wide as the universe. He sings of God, of Man, of Nature, and, as the result of these three, of Human Life, and they are all linked by thought, and through feeling, one to another; so that the result is a complete whole which one can study as if it were a world of its own. As such, the whole of his poetry is full, not of systematic theology, but of his own theology; and to bring this out, while at the same time analysing his work as a poet, is the object of the lectures I shall deliver upon him. My first subject will be the mode in which he conceives God in His relation to Nature, and necessarily what he means by Nature; the next will be the relation which Nature bears to Man, and the work of God on Man through that relation. Afterwards I shall speak fully of Wordsworth's poetry of Man and its theology. It may seem too much to those who know Wordsworth but little, to devote so many lectures to him alone, but the only feeling that one who loves this poet can have is, that too much time can scarcely be spent upon him; and that if only a few are induced not to glance over but to study his work, more good may be done than by a hundred sermons. For in truth his poetry is, as Coleridge said of the *Prelude*,

> an Orphic song indeed,
> A song divine of high and passionate thoughts
> To their own music chanted.

The term Nature, in Wordsworth's use of it, means,

sometimes, the Nature of Man, those inherent and inde-
structible qualities which are common to the whole race,
and which form together that which we call Human
Nature.  In the realm of the imagination Wordsworth
frequently conceives of this Human Nature as one person,
acting as if directly from himself; the male being of the
universe to whom Nature, that is, the spirit who informs
the outward world, is as the female being of the universe
wedded in love and holy marriage.

But the term he more commonly uses when speaking of
Human Nature is the *Mind of Man*.  For all the practical
purposes of my lectures I may take the meaning of the
term Nature to be concerned in Wordsworth's poetry
with the world outside of us.  In most of the previous
poets, as in ordinary talk, it means the outward universe
with its motions and laws, all that we know and feel
beyond ourselves, organic and inorganic; and in this
sense Wordsworth sometimes uses it.  But that would
not define his use of the term accurately, for then Nature
might be conceived of as dead, or as the image of our
own thought.  Wordsworth added Life to the outward
world, and separated it from our thought.

I traced in a previous lecture the growth of the concep-
tion of Nature as alive, and said that this conception
which had only been in germ in others, reached its full
growth in Wordsworth's poetry.  In what way?  The
outward universe lay before the poet's eye and ear.  He
felt it speak to him, through his senses to his soul, and
feeling this, he asked, What is it?  Who is it that speaks?
Is it only the matter of the universe, which by itself is
dead?  No, he answered; Matter is animated by a soul,
and it is this soul which thrills to meet me.  "An *active*
principle" subsists

> In all things, in all natures, in the stars
> Of azure heaven, and unenduring clouds,
> In flower and tree, in every pebbly stone
> That paves the brooks; the stationary rocks,
> The moving waters and the invisible air,
> .    .    .    .    .    .
>                    from link to link
> It circulates, the soul of all the worlds.

Now that which acts, lives; and the universe lives as much by its soul as we do by ours.

To this active principle, Wordsworth gave personality; that which all shared in was in fact one.  It was one life, one will, one character, one person.  And this personality he called Nature.

To Wordsworth as he wrote, she took a living form, and became the life-giving spirit of the world.   Day by day she built up the universe; it was she who, from her own vast life, gave to everything its special life, a separate soul to each:

> Yet whate'er enjoyments dwell,
> In the impenetrable cell
> Of the silent heart, which Nature
> Furnishes to every creature.

Each had from Nature not only its own distinct soul and character, but also its own distinct work to do; the elements had their business, " the stars have tasks, the silent heavens their goings on."

And not only had each separate thing the gift of a soul from Nature, but whenever a place, such as a lonely dell among the hills, had a special beauty and character of its own, it was it by reason of a special soul within it, of a more manifold soul than that which dwelt in a single flower or stone.[1]

The thought was still further varied; and the larger divisions of the world of Nature, the whole of the sky, the whole of the earth and of the sea, were gifted with distinct and more complex being:

> The gentleness of Heaven is on the sea:
> Listen!  the mighty Being is awake
> And doth with his eternal motion make
> A sound like thunder everlastingly.

And further still, the moving powers of Nature, the wind, when it dances over wood and hill, tossing trees and grass, bearing on its bosom the seeds of earth, becomes the

---

[1] " A spirit and pulse of good,
A life and soul to every mode of being
Inseparably linked."

" over-soul " of the things it touches, adds to them a
new pleasure and a new life, a life of reckless sport and
jollity.

Describing the dandelion seed, or the thistle beard in
their game upon the lake, Wordsworth writes—

> Suddenly halting now, a lifeless stand!
> And starting off again with freak as sudden;
> In all its sportive wanderings, all the while
> Making report of an invisible breeze,
> That was its wings, its chariot, and its horse,
> Its very playmate and its moving soul.

Nor is this all; Nature has her own personal pleasures,
emotions, thoughts, plans, such as we might have. She
chooses places, as we might do, for her special delight in
the universe which is her kingdom, quiet places such as
that " glade of water," and one green field hidden far
among the trees, of which the poet says—

> The spot was made by Nature for herself,

giving vivid personality by this touch of selectiveness to
the being he has created. She exercises watchful care
over the life of all things; she loves, with passion pure
and calm, all her children.

And her love passes from her own works to Man. She
pours herself into the poets, whom she chooses for her
special friends, and through whom she speaks to Man;
and Wordsworth felt that he was chosen by her from his
birth. Others there were whose souls, though unable to
express themselves, were yet a favoured haunt of hers.
Such was his brother, who had early gone to sea:

> Nature there
> Was with thee: she who loved us both, she still
> Was with thee; and even so didst thou become
> A silent Poet; from the solitude
> Of the vast sea didst bring a watchful heart
> Still couchant, an inevitable ear,
> And an eye practised like a blind man's touch.

There were others also, whom she chose not as persons to

express her, but as children on whom she could lavish all her love without asking from them a return. And no lovelier poem exists than that in which Nature makes her whole world unite to educate and make beautiful one little maiden:

> Three years she grew in sun and shower
> Then Nature said—" A lovelier flower
> On earth was never sown;
> This Child I to myself will take,
> She shall be mine, and I will make
> A Lady of my own.
> Myself will to my darling be
> Both law and impulse; and with me
> The Girl, in rock and plain,
> In earth and heaven, in glade and bower,
> Shall feel an over-seeing power
> To kindle and restrain."

There is no need to quote the rest, it is well-known; but nothing can be more living than the personality with which this poem invests Nature, nothing greater than the difference in feeling and thought between this conception and the mechanical Nature of Pope, or the dead universe of Cowper. We are in contact with a person, not with a thought. But who is this person? Is she only the creation of imagination, having no substantive reality beyond the mind of Wordsworth. No, she is the poetic impersonation of an actual Being, the form which the poet gives to the living Spirit of God in the outward world, in order that he may possess a metaphysical thought as a subject for his work as an artist. We know that this theological idea is at the basis of Wordsworth's representation of Nature from many passages. Here is one:

> Wisdom and spirit of the Universe:
> Thou Soul that art the Eternity of thought;
> And giv'st to forms and images a breath
> And everlasting motion; not in vain,
> By day or starlight, thus from my first dawn
> Of childhood didst thou intertwine for me
> The passions which build up our human soul.

This is God, living, moving, and rejoicing in all his works;
not God in Man, but God in Nature, a wholly distinct
manifestation of His life.   Again, he speaks of

> The Being that is in the clouds and air,
> That is in the green leaves among the groves.

And to this Being he allots the care also of the creatures
whom He loves.   Moreover, His

> Dwelling is the light of setting suns,
> And the round ocean, and the living air,
> And the blue sky, and in the mind of man
> A motion and a spirit, that impels
> All things thinking, all objects of all thought,
> And rolls through all things.

It is more, you observe, than a mere influence; it is a
conscious life which realises itself as a personality, in
realising itself within the sum of things.   In fact, this
Being, who is the life of the universe, is the all-moving
Spirit of God, the soul which is the eternity of Thought
in Nature.[1]   It may be the fashion to call this pantheistic,
but it is the true and necessary pantheism which affirms
God in all, and all by Him, but which does not affirm
that the All includes the whole of God.   It is true a
certain amount of what is called the personality of God
seems to slip away from Wordsworth when he speaks of
God being in Nature;  but we must separate, in speaking
of his theology, his idea of God in relation to man, which
he conceived of as distinctly a personal relation, from his
idea of God in relation to Nature, which he could not
conceive of as an absolutely personal relation.   In the
case of man, God entering into what we call personality

---

[1] A few lines in the *Prelude* express this clearly:

> Hitherto,
> In progress through this Verse, my mind hath looked
> Upon the speaking face of earth and heaven
> As her prime teacher, intercourse with man
> Established by the Sovereign Intellect,
> Who through that bodily image hath diffused,
> As might appear to the eye of fleeting time,
> A deathless spirit.
>
> Bk. v.

is thought of as personal—in the case of Nature, God entering into that which is impersonal is thought of as impersonal; or rather we are forced by our ignorance to use terms which imply impersonality, such as a motion, a Presence, and others.

Nevertheless Wordsworth's feeling of personality, that is, of distinct self-consciousness of Being in God, was so strong, that he uses also such terms as the " Being who is in the clouds and air," and he would probably have said that the personality of God in reference to Nature consisted in God's consciousness of Himself at every moment of time in every part, as well as in the whole of the universe.

But as this is a metaphysical and not a poetic thought, and as Wordsworth wanted a thought which he could use poetically,[1] he transferred this idea of God, realising His personality in the whole of the universe, to an actual person whom he creates, to a Being whom he terms Nature.

And hence there grew up in his mind the thought of one personal spiritual life, which had infinitely subdivided itself through all the forms of the outward world, which could realise an undivided life at any moment, but which also lived a distinct life in every part. It became possible then for him to have communication with any one manifestation of that life, in a tree, or a rock, or a cloud; to separate in thought the characteristics of any one form of it from another—or omitting the consideration of the parts—to think of or communicate with the whole, to realise the one spiritual life that conditioned itself in all,

---

[1] The closing lines of the sonnet written at sea off the Isle of Man show how keenly Wordsworth felt the necessity of conceiving of Nature and of all her forms as living, if any intense poetry of Nature was to be written, and how, as a poet of Nature, he resented the mechanical theory of the universe.

> O Fancy, what an age was *that* for song!
> That age when not by laws inanimate,
> As men believed, the waters were impelled,
> The air controlled, the stars their courses held;
> But element and orb on *acts* did wait,
> Of *Powers* endued with visible form, instinct
> With will, and to their work by passion linked.

as a Person with whom he could speak and from whom he could receive impulse, or warning, or affection.

And when this was done, when Nature seemed one Life, then the necessary spirituality of the thought made him lose consciousness of the material forms under which this life appeared; and that condition of mind arose in which Nature was unsubstantialised in thought. And we find Wordsworth in many passages representing this as his experience, nor is it at all an uncommon one. For there are times when the sense of this spiritual life in Nature becomes so dominant that the material world fades away, and we feel as if we ourselves were pure spirit, and all the objects of sense were not real things we could touch, but unsubstantial appearances. In certain physical states—when they are accompanied with that upper meditation, if I may so call it, in which one seems to float apart from the body—the outward world is not felt, but only the life which inspires it. We are forced to go to a tree to touch it, in order to realise that it is tangible. We receive, that is, images through the senses, and the senses give them to the imagination and the intellect to deal with. These powers turn the sensible images into ideas and emotions, and so vivid do these ideas and emotions become, that they push the sensible things which awaked them out of the field of our consciousness. Through the sense we lose the sense, through the visible we enter the world of the invisible. It is an experience many of us have gone through. It comes chiefly when the incessant small noises of Nature make less attack upon the ear, when we are high up on a mountain side, or when we sit at night by the sea when the low mist seems to hush the water into silence, or when in deep noon one sound alone, like the wandering voice of the cuckoo, smites on the ear. One knows how Wordsworth felt this last—how the invisible bird became to him only a voice, a mystery; till the whole world was taken out of the region of sense and made as visionary as this herald of the spring.

> O blessed bird; the earth we pace
> Again appears to be
> An unsubstantial faery place:
> That is fit home for thee.

It is an experience which often came to this poet as boy and man. It marked his youth, as he tells us in one of his letters; it marked his manhood, and then he knew better what it meant: then he felt that when the earth grew unsubstantial in this hour of ecstasy, it was to reveal the spiritual substance which lay within it, the life of the living God—the ineffable act and thought of God by which the universe consisted. He speaks of times when

> The gross and visible frame of things
> Relinquishes its hold upon the sense,
> Yea, almost on the mind itself, and seems
> All unsubstantialised.

And the living soul communes directly with the living soul of Nature, " spirit to spirit, ghost to ghost."

What is it then, to which we speak, with whom we have communion? Not with Nature the poetic creation of the imagination, but with the spirit of the God who abides as Life in all. Here are some lines from the *Excursion* which express it, which embody the grandeur of Wordsworth's theology of Nature in words as grand as the thought:

> Such was the Boy—but for the growing Youth
> What soul was his, when, from the naked top
> Of some bold headland, he beheld the sun
> Rise up, and bathe the world in light! He looked—
> Ocean and earth, the solid frame of earth
> And ocean's liquid mass, in gladness lay
> Beneath him:—Far and wide the clouds were touched
> And in their silent faces could be read
> Unutterable love. Sound needed none,
> Nor any voice of joy; his spirit drank
> The spectacle: sensation, soul, and form,
> All melted into him: they swallowed up
> His animal being; in them did he live,
> And by them did he live; they were his life.
> In such access of mind, in such high hour
> Of visitation from the living God,
> Thought was not; in enjoyment it expired.
> No thanks he breathed, he proffered no request;

Rapt into still communion that transcends
The imperfect offices of prayer and praise,
His mind was a thanksgiving to the power
That made him; it was blessedness and love!

I have now to ask, what are the special characteristics of this life of Nature, and how are they connected with the thought of a divine life?

The first characteristic of this life of Nature is, that it is a life of enjoyment. No instance of Wordsworth's belief in this is finer than the first poem upon the naming of places. I give it as one example, though the thought runs through the whole of Wordsworth:

It was an April morning: fresh and clear
The Rivulet, delighting in its strength,
Ran with a young man's speed; and yet the voice
Of waters which the winter had supplied
Was softened down into a vernal tone.
The spirit of enjoyment and desire,
And hopes and wishes, from all living things
Went circling, like a multitude of sounds.
The budding groves seemed eager to urge on
The steps of June: as if their various hues
Were only hindrances that stood between
Them and their object: but, meanwhile, prevailed
Such an entire contentment in the air
That every naked ash, and tardy tree
Yet leafless, showed as if the countenance
With which it looked on this delightful day
Were native to the summer.—Up the brook
I roamed in the confusion of my heart,
Alive to all things and forgetting all.
At length I to a sudden turning came
In this continuous glen, where down a rock
The Stream, so ardent in its course before,
Sent forth such sallies of glad sound that all
Which I till then had heard appeared the voice
Of common pleasure; beast and bird, the lamb,
The shepherd's dog, the linnet and the thrush
Vied with this waterfall, and made a song
Which, while I listened, seemed like the wild growth
Or like some natural produce of the air,
That could not cease to be.

Naturally, the same idea of frank enjoyment of life is given to things which have organic life. The hare runs races in her mirth, the flowers enjoy the air they breathe. The waves dance beside the daffodils, but they

> Outdid the sparkling waves in glee,
> A Poet could not but be gay
> In such a jocund company

The bluecap in the appletree cannot contain himself for glee, nor the lambs, in spring. Thus, he says of the linnet:

> Thou, ranging up and down the bowers,
> Art sole in thy employment;
> A Life, a Presence like the Air,
> Scattering thy gladness without care,
> Too blest with any one to pair;
> Thyself thy own enjoyment.

And though, when autumn had come, these gave no sign of open joy, yet it did not follow that they had no enjoyment, for other pleasures might be

> Sweeter e'en than gaiety.

And all this life was praise to God, natural, unconscious praise, praise because the givers could not help giving it; their enjoyment their greatest praise, as ours should be; full and deep as that with which each morning the lark sang its hymn to God.

> Happy, happy Liver!
> With a soul as strong as a mountain river,
> Pouring out praise to the Almighty Giver.

That was the religious aspect of this delight in life. But it passed from the religious to the theological when this infinite pleasure of the whole of Nature was felt to be by Wordsworth, not only symbolic of, but actually, the joy of God in His own life. It was God who renewed each moment in the boundless delight of all things, his " ancient rapture " in the continuous act of creation; it was God Himself who rejoiced in the brook and the tree, in the daisy and the lark. It is a thought which should

add a new element to our happiness.  For in our worst
sadness we ought not to be too morose to be glad of the
pleasure of all things—in our worst grief the sense of
God's enjoyment which we receive from the joy of Nature
ought to come with healing to our hearts.

The second characteristic of the life of Nature is its
quietude.  She has joy, ecstasy in her life, but it is
untroubled ecstasy.  We are " pressed by heavy laws,"
tormented by doubt, and rent by struggle against con-
ditions which we will not obey at once.   Nature's life is at
peace, for her children never wage a foolish strife with
her; nor does self enter their hearts to make them weary
of life.  Deep calm is at her heart, the mountains rest
in their own peace, the stars shine quietly, the sun " sinks
down in his tranquillity," the flowers keep a still silence,
and though there are storms which drive the clouds in
passionate course, and torrents which rend the earth,
and strong forces which sweep to and fro the elements
in bewildering and endless motion, yet in the higher
region of thought in which these things are seen in their
relation to the great whole, there is

> Central peace subsisting at the heart
> Of endless agitation.

And this, too—this tranquil being in each thing which
sends " its own deep quiet to restore our hearts," this
central peace, was not self-born in Nature—it was in
Wordsworth's thought the ineffable calm of God's exist-
ence which spoke to us and redeemed us.

The third characteristic is ceaseless intercommunion,
and that was founded on the unutterable love which
flowed through all things, and with which each thing
acted on each other.  The whole world was linked
together.  Every part, every element, gave and received,
honoured and did service to each other.  Each plant and
hill, cloud and stream, has its own life and character,
and they delight in social intercourse like friends who
love each other—there is no jar, no jealousy, no envy
there—their best joy is in being kind to one another.

This idea is the loveliest of all which Wordsworth

introduced into English poetry, and it flowed from his
conception of everything in Nature having its own
peculiar life. I might give a hundred instances of it,
for it runs like a living stream through all the woodland
of his poetry. It is varied in many ways; the waves are
brothers which run after one another; he says of the great
eminence which of all his hills last parleyed with the
setting sun that the meteors made of it their favourite
haunt, as if even those wild bodies had their power of
choice to love one cliff especially; the lake rejoices to
receive into her bosom the scenery which surrounds
her:

> Through all her depths St. Mary's lake
> Is visibly delighted,
> For not a feature of the hills
> Is in her mirror slighted.

And Windermere prepares herself, like a woman for one
she loves, to receive the evening:

> The lake though bright is of a placid blue
> As if preparing for the peace of evening.

In spring time the whole world gives and receives joy;
and earth and sky and man feel their communion each
with each:

> There is a blessing in the air,
> Which seems a sense of joy to yield
> To the bare trees, and mountains bare,
> And grass in the green field.
> .     .     .     .     .     .
> Love, now an universal birth,
> From heart to heart is stealing,
> From earth to man, from man to earth—
> It is the hour of feeling.

But the noblest passage out of many is in the *Excursion*
where the Solitary speaks of the two great brother peaks
which overpeered the glen. I read it: mark how the
wind rejoices in them, and they give back its wild pleasure;
how all the things which touch and haunt them get their
reply; how they are loved and love; how busy are the

mute agents there; how proud the stars to shine on them:

> "Those lusty twins," exclaimed our host, "if here
> It were your lot to dwell, would soon become
> Your prized companions.—Many are the notes
> Which, in his tuneful course, the wind draws forth
> From rocks, woods, caverns, heaths, and dashing shores;
> And well those lofty brethren bear their part
> In the wild concert—chiefly when the storm
> Rides high; then all the upper air they fill
> With roaring sound, that ceases not to flow,
> Like smoke, along the level of the blast,
> In mighty current; theirs, too, is the song
> Of stream and headlong flood that seldom fails;
> And, in the grim and breathless hour of noon,
> Methinks that I have heard them echo back
> The thunder's greeting.   Nor have Nature's laws
> Left them ungifted with a power to yield
> Music of finer tone; a harmony
> So do I call it, though it be the hand
> Of silence, though there be no voice;—the clouds,
> The mist, the shadows, light of golden suns,
> Motions of moonlight, all come thither—touch,
> And have an answer—thither come, and shape
> A language not unwelcome to sick hearts
> And idle spirits:—there the sun himself,
> At the calm close of summer's longest day,
> Rests his substantial orb;—between those heights
> And on the top of either pinnacle,
> More keenly than elsewhere in night's blue vault,
> Sparkle the stars, as of their station proud.
> Thoughts are not busier in the mind of man
> Than the mute agents stirring there:—alone
> Here do I sit and watch."

The deep underlying thought of all this belief in the love and intercommunion of all things—the thought which makes Nature, in this conception of her, divine—was that this endless interchange of life and joy was in reality, not the type of, but actually, the never-ceasing self-reciprocation of God.   He divides Himself into a myriad forms, and lives in each distinctly, and makes His own ineffable society and enjoyment by living with Himself from form to form, by loving Himself, and by self-communion through infinitely varied activity and beauty and sacrifice, giving and receiving Himself for ever in the universe. And yet, though I say self in these sentences, it is because we must so express it, in order to get the idea. There is no Self in our sense of the word in God, none except the consciousness of perfect Being: and we can best express what that consciousness of Being is by saying that it is for ever the unspeakable delight of everlasting thought unremittingly passing into creative activity, in which that which we call self is so lost as never to be known.

This is the idea of Life in Nature which Wordsworth has given to the world. It fills the heart of his readers; it makes of Nature a new thing to them; it makes the commonest walk in the woods a delight, a teaching, a society, it fills the world with life and energy and joy; it uplifts us sometimes when alone among the hills—when Nature is in one of her wild moods, and her life most intelligent and most eager, into a kindred ecstasy in which we long to be borne away with wind and cloud to join the mighty stream of rejoicing Life. So was it once at least with Wordsworth: and with this I close.

> Oh! what a joy it were, in vigorous health,
> To have a body (this our vital frame
> With shrinking sensibility endued,
> And all the nice regards of flesh and blood)
> And to the elements surrender it
> As if it were a spirit!—How divine
> The liberty for frail, for mortal man,
> To roam at large among the unpeopled glens
> And mountainous retirements, only trod
> By devious footsteps; regions consecrate
> To oldest time! and, reckless of the storm
> That keeps the raven quiet in her nest,
> Be as a presence or a motion—one
> Among the many there; and while the mists
> Flying, and rainy vapours, call out shapes
> And phantoms from the crags and solid earth
> As fast as a musician scatters sounds
> Out of an instrument; and while the streams
> (As at a first creation and in haste

To exercise their untried faculties)
Descending from the region of the clouds,
And starting from the hollows of the earth
More multitudinous every moment, rend
Their way before them—what a joy to roam
An equal among mightiest energies;
And haply sometimes with articulate voice,
Amid the deafening tumult, scarcely heard
By him that utters it, exclaim aloud,
" Rage on ye elements! let moon and stars
Their aspects lend, and mingle in their turn
With this commotion (ruinous though it be)
From day to night, from night to day, prolonged! "

## LECTURE VI

### WORDSWORTH—*continued*

In my last lecture I spoke of the meaning Wordsworth had for the term " Nature," of his conception of Nature as having a life of her own and of the characteristics of that life, its endless joy, central peace, and how all its forms, each having their own life, were knit together by unselfish love. But these are terms which are true of humanity also; we can say that human nature is capable of joy and peace and love, and Wordsworth does say that we see in Nature similar passions to our own. But though he thought them similar, he did not think them identical; he drew a clear distinction between them, between the life in Nature and that in Man. On this distinction I must now enlarge, in order that I may come to that part of my subject which treats of the education that Nature gives to man; a thought that pervades the whole of Wordsworth's poetry.

There are poets who impute to Nature their own moods and feelings, as when Tennyson makes the larkspur listen for Maud's footstep, or when Coleridge, giving to natural things the power of Man, makes the Wind an actor or a poet. This is what Ruskin calls the " pathetic fallacy; " and a few instances, such as the phrase " forlorn cascades," where the lonely waterfall seems to him abandoned by the world because he feels himself forlorn, exist in Wordsworth; but he always means to distinguish clearly between his own feelings and those which he believes belong to things outside himself. The Me and the not-Me are not the same. It is not the poet who makes Nature this or that by giving himself to her; it is she who builds up part of his being by communicating herself to him. It is not that the sea is in this or that special mood, because he is in it, or that the birds sing of certain things of which he is thinking, but that the sea has its own moods, and that the birds sing their own emotions:

> The birds around me hopped and played
> Their *thoughts I cannot measure :*

He does not define their thoughts: he is only certain that they do think, and have pleasure and pain of their own:

> But the least motion that they made
> It seemed a thrill of pleasure.

It is the same thing with flowers and rocks and clouds; he could not express their kind of existence, but he was certain of its being a feeling existence:

> And 'tis my faith, that every flower
> Enjoys the air it breathes.

He is, of course, obliged to use the same terms as we use about our thinking and feeling, when he speaks of the life which natural things live, but he does not identify their thoughts and feelings with ours. They are similar to ours but they differ from ours, being conditioned by the different material through which they work, in a much greater degree, though in the same way as the thoughts and feelings of a man differ from those of a woman.

It is important in reading Wordsworth to understand this clearly—this separate life of Nature and Man, this distinctness which enables a dramatic action to take place between them. We have wholly got rid of the thought of Coleridge that Nature lives by the projection of our self upon it: we do not receive what we give, we give and receive back something wholly different. It is not the reflection of ourselves which we have from Nature, it is the friendship of another than ourselves.

It is this which makes Wordsworth's poetry so fresh, so healthy, and of such a morning quality. He forgets himself in the beauty, joy, and life of things; he will not spoil Nature by tracing in her any likeness to his own moods; he would not willingly have written that stanza in *In Memoriam*, beginning with these lines:

> Calm is the morn without a sound,
> Calm as to suit a calmer grief:—

they would have contradicted his philosophy—nor traced in the gathering storm and looming cloud the " wild despair " of grief which filled Tennyson's heart for the loss of his friend. Nor would he, even by permitting human associations to cluster thickly in certain places, prevent these places from making their own natural impression upon him—a thing which Tennyson does frequently. The whole of the descriptions of Nature in *In Memoriam* are tinged with one or the other of these faults: skies, flowers, clouds, and trees, are full of the self of the poet, or of recollections of his friend; and the result is that a partly morbid impression is left on the reader, even in the triumphant passages at the end—an impression of the tyranny of Human Nature over Nature, of ourselves as being the only thing in the universe — which is a depressing element in the poem. It is painful to be deprived by this imposition of Man on Nature of the only chance we have of getting rid of ourselves, or of feeling another life than human life. It is the first excellence of Wordsworth that though he does not pass by this " pathetic fallacy " altogether, he only treats it as a transient and unhealthy phase.

The poem on the picture of Peele Castle in a storm has been so explained as to be an example of this pathetic fallacy, but Wordsworth is true in it to his philosophy.

He sees in it the Sea at peace, but he does not see it as the image of his own peace. It has its own quiet from its own nature, not from his. Being thus distinct, it sends its impression of calm to influence his heart. That being received, the powers of his mind take it up, and add their own work to it, " the consecration and the poet's dream." From both these things—from the impression passively received, and the active energy of thought upon it—another thing arises, the poetic picture, the work of art.

> Ah! then, if mine had been the Painter's hand,
>   To express what then I saw; and add the gleam,
> The light that never was, on sea or land,
>   The consecration, and the Poet's dream;
>
> I would have planted thee, thou hoary Pile,
>   Amid a world how different from this!
> Beside a sea that could not cease to smile;
>   On tranquil land, beneath a sky of bliss.
>
> Thou shouldst have seemed a treasure-house divine
>   Of peaceful years; a chronicle of heaven;
> Of all the sunbeams that did ever shine
>   The very sweetest had to thee been given.
>
> A Picture had it been of lasting ease,
>   Elysian quiet, without toil or strife;
> No motion but the moving tide, a breeze,
>   Or merely silent Nature's breathing life.
>
> Such, in the fond illusion of my heart,
>   Such Picture would I at that time have made
> And seen the soul of truth in every part,
>   A steadfast peace that might not be betrayed.

It is an illustration, in a small way, of what he means in the lines soon to be quoted, when he says that the individual mind and the external universe are fitted, in difference, to each other, and when wedded together accomplish a *creation*—something different from both—with blended might.

The latter part of the poem is another side of the same thought, only the Art work which he wished to do for the calm, is done by Beaumont for the storm. He can no longer look on a calm sea and find the impression of calm. Something has happened which forbids it; the sea has engulphed his brother. But he neither imposes the storm in his own heart on the calm, nor sees the sea in the storm as in sorrow for his loss. The sea has *its own* anger and fury. But Beaumont has seen it in storm, and receiving from it an impression of anger, has added to that impression, by imagination, correlative human emotion, and composed both into one creation by Art. And on this creation Wordsworth loves to look. It, the human work, the artistic result of the blended might of Nature and of the human mind, consoles him by its sympathy with his sorrow. The conclusion follows easily from this analysis.

Nothing can be more remote than all this from the faded sentiment which we found in Warton and the other poets of his class. To sit in the shade of yew trees, and feel a charm in their gloom reflecting our own—as was the case with the youth on whom Wordsworth wrote his *Lines near Esthwaite*—to trace in the barren landscape an emblem of our own unfruitful life, is the most sickly of all pleasures:

> The man whose eye
> Is ever on himself, doth look on one
> The least of Nature's works, one who might move
> The wise man to that scorn which wisdom holds
> Unlawful, ever.

And he went further still: not only were we bound to resist this tendency, but Nature herself had against it a sad resentment. Against it she continually fought, her one effort being to redeem us from this self-consideration, to lead us to lose our stormy passions in her quiet, our consuming sadness in her joy. An instance of this in his own experience occurs in the Ode on the intimations of Immortality. He begins by feeling that a glory has passed from the earth since he was young: grief falls on him, and in the shade of disenchantment the splendour leaves the grass, and the freshness the sunlight. But with the very utterance of the thought he springs away from this diseased condition. Nature speaking to him, he hears her voice; and joy returns, not the joy of early life, but a stiller, more grave delight. " No more shall grief of mine the season wrong," he cries; it would indeed be an evil day if he were sullen,

> While the earth is herself adorning
> This sweet May morning.

There shall be no severing of his love from fountains, meadows, hills, and groves:

> Yet in my heart of hearts I feel your might;
> I only have relinquished one delight
> To live beneath your more habitual sway;
> I love the brooks which down their channels fret
> Even more than when I tripp'd lightly as they;
> The innocent brightness of a new-born day
>     Is lovely yet.

The lines have their own special connection, but through them also runs the thought of which we speak—of the distinctness of the being of Nature from the being of Human Nature, and of the work which Nature, as distinct, does on Man. His own mood of morbid melancholy which he tried to lay on Nature, she had refused to receive; she sent him back, on the contrary, her mood of joy. When he had opened his heart to that influence, though the melancholy did not wholly depart, it was freed from weakness and selfishness. His heart was opened, his sadness was filled with strength and the hope which comes of delight in other things than our own emotions.

All this may not be theological, but it is distinctly religious. It is the very element in which a high religion becomes possible, a freedom from looking into self which enables men to love and lose themselves in others; to win power by taking into themselves a thousand influences; to conquer life by the possession of that sound mind which, in freedom from the prejudices to which self-consideration gives birth, can see things and opinions directly as they are. Hence, and especially because of this, the religion of Wordsworth is the noblest we possess in our poetry, and the healthiest.

And, apart from personal religion, if we pass into the realm of theology, we are rescued in Wordsworth's poetry from the sight of our self in Nature, and enabled to see God in it. The man who finds in Nature only the reflection of his own passions and thoughts can only find God therein in His relation to himself, or his fellow-men. He sees God only as human, and missing thus all the absolute side of the Deity, his idea of God is very imperfect. But he who, escaping through passionate love of Nature from self, looks straight into Nature and sees her as she is, beholds God not only as personal, but as impersonal, not only as the human God, but as far beyond humanity; and realises that there is an infinite sublimity, an eternal calm, a glory of order, beauty, and variety, to which he dare give no name nor allot a human personality, but which he truly knows is active and loving, wise and of unweariable power. And our modern theology bitterly wants that conception. It would tend to free it from its ceaseless and diseased insistence on humanity alone, and let us loose a little from ourselves.

II. Having now spoken of Wordsworth's separation of Man fr m Nature, and its moral result on his poetry, I ask what philosophic conception he founded on it. I shall try to approach it by an analogy. We get a hint in the first chapter of Genesis that God conceived of man and woman as originally one being, as Man—who held in one person all the male and female qualities, and as such, was a perfect ideal of Human Nature; that afterwards He divided this one Being into two persons, having similar passions, volitions, and appetites, but differently conditioned by sex; that each of these was the complement of the other and fitted to unite with one another, in order that by the mutual play of the divers qualities of each on the other the education of both might take place; and that when both, through this mutual action on each other, became at one, Human Nature would be again, as it was at first, complete.

The conception of Wordsworth with regard to Man and Nature is much the same. The spirit which lives in each differs as Man differs from Woman, not indeed in the same, but in a similar manner, but—they differ for the purpose of union, and there is between them a preordained fitness. Each educates the other, and in their final marriage is the consummation of the perfection of the human mind and Nature. Here are the lines in which Wordsworth sketches this conception. It lies at the root of his philosophy:

> For the discerning intellect of Man,
> When wedded to this goodly universe
> In love and holy passion, shall find these—

that is, Beauty, Paradise, the Elysian Fields, all ideal dreams of men—

> A simple produce of the common day.
> —I, long before the blissful hour arrives,
> Would chant, in lonely peace, the spousal verse
> Of this great consummation—and by words
> Which speak of nothing more than what we are,
> Would I arouse the sensual from their sleep
> Of Death, and win the vacant and the vain
> To noble raptures; while my voice proclaims
> How exquisitely the individual Mind
> (And the progressive power, perhaps no less
> Of the whole species) to the external World
> Is fitted:—and how exquisitely, too—
> Theme this but little heard of among men—
> The external World is fitted to the Mind:
> And the *creation* (by no lower name
> Can it be called) which they with blended might
> Accomplish:—This is our high argument.[1]

So the whole grand idea is that God has made these two —Man and Nature—for one another and to develop each other, and His mighty object is that we should realise in the marriage of the mind and the external world the pre-arranged harmony. It is a sketch which is filled in in various ways in the minor poems. It forms the true burden of the *Excursion* and the *Prelude*. To reveal, to explain this underlying unity, to urge us to realise it by revealing the beauty in Man and Nature, is, in Wordsworth's thought, the special work of poetry. "Poetry is the image of Man and Nature," and the object of the poet is to produce such pleasure in the individual man by his imaging of Nature and Man as to induce love of

[1] Preface to the *Excursion*. See also the preface to the *Lyrical Ballads*, where he says that the poet is one " pleased with his own passions and volitions, and who rejoices more than other men in the spirit of life that is in him; delighting to contemplate similar " —observe, he says similar, not identical—" volitions and passions as manifested in the goings-on of the universe, and habitually impelled to create them where he does not find them."

Nature and union with her. " He considers Man and the objects which surround him as acting and reacting upon each other, so as to produce an infinite complexity of pain and pleasure." " He considers Man and Nature as essentially adapted to each other, and the mind of Man as naturally the mirror of the fairest and most interesting properties of Nature." [1]

And when we look into our intuitions and emotions, when we are with an open heart alone with Nature, we seem to know that this is a true philosophy. We ask if Nature, so distinct from us, has no longing to unite herself to us, to find the complement of her Being in ours; and we cannot but trace this desire in the animals which love us, in the pleasure all of them, when we are kind, take in our company. And what we trace in the animals we need not fear to apply further, at least in the sphere of poetic feeling. There is a way in which things seem to look at us, and beg for our affection and sympathy. The trees nod to us, and we to them, as Emerson said. In hours when we have most shaken off the coil of self and the troubles of the world, we are impressed with delight by the love which all things seem to bear to us. A real emotion, as deep, but more clear and pure than that awakened by human love, is kindled in us by the knowledge that the trees are whispering their affection in our ear, and the brook singing its song to us, and the flowers adorning themselves to please our eye. Nor is there an atom of selfishness in this. We are frankly delighted with it, and accept it with healthy joy. We rejoice as much in the pleasure which Nature feels in uniting herself to us as in the pleasure she gives us. And when we feel so, we are ourselves purer and kinder, and less envious than at other times. She loves us and desires the time when her " marriage " with us shall be complete; and when we are most conscious of that and most give back the wish, then we know best what St. Paul meant when he said — " The earnest expectation of the creature waiteth for the manifestation of the sons of God."

[1] Preface to the second edition of the *Lyrical Ballads*.

And we, on our part, we also possess this desire of union. Most of us have felt it at times to be unutterable, so secret and deep is its passion; and when—rarely, indeed, for they are the most consecrated moments of life—we have realised the emotion of harmonious alliance with the world, I know not if any purely human joy can be so exquisite. When we cannot realise it, the way in which our whole nature chafes against the secrecy and reticence of Nature shows how much the feeling partakes of true passion, while the very existence of such a passion prophesies the time when the marriage of the soul to the soul of Nature shall be accomplished. Men have tried to explain this longing by saying that it is the human element which we have projected into Nature, or that it is our own thought there to which we desire to reunite ourselves. It may be, they say, that the trees and the stream are really we, and that we love ourselves in loving them; and philosophy claps her hands and says that she has settled the question for poetry. But the contradiction of that is rapid and instinctive; in the realm of feeling it is impossible to believe it; one cannot love oneself in that manner. Moreover, whenever we are in that humour, when we try to say that the life of waters, clouds, and leaves is but "the eddying of our living soul," it is curious with what a mocking spirit they look upon us: walk in the woods with only that idea, or by the sea, and every tree and wave will say to you—"*You* find my secret, little fellow!"[1]

But a single rush of love to the great spirit who lives there will make her open her arms and heart to you. Turn to the trees and waves, as to friends, in that sudden expansion which one feels at times to human friends and in which all barriers melt, and there will not be a blade of grass nor a drift of cloud which will not partake its life with you, teach you its lesson, interpose between your

---

[1] One remembers Emerson's phrase—"Nature will not have us fret or fume. She does not like our benevolence or learning much better than she likes our frauds and wars. When we come out of the Caucus, or the bank, or the Abolition Convention, or the Transcendental Club, into the fields and woods, she says to us, 'So hot, my little sir.'"

heart and yourself its kindness, whisper to you infinite secrets and fill you with joy and calm.

> How bountiful is Nature; he shall find
> Who seeks not, and to him that hath not asked,
> Large measure shall be dealt.

This is the task of Nature, and she fulfils it at the command of God, or rather it is God himself who in all her life gives us this education and help; and teaches us of Himself through her.

In the *Excursion*, Book iv., Wordsworth traces this work of hers into distant times. Long, long ago it began: Man was not left to himself to corrupt in apathy;

> to feel the weight
> Of his own reason, without sense or thought
> Of higher reason and a purer will,
> To benefit and bless, through mightier power.

The Persian, when he sacrificed "to moon and stars, and to the winds, and mother elements," felt through them "a sensitive existence and a God." The Chaldæan shepherds entered the invisible world through the thoughts which the moving planets and the still star of the Pole awakened in their minds; the Greek idolatrously served a hundred gods:

> And yet—triumphant o'er this pompous show
> Of art, this palpable array of sense,
> On every side encountered; in despite
> Of the gross fictions chanted in the streets
> By wandering Rhapsodists; and in contempt
> Of doubt and bold denial hourly urged
> Amid the wrangling schools—a *spirit* hung,
> Beautiful region! o'er thy towns and farms,
> Statues and temples, and memorial tombs:
> And emanations were perceived;—

For Nature spoke through the things of sense and told of spirit; and when the votary, thankful for his son's return, shed his severed locks upon Cephisus' river, then

> Doubtless, sometimes, when the hair was shed
> Upon the flowing stream, a thought arose
> Of Life continuous, Being unimpaired;
> That hath been, is, and where it was and is
> There shall endure.

This was the work of Nature teaching an indefinite
religion, telling of God to men who knew Him not, speak-
ing of the infinite world beyond, through the emotions
which the finite roused.

And now, in our later times, such training has gone so
far that we would not give to the trees or brook a wild
half-human soul, and make a Dryad or a Naiad take their
place; for that would be to lose the tree or the brook
itself. We keep the natural object, but we know within it
is the life of God. It tells us in its own way part of the
character of our Father. It is one of the forms He takes
to us. Listen to Wordsworth speaking of the brook that
the poet and the painter sought:

> If wish were mine some type of thee to view,
> Thee and not thee thyself, I would not do
> Like Grecian artists—
> No Naiad shouldst thou be—
> It seems the Eternal Soul is clothed in thee
> With purer robes than those of flesh and blood,
> And hath bestowed on thee a safer good,
> Unwearied joy, and life without its cares.

Then transferring in another place the same thought from
one object to all objects, he sees in the whole universe
the revealer of God to Man—the great Evangelist to Man.
" I have seen "—the lines are well-known—

> A curious child, who dwelt upon a tract
> Of inland ground, applying to his ear
> The convolutions of a smooth-lipped shell.
> To which, in silence hushed, his very soul
> Listened intensely; and his countenance soon
> Brightened with joy; for from within were heard
> Murmurings, whereby the monitor expressed
> Mysterious union with its native sea.
> Even such a shell the universe itself
> Is to the ear of Faith; and there are times
> I doubt not, when to you it doth impart
> Authentic tidings of invisible things;
> Of ebb and flow, and ever-during power;
> And central peace, subsisting at the heart
> Of endless agitation. Here you stand,

Adore, and worship, when you know it not;
Pious beyond the intention of your thought;
Devout above the meaning of your will.

It is God then who unites Nature to us, and directs her teaching; it is His life acting on ours.

But in order to be able to receive her training there must be certain qualities in us. What are these in Wordsworth's philosophy? They are the qualities of the child. The first is the simple heart which loves, and to which the world is sweet, it knows not why. We then accord the measure of our hearts to the music of His power who attunes the world to love; and loving things we know them. But our meddling intellect, working without love, misshapes the beauty of the world. It can only divide and subdivide, and isolate for discussion thing from thing, element from element. It cannot see the living, thinking, feeling whole:

It substitutes an universe of death
For that which moves with light and life informed,
Actual, divine, and true.

The world, which science " examines, ponders, searches, vexes, criticises," is not the real life of things; and Nature refuses to speak to those who prize

the transcendent universe
No more than as a mirror that reflects
To proud self-love her own intelligence.

But to those who enter her kingdom with that listening love of a child which watches and receives, she gives her teaching:

One moment now may give us more
Than years of toiling reason;
Our minds shall drink at every pore
The spirit of the season.

But Wordsworth never meant to depreciate the nobler science, but only that which, striving after no vast ideal conception of the whole, pored alone over what it could hold in its hands, and fixed itself exclusively on phenomena.

Wordsworth disliked, as much as Socrates did, the people who would believe in nothing or consider nothing but that which lay before their eyes. But the larger science of to-day, such as Faraday practised, which works through imagination as well as through experiment and observation, he would not have disliked. From geometric science, for example, he drew

> A pleasure quiet and profound, a sense
> Of permanent and universal sway,
> And permanent belief—there, recognised
> A type, for finite natures, of the one
> Supreme existence, the surpassing life
> Which—to the boundaries of space and time,
> Of melancholy space and doleful time,
> Superior and incapable of change,
> Not touched by welterings of passion—is
> And hath the name of God.

Another quality which fits us to receive the training of Nature is reverence, the food and source of admiration. The scornful spirit is the blind spirit and the unthoughtful one; and to its blindness Nature displays in vain her beauty, and Man his wonderful life; contempt sees nothing, and seeing nothing has no materials for thought. He who feels it for any living thing—and when Wordsworth says "living thing" he means things which we call inanimate, as well as things animate—

> hath faculties
> Which he hath never used, and thought with him
> Is in its infancy.

But he who bends in loving reverence before the beauty and majesty of the universe, receives its teaching at every pore.

But of all qualities, the two most necessary were purity of heart and unworldliness of character, and in Wordsworth's thought they mingled into one. There is one well-known sonnet which enshrines this belief of his in a statement of its opposite.

> The world is too much with us; late and soon,
> Getting and spending, we lay waste our powers:

> Little we see in Nature that is ours;
> We have given our hearts away, a sordid boon!
> The Sea that bares her bosom to the moon;
> The winds that will be howling at all hours,
> And are upgathered now like sleeping flowers;
> For this—for everything, we are out of tune;
> It moves us not.

And in a letter he says the same thing—" It is an awful truth, that there neither is, nor can be, any genuine enjoyment of poetry among nineteen out of twenty of those persons who live, or wish to live, in the broad light of the world—among those who either are, or are striving to make themselves, persons of consideration in society. This is a truth, and an awful one, because to be incapable of a feeling for poetry, in my sense of the word, is to be without love of human nature and reverence for God."

Now as these qualities are found chiefly in their purity in the child, it is then that the work of Nature, as education, begins. Of what that work is, and how it is carried on, he has given two examples—one in the first book of the *Excursion*, another in tracing his own growth under the influences of Nature in the *Prelude*. Of these two I will give an analysis.

He traces in the first the history of a Highland child, early thrown into solitary life among the hills. As he came home at evening and saw the hills grow larger in the mist, and the stars steal out in the infinite expanse, and felt the horror of the pine wood in his heart, he received impressions of greatness and its power, indefinite, but full of force to awaken and develop feeling. These feelings, in their turn, reacted on the forms of Nature till the impressions they made became like real existences in his soul. Image after image thus received and made into living things, soon made him unconsciously mingle up the living image in his soul with the natural image of which it was the counterpart; till he slowly began to feel that every image became living in him, not only because he gave it life, but also because the object which produced it possessed a life of its own which, coming to the life in him, stirred and kindled it into creation.

> And 'mid the hollow depths of naked crags
> He sate—and e'en in their fixed lineaments—
> Or from the power of a peculiar eye,
> Or by creative feeling overborne,
> Or by predominance of thought oppressed,
> Even in their fixed and steady lineaments
> He traced an ebbing and a flowing mind,
> Expression ever varying.

This was the work of the awe which Nature produces in the child—a sense of sublimity, and of life as the source of that sublimity.

As he grew, the fear which somewhat spoiled the awe died away; and when it perished and awe alone was left, then the whole vast world Being, when, at the sunrise, it appeared to him from the mountain top, drenched in light as with joy, and all its glory seeming to him—trained as he was to feel that Nature was alive—not glory only but love, awoke unspeakable love in him. His mind became one mighty sacrifice of gratitude and love to God. And this reacted on the religion he had learnt and added to it the element of feeling. He had received revealed religion at his mother's knee, had given it his reverence, but it yet was cold to emotion. But it was different now; emotion had come to him from Nature, and his spirit was stirred to feel it towards the things of Faith.

> A Herdsman on the lonely mountain tops,
> Such intercourse was his, and in this sort
> Was his existence oftentimes *possessed*.
> O then how beautiful, how bright, appeared
> The written promise! Early had he learned
> To reverence the volume that displays
> The mystery, the life which cannot die;
> But in the mountains did he *feel* his faith.
> All things responding to the writing, there
> Breathed immortality, revolving life,
> And greatness still revolving; infinite:
> There littleness was not; the least of things
> Seemed infinite; and there his spirit shaped
> Her prospects, nor did he believe,—he *saw*.

That is the sketch given of this early education by Nature in the *Excursion*. It resembles in one or two points the more elaborate one given in the *Prelude,* which I analyse now, and which is the history of Wordsworth himself. Even from his birth he holds that Nature was his friend. The " ceaseless music " of Derwent flowed through his infant dreams, and gave him an unconscious foretaste, a dim earnest of the calm

> That Nature breathes among the hills and groves.

Then, as he became a boy her real work began to tell. As before, it began with vague impressions of fear. When at night upon the moors, so profound was the vast impression of peace, he felt his bustling presence almost a trouble in the calm of skies and earth. There, when conscience touched him (having robbed the prey of another's trap than his own), Nature herself was felt as the avenger. Low breathings came after him, and steps, " silent as the turf they trod," were heard among the solitary hills.

Did he, as cragsman, shoulder the naked crag and cling to the perilous ridge?—then, if his courage held, Nature was his companion; if it gave way, she became his destroyer. Did he, half by stealth, row on the lake when evening fell?—then, the huge peak which suddenly rose upon his view seemed to be instinct with voluntary power, and stride after him with a purpose of its own; and for days afterwards his brain

> Worked with a dim and undetermined sense
> Of unknown modes of Being,—

half glimpses of the dweller on the threshold.

These were the vague impressions, mostly of dim yet delightful fear, which, repeated in many forms and woven together, not confusedly but as notes which fell into harmony, began to build up his character. For such impressions stirred in him germs of feeling—the sense of moral wrong, the sense of indefinite sublimity, the sense of a vast and invisible *life* without himself. And these germs of emotion, becoming conscious of themselves, were sent back to Nature, and made the impressions which were afterwards received from her more vivid, more infinite, more overwhelming: and they in turn stirred deeper emotion in him, and the deeper emotion again found itself met by a mightier answer—till in the mutual play of action thus established, his character grew daily into form. His mind *began* to be married to the external world and the external world to it; the first steps of that union were made which, when fulfilled, should make up that " calm existence which was to be his when he was worthy of himself."

It was the living Soul of the universe which was doing this work; a personal Being, ever melting on the skirts of consciousness into the impersonal. The eternal Thought that watches over the thought of men, watched over his development; and itself linked to the majestic forms and scenes of Nature, acted through them upon his soul, and wrought in him the passions that build up character, and the ideals that ennoble it.

> Wisdom and Spirit of the universe!
> Thou Soul that art the Eternity of thought,
> That giv'st to forms and images a breath
> And everlasting motion, not in vain
> By day or starlight thus, from my first dawn
> Of childhood, didst thou intertwine for me
> The passions that build up our human soul;
> Not with the mean and vulgar works of man,
> But with high objects, with enduring things—
> With life and nature—purifying thus
> The elements of feeling and of thought,
> And sanctifying, by such discipline,
> Both pain and fear, until we recognise
> A grandeur in the beatings of the heart.

Nor did this mutual intercourse cease its movement for a moment. By day and night, summer and winter, the silent education went on till at last he felt the " presence of Nature in the sky and on the earth," and saw the " visions of the hills," and spoke with the " souls of lonely places," and, in dim perception—but without an intellectual form being given to the feeling—felt that the whole world was alive and speaking to him as his companion, greater than himself, but yet at one with

him. Each of these presences, visions, souls, ministered
to him, haunted him, partook of his danger and desire,
and had a distinct desire and danger of their own; till, at
last, as examples multiplied of this intercommunion (and
what the forms of nature said were met at once by a
response in his own heart, that fitted the impressions
made), the whole earth became like a great Being and,

> With triumph and delight, with hope and fear,
> Worked like a sea.

The whole of this is an explanation given in after life of
that which he insensibly felt as a child. There was no
reasoning possible then. It was a wild tempestuous time,
full of giddy bliss, and the physical joy of being: and the
images he received from Nature partook of this wild and
even vulgar character, images undignified by any associa-
tion, made quiet by no thoughtfulness.

But (and here is another element in the education
Nature gives the child) in the midst of this wild extrava-
gance of boyish life with Nature, there were moments of
quietness in which a calmer beauty, of which he was then
unconscious, entered into his soul and took up there its
dwelling.

Looking back on them, he sees them as a part of that
great work by which the universe and the mind of Man
are wedded together. They are the result of that pre-
established harmony which God has set between His
thought in us and His thought in Nature. He calls them,
in lines as beautiful as they are profound,

> Those hallowed and pure motions of the sense
> Which seem, in their simplicity, to own
> An intellectual charm: that calm delight
> Which, if I err not, surely must belong
> To those first-born affinities that fit
> Our new existence to existing things;
> And, in our dawn of being, constitute
> The bond of union between life and joy.

By both were sown the first seeds of a deep love of Nature
which now began to take the place of a dim dread of her.
The quieter impressions remained as they were; the

common and vulgar joys through which the others were received slowly died out of the memory; but the impressions remained and their beauty. His mind became filled with solemn and lovely images; he linked those images to the places from which he had received them, and loved the places for their sake. In this way, year by year, Nature grew more dear, and with his love to her his soul grew into completer being.

It was thus the poet's education began. How it went on, I shall tell in my next lecture. But does it not do one good to read of it? How pure and fresh it is; how healthy and natural, how true to Nature and how near to God. For so ought always to begin, if possible, the building of the soul. Natural religion should go before spiritual; vague feelings of joy and calm in the presence of One whom we know not yet, but who knows us—in these best begins the religion which afterwards, in the sadness and trouble of life, teaches us to know that Presence in Nature as the Father in our hearts; in these best arises that spiritual life which, at first content with nature-worship, learns, when it has become sadly conscious of sin and sorrow, to love God as the Redeemer, and to trust Him as the Comforter.

## LECTURE VII

### WORDSWORTH—*continued*

THE simple ways in which the childhood of Wordsworth walked, and how he was taught by the rivers, woods, and hills, were spoken of in my last lecture. The education thus begun by Nature was carried on steadily, and I shall explain its further course to-day. It divides itself into two parts, the first period when the influences of Nature were unconsciously received; the second, when the new element of the relation of his own soul to Nature slowly introduced itself. For, becoming conscious of his own being, he became also conscious of its distinctness from the external world, and of the power and life which he was able to project from it over Nature—conscious, that is, of that action and reaction between the mind and the world without, the possibility of which was contained in the prearranged harmony which God had established between them. This point I shall fully speak of, and also how far this consciousness of the soul of its relation to Nature modified the continuous education which Nature gave him.

And throughout, and after nearly every point, I shall mark how the various lessons he learnt influenced or were likely to influence the poetic character of Wordsworth, the growth of his religious life, and those theological ideas which he held with regard to the relation of God and Man to the natural world.

Wordsworth begins the second book of the *Prelude* by a description of the tumultuous joy and eagerness of boyhood in its sports among a rich and varied scenery. Looking back in tranquil manhood to this unconscious time, he half sighs to think that these things are no more.

It tames our " pride of intellect and self-esteem of virtue,"
to think how little we can give

> to duty and to truth
> The eagerness of infantine desire.

So that an ideal of eagerness in pursuit of things, and a
respect for the enthusiasm which makes us unconscious of
self, are part of the indirect teaching which we receive
from Nature in boyhood.  They were two lessons which
formed part of his poetic training, for a poet is one who
is bound to lose himself in Beauty and Truth, and to see
things more eagerly than other men.  And they have
also their moral influence, for it inspirits a man who has
strength enough for self-restoration, to know in after-life,
in times of depression and pain, that he has once possessed
joy and force; for then he believes in their existence in
his nature, and works towards their recovery.  And this
is one of the continually recurring moral ideas of Words-
worth.  You will find it running through a hundred
poems.

But this kind of teaching that Nature now gave him
was not consciously received by the boy; nor was it direct,
but incidental.  It could not be consciously sought for;
but it came suddenly, in flashes of impulse in the midst
of holiday delights.  On Windermere were lovely and
lonely islands, and to these he and his companions rowed
in rivalry.  But when they landed and wandered among
the lilies or beneath the oaks or by the ruined shrine,
emulation, jealousy, and pride were insensibly tempered
by the stillness of the place, so that they did not care, after
a time, whether they had the crown of boyish fame or no.

It was such silent influences of Nature frequently
repeated that instilled drop by drop into Wordsworth's
being that " quiet independence of the heart," that
sense of

> The self-sufficing power of solitude,

so remarkable in him afterwards as man and poet.

Again, in the midst of noisy sport, a single, sharp
impression came, the voice of Nature, not in rebuke of

their delight, but in her desire to make herself felt, which stilled them for a moment into thoughtfulness. Once in St. Mary's nave the sudden song of the wren singing to herself, invisible, made one of those hushed surprises which no one can ever forget. Sometimes, pausing for a moment when racing home, the sound of streams among rocks and the " still spirit shed from evening air " made their presence felt in his heart. Sometimes, when the games were over, and the minstrel of their troop blew his flute alone on the island, and they lay resting and listening upon the lake, the whole scene entered into his soul:

> The calm
> And dead still water lay upon my mind
> Even with a weight of pleasure, and the sky,
> Never before so beautiful, sank down
> Into my heart, and held me like a dream.

He imputes the same experience to the boy, his playmate who lived by Winander, and of whom he tells in a famous passage. After describing him as in wild mirth he stood by the shore of the lake and blew hootings to the owls that answered till all the hills re-echoed—he marks how, suddenly, in the midst came a lengthened pause of silence. Then it was that the invisible quiet Life in the world spoke to him.

> Then sometimes, in that silence while he hung
> Listening—a gentle shock of mild surprise
> Has carried far into his heart the voice
> Of mountain torrents: or the visible scene
> Would enter unawares into his mind,
> With all its solemn imagery, its rocks,
> Its woods, and that uncertain heaven, received
> Into the bosom of the steady lake.

Those are the lines of which Coleridge said, " Had I met these lines running wild in the deserts of Arabia, I should instantly have screamed out—Wordsworth." But the deep meaning of them is, that there is in the material universe a spirit at work on us, to calm, to exalt, and to suggest to our boyhood thoughts which sleep within, like seeds, till future events develop them.

**H**

And now, accumulating from every quarter, these accidental impressions enlarged his sympathies till every day some new scene in Nature becoming dear, the conception of Nature as an organic Being, having a life beyond his, and existing in a direct relation to him, began, not to be realised, but to quicken in his mind.

A change then took place. Nature had been secondary in his life; his boyish sports were first, and she had intervened among them with these surprises. She was the seeker, he the sought. But now, he sought her directly for the pleasure she gave. She had conquered his unthinking pleasure in play and replaced it by the enthusiasm of herself. He did not know well why he sought her, but a trouble came into his mind, which drove him away from the sports of boyhood. They had been the props of the impressions he had received from Nature. But, behold, when the scaffolding was removed, there was the building, sustained by its own spirit, the building of the love of natural Beauty and Life, a house not made with hands. Hence, the trouble was the first trouble of a youth who was leaving boyhood and who had begun to realise consciously all he had learnt unconsciously. It was such a trouble as moved the waters of the Bethesda spring.

The sensibility of his soul to Nature now went directly and with known purpose to commune with her. It was like two lovers who had seen one another only at intervals meeting at last for daily communion. Every hour brought new happiness, because it brought new knowledge of the life of things. And the source of the knowledge was love, refined to intense watchfulness by desire. Formerly he had received large indefinite impressions, now he saw into the " transitory qualities " of things, such as, if I may explain the phrase by an illustration, the subtle changes in colour of the lime-tree leaves as summer draws on day by day from spring, or the difference of the sound of a brook in winter and summer, or the way in which a passing cloud will alter the whole sentiment of a landscape, or even closer still, the way in which a sudden stroke of life will enlighten a lonely place;

as when, in one of his own inimitable touches, he says of
a lonely mountain lake—

> There sometimes doth a leaping fish
> Send through the tarn a lonely cheer.

Running along with these numberless small impressions,
and derived from them, were " gentle agitations of the
mind " from observation of these manifold differences,
so that whatever came from Nature was answered by a
different but correspondent feeling, and that marriage
of the soul and the world began to grow towards its
fulfilment.

One might object that this minute habit of observance
would take away from the poet the power of receiving a
grand impression of the whole. On the contrary, when
the soul is freely receiving, and this sort of work is done
by the feeling, and not by the understanding, it prepares
the soul, by kindling and quickening emotion, for a
sublime impression. Nay more, since it brings the know-
ledge of particulars, it educates us for the moment when
the vast, single conception of the Whole dawns like a
sun upon the mind.

But this has its stages of growth in single impressions,
made by separate scenes of sublimity and calm, and
Wordsworth dwells on both. I would walk alone, he says,

> Under the quiet stars, and at that time
> Have felt whate'er there is of power in sound
> To breathe an elevated mood, by form
> Or image unprofaned; and I would stand,
> If the night blackened with a coming storm,
> Beneath some rock, listening to notes that are
> The ghostly language of the ancient earth,
> Or make their dim abode in distant winds:
> Thence did I drink the visionary power.

These moments were the origin of an ideal of sublimity.
In after life, we forget what we felt, but not *how* we felt
at such times: remembrance of the way in which we have
been impressed creates and supports the obscure sense of

a sublimity possible to the soul, to which with growing faculties the soul inspires—

> feeling still
> That whatsoever point they gain, they yet
> Have something to pursue.

To have such an ideal is in itself a kind of religion. And Wordsworth, in the *Excursion*, taking up the same point, shows how an ideal of sublimity, won in early life from Nature, will make a man impatient of any pettiness of temper or life, of any wanting in noble simplicity, of any want of directness, of any of those meannesses, which, though they seem only paltry, have their root in some foulness or other. Nor will he ever become basely content. He shall feel

> congenial stirrings late and long
> In spite of all the weakness that life brings—

however tranquil—

> Wake sometimes to a noble restlessness.

Correlative with sublimity is calm; it is the other side of the shield. The power which, in Nature, moves the mind to delight, and which arises from her inner order, made her hours of calm produce calm in him. And a certain love of calm in himself strengthened the impression. When, in early morning walks, he saw beneath him the valley sleeping in the lonely dawn—" How shall I seek the origin," he breaks out:

> Where find
> Faith in the marvellous things which then I felt?
> Oft in these moments such a holy calm
> Would overspread my soul, that bodily eyes
> Were utterly forgotten, and what I saw
> Appeared like something in myself, a dream,
> A prospect in the mind.

This was also destined to grow into an ideal, and it was necessary for his poetic work. One must have the power of compelling rest in the soul in order to work nobly. Nor is that self-control which can use passion and not be used by it, less needful for the man than for the poet. It is not the calm of indifference which we want in order to be great, but the calm which will and temperance produce in a nature capable of storm. The perfect moral work of life is done by him who has passion, but who subdues it to the workable point of heat.

From the time, now, that he had sought Nature directly, he had gained two things; a multitude of minute impressions awakening a multitude of thoughts: a sense of sublimity and of calm, which the work of his own soul was to change into moral ideals of them. So far the preparation for the grasp of Nature as a great whole had gone.

But something more was needed, *the influence of his own soul on Nature;* and this now began to be felt. Looking back, as he writes, on that time, he knew that his soul had been insensibly at work on the impressions Nature had given it. This was true, he thought, even of his infancy. The infant is frail and helpless then, yet he is

> An inmate of this active universe:
> For feeling has to him imparted power
> That through the growing faculties of sense
> Doth like an agent of the one great Mind
> Create, creator and receiver both,
> Working but in alliance with the works
> Which it beholds.

The lines re-illustrate the philosophic view of the distinctiveness of Nature and man on which I have dwelt, and in this mutual reaction of the two, and in having it, consciously in manhood, unconsciously in childhood, is the poetic spirit:

> Such, verily, is the first
> Poetic spirit of our human life,
> By uniform control of after years,
> In most, abated or suppressed; in some
> Through every change of growth and of decay,
> Pre-eminent till death.

In becoming conscious, then, of this interaction he first
began to be a poet.

Therefore he now knew that, unsubdued by the torrent
of natural glory and beauty poured into his heart, he
retained a plastic power to form and shape the images he
received.   Nay more, though his mind was still subservient
to Nature, it gave back a glory of its own to Nature:

> An auxiliar light
> Came from my mind, which on the setting sun
> Bestowed new splendour;
>                    And the midnight storm
> Grew darker in the presence of my eye.

Added to this was the power of imagination, which brought
into poetic relation remotely connected objects, and which
transferred his own enjoyments and passions to inorganic
natures.   Yet when he says that he did that, he feels that
he is partly untrue to his special view of the difference
between man and Nature;   and he says that this trans-
ference of himself to Nature was perhaps due to an excess
in the great social principle of life which naturally coerced
all things into sympathy—or, on the other hand, that he
did not really impose himself on Nature, but conversed
with things as they really were, with the enjoyments and
passions, that is, of Nature herself.   But however that
might be, the end of all this was, that what he had uncon-
sciously felt as a boy became at last a conscious possession;
he realised that all Nature was one great organic Being,
with whom he could commune through the means of love,
who directly communed with him, and whose ceaseless
prayer and anthem was the adoration and love of God.

> Thus while the days flew by and years passed on,
> From Nature and her over-flowing soul,
> I had received so much that all my thoughts
> Were steeped in feeling.   I was only then
> Contented, when with bliss ineffable
> I felt the sentiment of Being spread
> O'er that all moves and all that seemeth still;
> O'er all that, lost beyond the reach of thought
> And human knowledge, to the human eye
> Invisible, yet liveth to the heart.

> Wonder not
> If high the transport, great the joy I felt,
> Communing in this sort through earth and heaven
> With every form of creature, as it looked
> Towards the Uncreated with a countenance
> Of adoration, with an eye of love.
> One song they sang, and it was audible,
> Most audible, then, when the fleshly ear,
> O'ercome by humblest prelude of that strain,
> Forgot her functions, and slept undisturbed.

It is a wonderful picture of a youthful life—this young and solitary creature, living in communion only with the Being of the World, in a world which only lived to him and to God who sees the heart.

He had now reached his seventeenth year, and the results of his experience were these—he was conscious of the direct influence of Nature on him; of his own mind and the power it had to speak with and to answer Nature; and of both Nature and himself as living powers acting on each other. With these was united a vague sentiment of religion, which chiefly appeared in a simple, pure, and manly morality of life. This, he held, was the direct result of the work of Nature upon his soul, and looking back on his life then and afterwards, and summing up the result, it is to this early association with the beautiful and sublime things of the outward world that he traces the whole quiet, and faithful, and temperate character of his life, and of his self-training as a poet. The passage is long, but it is necessary to quote it, and it completes the history of his boyhood. It follows directly on the last quotation.

> If this be error and another faith
> Find easier access to the pious mind,
> Yet were I grossly destitute of all
> Those human sentiments that make this earth
> So dear, if I should fail with grateful voice
> To speak of you, ye mountains, and ye lakes
> And sounding cataracts, ye mists and winds
> That dwell among the hills where I was born.
> If in my youth I have been pure in heart,
> If, mingling with the world, I am content

With my own modest pleasures, and have lived
With God and Nature communing, removed
From little enmities and low desires,
The gift is yours; if in these times of fear,
This melancholy waste of hopes o'erthrown,
If, 'mid indifference and apathy,
And wicked exultation when good men
On every side fall off, we know not how,
To selfishness, disguised in gentle names
Of peace and quiet and domestic love,
Yet mingled not unwillingly with sneers
On visionary minds; if, in this time
Of dereliction and dismay, I yet
Despair not of our nature, but retain
A more than Roman confidence, a faith
That fails not, in all sorrow my support,
The blessing of my life; the gift is yours,
Ye winds and sounding cataracts! 'tis yours,
Ye mountains! thine, O Nature! Thou hast fed
My lofty speculations; and in thee,
For this uneasy heart of ours, I find
A never-failing principle of joy
And purest passion.

*Prelude*, Bk. ii.

He now passed, thus educated by Nature, out of her special guidance, and went to Cambridge as a student. It was a strange change from the solitary glen. He was excited, full of spirit and hope, and when he saw the turrets of the University rising in the distance, he felt his heart racing before him. He puts with one of his characteristic touches his own feeling into the place itself:

As near and nearer to the spot we drew
It seemed to suck us in with an eddy's force.

He entered, and was at once full of the blithe delight of a young fellow, fresh from the hills, to whom everything was new. "I was the dreamer, they the dream"—His new dress—and he became a dandy—the society, the lecture-rooms, the motley spectacle, the sound of frequent bells at night, the ante-chapel of Trinity where the statue stood—

Of Newton, with his prism and silent face,
The marble index of a mind for ever
Voyaging through strange seas of Thought, alone—

all dazzled him at first, and he forgot his early aspirations. But he soon returned to his more natural self, and felt even the more for this short forgetfulness how native were his poetic instincts. Prizes, examinations and their fame, for these things he had no care; and the little interests of the place were not great enough for one accustomed to the solemn and awful interests of Nature. He was not, he felt, for that hour nor for that place. And we must hold that he was right. Special gifts have special duties, and they override the duties incumbent on ordinary men. It might be the duty of this or that youth to read for a prize; it was Wordsworth's instinct, and the instinct may be called a duty, not to do so. It marks the strong and independent character of his mind that he felt so early in life, that the bent of his genius set him apart, and must be followed. The mountains had taught him wisdom, and he turned — even in the fen-country, and among men — to Nature again, and looked in her for universal things, and called on the earth and sky to "teach him what they might." And when they spoke he turned into himself, and asked what their revelations were in him, till he felt, as he had felt in his native glen, that they were in truth "visitings of the Upholder of the tranquil soul." And receiving these, he recognised with joy a new power in his own soul, and sending it forth to work on Nature, found in her life enjoyments and passions similar but not identical with his own.

To every natural form, rock, fruit, or flower,
Even the loose stones that cover the highway,
I gave a moral life: I saw them feel,
Or linked them to some feeling: the great mass
Lay bedded in a quickening soul, and all
That I beheld respired with inward meaning.
And that whate'er of Terror or of Love
Or Beauty Nature's daily face put on
From transitory passion, unto this
I was as sensitive as waters are

> To the sky's influence in a kindred mood
> Of passion; was obedient as a lute
> That waits upon the touches of the wind.
> Unknown, unthought of, yet I was most rich—
> I had a world about me—'twas my own;
> I made it, for it only lived to me,
> And to the God who sees into the heart.

> *Prelude*, Bk. iii.

Sometimes he betrayed his joy in all this by gestures, and those who saw him called it madness. And it was madness, he says—

> If childlike fruitfulness in passing joy,
> If steady moods of thoughtfulness matured
> To inspiration, suit with such a name.

Nor could that be well called madness in which there was so intense a development of what one might call the logic of the eye—

> For the bodily eye
> Amid my strongest workings evermore
> Was searching out the lines of difference
> As they lie hid in all external forms,
> Near or remote, minute or vast; an eye
> Which, from a tree, a stone, a withered leaf,
> To the broad ocean and the azure heavens
> Spangled with kindred multitudes of stars,
> Could find no surface where its power might sleep;
> Which spake perpetual logic to my soul,
> And by an unrelenting agency
> Did bind my feelings even as in a chain.

Is not that a splendid commentary upon the passionate minuteness of his natural description—" Could find no surface where its power might sleep? "

It was thus that Nature continued to exercise her power over him, and moulded even his university life. He was kept, by the continuance of her influence, from overwork, and from that tendency of a college career to lessen originality. At the same time, the lively society, the first clash of life with other men, lessened the somewhat overwhelming influence of Nature, and not only prepared him for his future interest in mankind, but stirred to life those germs of it which had been insensibly sown in the north. The idle life was also, I think, good for him; he wanted idleness and repose; there was no need for him to do anything but drift and have that " wise passiveness " which he afterwards recommends, but which he took then as unconsciously as a child. In these first months, then, he read the face of Nature, he read Chaucer, Spenser, Milton, he amused himself and rested—and since he was Wordsworth, he could not have done better.

But the time spent at Cambridge was not without its special influence: a human element, as I said, crept into his life. When, then, after eight months' absence, he returned to his mountain home, he found that certain changes had been wrought in his relation to Nature. He had a human-heartedness about the love he bore to objects lately the absolute wealth of his own private being. He had loved rocks and brooks and stars as one angel might love another—now human feelings and changes were connected with them, and a pensive shade stole over Nature. It was no longer only sublimity or calm which he felt, but something kinder, sweeter — an inner touch of love, delight, or hope. His human soul, awakened by life among men, began to wed Humanity to Nature, and out of that came the first emotional feeling of a personal religion. It was on a day when the hour of evening was " sober, the air untuned." It influenced him like the face of a friend in trouble, thrilling him through and through with love and pain. And in the air of this emotion, strength and comfort, which " he only knew he needed when they came," entered his heart, and with them came " inward hopes, and swellings of the spirit,"

> glimmering views
> How life pervades the undecaying mind—
> How the immortal soul with godlike power
> Informs, creates, and thaws the deepest sleep
> That time can lay upon her;
>
> *Prelude*, Bk. iv.

—the sense of the majestic strength of man if he will but

live in the "light of high endeavour," and the glory of the close that endurance wins.

The second religious impression was a deeper and more important one. It made a crisis in his life, and it is worth remarking that it came not as the first in the sombreness of evening, but in the freshness of dawn.

When he returned from Cambridge he had felt not only more human, but also an inner falling off; less fiery aspiration in his soul, some taint of the world, some touch of vanity and its corruption. He could not, as before, forget himself in Nature. But he was wrong in this regret. It was a backward motion, but had it not been, love of Nature could never have passed into love of Man. We must often reach the higher by going back a little, and Wordsworth's "boundless chase of trivial pleasure" was a necessary parenthesis in his education. Through it the image of mankind had room to creep into his heart, and in reaction from it he drew nearer to God. It was in the very midst of this light and thoughtless gaiety, returning from a rustic ball—just as impressions of calm and beauty came on his boyhood in the midst of careless sport—that his highest early revelation broke upon him. For often in these opposing currents of the life of Man—and Wordsworth's life was now a parti-coloured show of grave and gay—at a moment when the force of the currents being equal, calm ensues, we are surprised by the voice of God in the hush of exhausted excitement. It is then that Solitude and Nature do their work, and we never can forget the surprise. I quote the lines in which he describes this baptismal hour when he was consecrated to his lofty work. He is going home after a night of merriment:

> Magnificent
> The morning rose, in memorable pomp,
> Glorious as e'er I had beheld—in front
> The sea lay laughing at a distance; near
> The solid mountains shone, bright as the clouds,
> Grain-tinctured, drenched in empyrean light;
> And in the meadows and the lower grounds
> Was all the sweetness of a common dawn—

Dews, vapours, and the melody of birds,
And labourers going forth to till the fields.
Ah! need I say, dear Friend! that to the brim
My heart was full; I made no vows, but vows
Were then made for me; bond unknown to me
Was given, that I should be, else sinning greatly,
A dedicated Spirit. On I walked
In thankful blessedness, which yet survives.

This was the God of Nature speaking in solitude. But solitude is still more solitary, says Wordsworth, where it has a human centre, and he finishes his account of his vacation time by narrating a dull story of his meeting an old soldier in a lonely road, and how far more deeply the loneliness sank into his soul, and with benign power separated him from worldliness, when this appropriate human centre impressed it on his mind. That would not have been the case some years before. I note it now to show how his mind was veering towards interest in Man as well as in Nature.

The next great religious impressions received through Nature were made on him during his journey on the Continent, and were more distinctly connected with Man; one was sublime when he crossed the Alps, the other beautiful as he wandered through the Italian lakes. They were prefaced by a certain growth in his own soul; gladness and tenderness alike had made the air of thought more fine and pure. And further, the capacities of his own soul had now been so stirred that it began to assert itself as creator: the expressing power had begun to dawn.

It was then that, inspired with desire to see the larger forms of Nature, he went abroad. There his interest in Man was still further aroused, for he landed at Calais and went through France when the land was thrilling with the first youthful passion of the Revolution. He joined with the frank pleasure of youth in all the delight of the land, he felt the excitement of the ideas of the time even in the midst of the dark solitudes of the Chartreuse, he looked with the pleasure of a natural Republican on the quiet valleys of Switzerland where

men were free. But these things were but incidents in
the devotion he gave to Nature and in the interest with
which he watched his own soul working upon her. First,
in lighter scenery, it was only that fantastic pensiveness
which we all have felt that came upon him. There were
hours of delightful dejection, like flowers " gathered from
formal gardens of the Lady Sorrow." But these in turn
were mixed with others in which a different impression
came, not of the fancy, but wholly of the imagination.
He crossed the Alps, and swept downwards towards Italy
through the gorge of Gondo. There the stupendous powers
of the world of the higher mountains spoke one language
to him:

> The immeasurable height
> Of woods decaying, never to be decayed,
> The stationary blasts of waterfalls,
> And in the narrow rent at every turn
> Winds thwarting winds, bewildered and forlorn,
> The torrents shooting from the clear blue sky,
> The rocks that muttered close upon our ears,
> Black drizzling crags that spake by the wayside
> As if a voice were in them, the sick sight
> And giddy prospect of the raving stream,
> The unfettered clouds and region of the Heavens,
> Tumult and peace, the darkness and the light—
> Were all like workings of one mind, the features
> Of the same face, blossoms upon one tree:
> Characters of the great Apocalypse,
> The types and symbols of eternity:
> Of first and last and 'midst and without end.
>
> *Prelude*, Bk. vi.

The majesty and awfulness of the place seized on him
and ravished him beyond himself—he was lost in the
revelation. The same note is struck in the last verse of
the hymn of the spirits to Asia in the *Prometheus* of
Shelley:

> Lamp of Earth, where'er thou movest,
> Its dim shapes are clad with brightness,
> And the souls of those thou lovest
> Walk upon the winds with lightness,
> 'Till they fail as I am failing,
> Dizzy, lost, yet unbewailing.

That was something of Wordsworth's feeling. Nature came upon him, imagination rushed into union with Nature, and in the fierce ardour of their creative embrace within him he lost all consciousness of self. Shelley could have stayed there, did stay there; the passionate pleasure of being lost in the Spirit of Nature through love of it would have been enough for him. He would have kept all his life the memory of that hour of rapture, and felt it over and over again without ever subjecting it to thought. It was different with Wordsworth; having felt this wonderful emotion, and wholly lost himself in it at the time, he returned to it afterwards that he might discover its meaning. It is perhaps less poetical, it is certainly less characteristic of the pure artist to do this; but it is just as well that all poets are not like Shelley, and instead of contrasting the two methods to the disadvantage of either, we may be thankful to have the delight of both.

Afterwards, then, Wordsworth looked back on this experience, and saw in it the glory of the soul in union with God. It can usurp sense, and joining itself as brother to the invisible and spiritual world, enter into that infinitude of God of which Nature is the voice and symbol. This is its greatness, this power bespeaks that its true home is in the Eternal, that its rightful world is the world of aspiration, desire, undying hope,

> And something evermore about to be.

And in this the soul is blest in thoughts,

> That are their own perfection and reward,
> Strong in herself and in beatitude
> That hides her.

It was here, then, that through a sublime impression of Nature, the knowledge of the super-eminent power of the human soul which had been growing up in his mind was fixed and recognised.

Descending into serener beauty, a tenderer revelation came on him from a tenderer Nature. He felt the loveliness and calm of the world as similar to moral loveliness and calm. The things he saw were gracious as virtue and goodness, sweet as love or the memory of a generous deed, or those visitations of pure thought,

> When God, the Giver of all joy, is thanked
> Religiously in silent blessedness.

Nor were such scenes only analogous to moral qualities; he seems—and it is a thought which, though fantastic, has its ground in his theory—to imagine that characteristic types of landscape had the power of suggesting each their correspondent virtue to the mind, and of giving to the heart the sensation, as it were, of that virtue.

So far Nature acted directly upon him, but in all these new scenes, as in the previous case, it was not without his own action on her work. He asserts his right as poet and man to offer no slavish worship in this temple. He was not prostrate, overborne as Shelley was, by the splendour of Nature; he never let loose the right of his own mind to co-operate with her. He began to feel that she was the complement of his soul, as natural religion is the complement of spiritual. He drew on still further to the full conception of that marriage of the mind of Man to the external world which he afterwards fulfilled. Whatsoever he saw or heard or felt was but " a stream which flowed into a stream kindred " to it in his own mind:

> A gale,
> Confederate with the current of the soul,
> To speed my voyage; every sound or sight,
> In its degree of power, administered
> To grandeur or to tenderness—to the one
> Directly, but to tender thoughts by means
> Less often instantaneous in effect;

And the action of all, in Wordsworth's deep religion, was to lead him, at last, to reach the point marked out for him by God.

One might say that having now become so conscious of the power of his own soul, he would naturally begin to have interest in Man more than in Nature. Everything that was then happening—the expectancy of the whole world, the sudden waking of the nations, the wonderful emotion of mankind—was, one would think, calculated to place Man first. But Wordsworth grew slowly; he reached that point afterwards, but not now. Nature was still predominant in his life. "Among the more awful scenes of the Alps," he says in one of his letters, " I had not a thought of Man, my whole soul was turned to Him who produced the terrible majesty before me." It was the same in the peaceful beauty of the lakes. The happy, glorious time, and the universal cry for liberty that strengthened his interest in Man, were but an additional gleam of sunshine which enhanced his sense of the beauty of the world. He was touched, "but with no intimate concern." He did not seem to need any human joy, for

> the ever-living Universe,
> Turn where I might, was opening out its glories,
> And the independent spirit of pure youth
> Called forth, at every season, new delights
> Spread round my steps like sunshine o'er green fields.

This is the close of the early education given him by Nature. What had it done for him? It had made him conscious of the might and dignity of his soul. It had shaped the views and aspirations of his soul to majesty. It had made him realise a Soul of beauty and enduring life without himself, and he knew, from the power by which it moved him, that that Soul was God. It had awakened in him ideals of sublimity in which self was lost, of calm and " ennobling Harmony " in which moral strength was gained, of tenderness in which joy and hope were born; and the sublimity and calm and tenderness were God. It had so spoken to him that he had separated himself for his work, and felt that he was a dedicated spirit, and the Power that had done this through Nature was God. He had secured in this way a noble natural religion.

But Nature had not only educated his soul, it had also done service to his intellect. In scanning the laws and watching the forms of Nature, by seeing things at first hand, he had gained a standard for measuring the value of things and thoughts; and he could now tell, as if by intuition—what in books " carried meaning to the natural heart "—

> What is passion, what is truth,
> What reason, what simplicity and sense.

Again, her order, which made itself felt within him, taught him to reverence the abstract truths of science and filled them with the spirit of imagination.  As he worked at geometric science, he was able to clothe the nakedness of its austere truths with the hues and forms and with the spirit of the forms of Nature.  The same calm which was impressed on him by Nature, in which he felt the ineffable oneness of its life—a thought created by the calm of Nature, and yet its source—he found again in the permanent and universal sway of law, that type of the supreme existence of God in whom all discords, untouched by passion, were harmonised and mingled.

The laws themselves were also made more interesting by being taken into the world of imagination.  It did no harm to his work in the sphere of science, that when away from it he clothed its laws with life, and asked, as he wandered and wondered among the hills, how did it happen that these great genii came to serve Man?

Again, as the solemn and simple aspects of Nature gave grandeur to Man's mind, and wrought to kindle and exalt the soul—so the changes of Nature, rapid and forceful, which told of life, were powerful to stir and train the intellect:

> Like virtue have the forms
> Perennial of the ancient hills; nor less
> The changeful language of their countenances
> Quickens the slumbering mind, and aids the thoughts,
> However multitudinous, to move
> With order and relation.
>
> *Prelude*, Bk. vii.

And now that imagination and intellect were awakened, they could not rest content with Nature only, or their own work; they turned to seek their food in books.  And in this sphere also Nature intervened.  He thanks God that he was allowed to run wild, and saved by Nature from a forced and artificial education; that he was handed over to the natural training of wild Nature and took up things as the external world woke interest in them. He lit by chance on books, and faëry tale and legend seemed more in harmony with Nature than manuals of science. She taught him not to lose her in over-education, so that at least in his case old Grandame Earth had not to grieve that the

> Playthings which her love designed for him

were unthought of, that the flowers and the river-sides were neglected. The pupil of Nature, his was a larger, grander teaching than that which merely trains the understanding. Books were good, he thought, yet how much less good than that invisible lesson which comes to us through the visible universe, even to the wild and careless child. But who gives that lesson, whose is the voice that works so silently? In Wordsworth's deep religion it is God:

> A gracious spirit o'er this earth presides,
> And o'er the heart of man—invisibly
> It comes—to works of unreproved delight,
> And tendency benign, directing those
> Who care not, know not, think not what they do.
>
> *Prelude*, Bk. v.

And surely he is right. When we cram our children to the throat with mere instruction, or make them move over roads of learning like machines, we are really shutting out from them God and God's teaching; we are forgetting the wisdom that is gained by freedom; we are killing originality and the poetic spirit. True force and grandeur of character have their roots in early freedom to drink in other lessons than those that instructors give, and come in the child and man, as they come in the forest tree:

> Not by casting in a formal mould
> But by its own divine vitality.

We have no need to trouble ourselves to give so much to

our children, nor would we do so if we believed, as we ought, that God is educating them Himself, that,

> In the unreasoning progress of the world
> A wiser spirit is at work for us,
> A better eye than theirs, most prodigal
> Of blessings, and most studious of our good
> Even in what seem our most unfruitful hours.
>
> *Prelude*, Bk. v.

And lastly, as Wordsworth passed from childhood into youth, the books that most attracted him were naturally the poets; and Nature stepped in here also and gave him a deeper insight into them. It is a splendid thought of his when he describes how he, who had been intimate with Nature in his youth, sees something more in the work of the great masters of song than mere glittering verse: he sees in them great Nature herself. Their words are viewless winds which visionary power attends; darkness and all the host of shadowy things make their abode in their poetry. In it, things, as in Nature, weave and unweave, change in shadow and sunshine of thought. That is one of the finest thoughts of Wordsworth, and the finest thing ever said of poetry. But it was Nature who taught him to feel and say it. It completes the history of this early education of Nature, and I quote it in conclusion:

> Here must we pause: this only let me add,
> From heart experience, and in humblest sense
> Of modesty, that he, who in his youth
> A daily wanderer among woods and fields,
> With living Nature hath been intimate,
> Not only in that raw unpractised time
> Is stirred to ecstacy, as others are,
> By glittering verse; but further, doth receive,
> In measure only dealt out to himself,
> Knowledge and increase of enduring joy
> From the great Nature that exists in works
> Of mighty Poets. Visionary power
> Attends the motions of the viewless winds,
> Embodied in the mystery of words:
> There, darkness makes abode, and all the host,

Of shadowy things work endless changes,—there,
As in a mansion like their proper home,
Even forms and substances are circumfused
By that transparent veil with light divine,
And, through the turnings intricate of verse,
Present themselves as objects recognised,
In flashes, and with glory not their own.

*Prelude*, Bk. v.

# LECTURE VIII

## WORDSWORTH—*continued*

I FINISHED in my last lecture our discussion of the early education which Nature had given Wordsworth, and traced its influence on his poetry of Nature. But Wordsworth was as much, if not more, the poet of Man as of Nature, and the poetry of Man took in his hands as great a development as the poetry of Nature. My task to-day will be to show—always taking the *Prelude* as our guide —how the love of Man grew up in his soul.

I begin by a quotation from an Essay of Wordsworth's in *The Friend*, which resumes a great part of that which we have been saying in the two last lectures with regard to the teaching of Nature.

"We have been discoursing of infancy, childhood, boyhood, and youth, of pleasures lying in the unfolding intellect plenteously as morning dewdrops, of knowledge inhaled insensibly like a fragrance, of dispositions stealing into the spirit like music from unknown quarters, of images uncalled for arising up like exhalations, of hopes plucked like beautiful wild flowers from the ruined tombs that border the highways of antiquity, to make a garland for a living forehead; in a word, we have been treating of Nature as a teacher of truth, through joy and through gladness, and as a creatress of the faculties by a process of smoothness and delight. We have made no mention of fear, shame, sorrow, nor of ungovernable and vexing thoughts ; because, although these have been, and have done mighty service, they are overlooked in that stage of life when youth is passing into manhood, overlooked or forgotten. We now apply for succour, which we need, to a faculty which works after a different course; that faculty is Reason; she gives much spontaneously, but she seeks for more; she works by thought, through feeling; yet in thoughts she begins and ends."

The way in which Nature works, then, is this: She makes an impression on the poet's mind, an impression of calm, for example. That after a time insensibly touches his sympathies, and the thought of his father's serene old age or his child's peaceful sleep is awakened in his heart; and led on in this process of soothing thought now quickened by human tenderness, he thinks of other things that belong to the sphere of calm—of the quiet balance of the powers of his own being, of the mighty rest of God; and these in turn create the resolve to attain calm of heart, to reach, through endeavour and watchfulness, the peace which passeth all understanding. " This is Nature," as Wordsworth says, for I have used a different illustration from that he uses, " teaching seriously and sweetly through the affections, melting the heart, and through that instinct of tenderness, developing the understanding."

" Let, then, the youth go back, as occasion will permit, to Nature and solitude, thus admonished by reason, and relying on this newly acquired support. A world of past sensations will gradually open on him as his mind puts off its infirmities: and he makes it his prime business to understand himself. In such disposition let him return to the visible universe and to conversation with ancient books—and let him feed upon that beauty which unfolds itself, not to his eye as he sees carelessly the things which cannot possibly go unseen, but to the thinking mind; which searches, discovers, and treasures up, infusing by meditation into the objects with which it converses an intellectual life, whereby they remain planted in the memory, now, and for ever."

This was the point which Wordsworth had reached when we left him. He had realised, through the affections which Nature had awakened, his own reason in its relation to God and Nature, and he had felt the immense delight of redoubling the charm and sublimity of Nature by throwing upon it the force of his own mind. By this work the interest of more than half of his life was concentrated round the growth of his own being, and he studied himself with eagerness. But he did this in connection with the influences of Nature upon him, not in connection with the influences of Man. From these he was, at this time, nearly altogether free, or at least not consciously influenced by them. Nature and God were first, Man second.

But the transition from the contemplation of his own being as a man to the contemplation of mankind itself was an easy one, and it now began to be made. His residence in London, in the midst of this great hive of workers, laid upon his soul the weight of humanity: the residence in France which followed finished the work. Man became the first, and Nature the second.

This was the great change, and he was bound to explain it. It seemed sudden. Was it really so? And he looked back on his life in order to answer the question. To say that it was sudden would have contradicted his philosophy. For no one has seen more clearly than Wordsworth that the operations of the soul are gradual, that ideas do not spring to life at once, but grow, so that when they are recognised as conscious possessions we find that they have been already for years developing themselves. We recognise them when they flower; we are not conscious of them in shoot, and stem, and leaves. But when they have flowered, we can go back and trace their origin and their growth. And Wordsworth now made it his business to ask how this idea of Man as the centre of the universe grew up in his mind; and to describe the religious aspect it finally took.

Looking back, he sees that it began in his childhood, and that just as interest in his own being was stirred in him by the love of Nature, so in this case also it was the love of Nature which from the earliest times led him onwards to the love of Man. His childhood was passed among magnificent natural scenery, not so enchanting as the Eastern paradises which he describes, but in this far lovelier that, unlike their gorgeous landscapes, its sun and sky and seasons found Man a worthy fellow-labourer among them; free, working for himself, led by all that

surrounded him to individual and social ends of his own
frank choosing, and educated through the simple gracious
life of home. The men and mountains were at one in
noble character. For the beauty of a country is elevated
by the freedom of its inhabitants. No one can walk
through Switzerland without feeling that the long, almost
unbroken, liberty of soul which marked her people, that
the grave republicanism which marks them now, add a
new element of greatness to her scenery. It is something
to stand in the churchyard of Altdorf, as I stood two years
ago, and look up the lake glittering blue in the morning
light, and say to oneself, " This land has never been other-
wise than free." It made wretched to many the loveliness
of Italy, and Arnold records the feeling in his letters, to
think that man was daily degraded there by a vile oppres-
sion; it adds a new brightness now to her appealing
beauty to think that she is mistress of herself. So to
Wordsworth the meadows beneath Helvellyn were lovelier
far than the Paradise of Gehol, because, in one, the freedom
of Nature's heart was in harmony with human freedom;
in the other, her freedom was ceaselessly jarred by human
slavery.

It was in this free pastoral life that the roots of Words-
worth's love for Man struck deep. Shepherds were the
men who pleased him first, not the Arcadian shepherd,
nor such as Spenser fabled, but men " intent on little but
substantial needs," whose life was yet full of beauty that
the men had hearts to feel. In such a rude life imagina-
tion had much food from things connected with Man, for
there was continually presented to the child (however
unconscious of what he felt) the awful problem of the
seeming helpless subjection of mankind to the wild powers
of Nature. There was not a rock or stream or deep
valley in the hills which was not vocal, in the traditions
of the neighbourhood, with some tale of human suffering
or human daring. Wherever the boy roamed, Man and
his battle with Nature spoke to him. For here, where
he lived, it was no " smooth life" the shepherd led, no
piping by rivulets among sunny meadows, but a toilsome
struggle for existence among hills where the snow buried

sheep and shepherd, and where the winds howled around
the companionless man who daily waited on the storms.
Wordsworth saw him frequently when

> the lingering dews of morn
> Smoke round him, as from hill to hill he hies,
> His staff protending like a hunter's spear:

And followed him in thought throughout the day, till he
felt

> his presence in his own domain
> As of a lord and master, or a power
> Or genius, under Nature, under God,
> Presiding: and severest solitude
> Had more commanding looks when he was there.

In certain aspects he became to the imagination like an
elemental genius, seen through the thick mist a giant
form stalking on the hill; or as he stepped from the
shadow of the rock, glorified " by the deep radiance of
the setting sun; " or descried in distant sky,

> A solitary object and sublime,
> Above all height! like an aerial cross
> Stationed alone upon a spiry rock
> Of the Chartreuse, for worship.[1]

In this way Man became ennobled outwardly before his
sight, his heart was introduced

> To an unconscious love and reverence
> Of Human Nature.

" The sanctity of Nature was given to Man: " and yet

---

[1] It is interesting to find the origin of this passage in the *Prelude*
in Miss Wordsworth's diary.   She and her brother are walking to
Tarbert in mist and rain, and hear suddenly a loud hooting in the
fields.   " It came from a little boy whom we could see on the hill
between us and the lake, wrapped up in grey plaid.   He was pro-
bably calling home the cattle for the night.   His appearance was in
the highest degree moving to the imagination: mists were on the
hill sides; darkness shutting in upon the huge avenue of mountains;
torrents roaring; no home in sight to which the child might belong;
his dress, cry, and appearance, all different from anything we had
been accustomed to: it was a text, as William has since observed
to me, containing in itself the whole history of the Highlander's
life; his melancholy, his simplicity, his poverty, his superstition,
and, above all, that visionariness which results from a communion
with the unworldliness of nature."

this creature so glorified by the imagination was a man
with the most common, a husband, father, one who
worked, rejoiced and suffered; and there was as much
poetry in him, and his simple human relations, as there
was in his relations to the imaginative world of Nature.
It is one of Wordsworth's poetic customs to see things in
the ideal and the real, and to make each make the other
poetical. He places the lark in a "privacy of glorious
light," but he brings him home at last to his "nest upon
the dewy ground." It is the very thing that he always
does for Man.

This was the first step whereby love of Nature led to
love of Man. To some it may seem far-fetched, but
Wordsworth blessed God that in his childhood he started
with faith in the nobleness of Man, that he began with
an ideal of human nature. Were it otherwise, he says:

> And we found evil fast as we find good
> In our first years, or think that it is found,
> How could the innocent heart bear up and live!

It was well for him that he first saw his race through
beautiful and noble objects, that he read the first pages
of the book of man through Nature. For he had thus
a safeguard against too rapid a disillusion of the sanctities
of faith in human nature; he could resist

> The weight of meanness, selfish cares,
> Coarse manners, vulgar passions, that beat in
> On all sides from the ordinary world.

His face was turned towards the truth that though Man
is base and sinful, yet that he is greater than his baseness
and his sin; that though at times we may despise him
as the slave of his meaner self, yet that we must reverence
him as destined to triumph over it, and claim his inherit-
ance of Heaven. For true knowledge of human nature is
the product, first, of a lofty but undefined ideal of Man;
secondly, of that ideal disappointed; and thirdly, of that
disappointment corrected by the calm judgment of a life
which has never let love go, nor faith in a God who is the
Father and the Saviour of men.

This was the root of Wordsworth's love of Man.  But as we have seen, Nature was at first pre-eminent.  Man was only an " occasional delight, an accidental grace " among the passion and the rapture in which Wordsworth moved, inspired by the beauty of the world.  As he passed on from childhood and left its sports behind, and began to directly commune with natural objects, another step in this love of Man was made.  When an inner impulse first urged him to embody in words his feelings, Fancy awoke and linked to Nature and her scenes human sentiment and human pictures.  He could not see a grave without placing a widow there to weep; nor the fox-glove dismantled of its bells without thinking of a vagrant mother whose children, careless of her sorrow, played around her; nor a rock, water-wet with springs and sparkling in the sunshine, without fancying it the silver shield of a knight hung over his tomb, or an entrance into some fairy palace.  Thus " wilful and busy Fancy "

> Engrafted far-fetched hopes on feelings bred
> By pure imagination—turned
> Instinctively to human passions.

And though Wordsworth did not understand the cause of this, nor see that he was being slowly led towards that which he calls the point

> Of sound humanity to which our Tale
> Leads, though by sinuous ways—

he had now arrived through these earlier and later impressions at a vague ideal of Man, in which he unconsciously reverenced and loved him as sublime or good, and threw around his vague ideal the brilliant or pensive drapery of Romance.  It was at this stage in his progress that he went to Cambridge, and found in the university life a point of transition between his early remoteness from social life and the great human disturbance into which he was soon to plunge.  It was, as he calls it, something that resembled " an approach to human business, a privileged world within a world, a midway residence with all its intervenient imagery, that suited far better his visionary mind than to be thrust out at once into the conflicts of substantial life." He saw in it an image of the great world, and it touched him into that distant interest in humanity of which I have already spoken. But it was not at Cambridge, but afterwards, on his return to the mountains, that the interest took a conscious form. The power and the life which lay in Man, as the crown of Nature, broke upon him at the very moment when he became through Nature a dedicated spirit. You will remember the passage already quoted, in which he describes the deep religious impression made on him by an early morning, his first clear realisation of his mission in life. In an after passage in the *Prelude* he refers to the intense emotion of that hour. We then find that he not only realised himself, but also—in the excitement of the hour, being uplifted by the strength of the emotions that had wrought in him—rose into that conception of Man, as an ideal Whole, which a boy often conceives from history and poetry. Recall, he cries,

> My song! those high emotions which thy voice
> Has heretofore made known; that bursting forth
> Of sympathy, inspiring and inspired,
> When everywhere a vital pulse was felt,
> And all the several frames of things, like stars
> Through every magnitude distinguishable,
> Shone mutually indebted, or half lost
> Each in the other's blaze, a galaxy
> Of life and glory. In the midst stood Man,
> Outwardly, inwardly contemplated,
> As, of all visible natures, crown, though born
> Of dust, and kindred to the worm; a Being
> Both in perception and discernment, first
> In every capability of rapture,
> Through the divine effect of power and love;
> As, more than anything we know, instinct
> With Godhead, and, by reason and by will,
> Acknowledging dependency sublime.

With the dream of this conception in his mind he went for the second time to Cambridge, and there a more practical contact with Man dispelled his ideal. Vice and folly were thrust upon his view, and he lost much of his early faith in human goodness: small characters, and the little bustling passions and the isolated aims of university life broke up the large impersonated idea of mankind. Yet the ideal was not quite lost, for first, Antiquity threw its solemn shadow over the present college life, and filled it with the shapes of the great men of the past, by whose life human nature was dignified; and secondly, the very vice and folly he beheld showed how lofty must be the nature which could fall so low. Nor was it possible for him to think of human life in its career to sorrow and guilt without a deeper and similar sense of that old indefinite terror and dismay which once the storms and angry elements had wrought within him. He began to see mankind as he had seen Nature. Though then the old imaginative ideal of simplicity and joy in human life had passed away, yet, through this new awfulness, another and a vaster thought of Man began to grow, which took to itself from the terror in it a touch of sublimity.

The journey to the Continent, through France and Italy trembling with the first revolutionary excitement, added something to his interest in Man, and balanced, by the passing joy which he felt in that glorious time, the unhappy impression he had received at Cambridge. But Nature was still " sovereign in his mind " when he arrived in London. There his ideal was further shattered. The exposure of innocent life to shame, the degradation of womanhood, the tragic sufferings of men, the vast follies, the triviality mixed with horror, the vulgar thought, the mean interests, the sight of men unfaithful to their work—these broke down the unsubstantial palace of his ideal. But even as it was broken down, another building began to be raised. At his very first entrance a truer, loftier thought of Man arose—a tremendous sense of power as belonging to mankind—

> A weight of ages did at once descend
> Upon my heart—no thought embodied, no
> Distinct remembrances, but weight and power—
> Power growing under weight.

The "endless stream of men and moving things," the everyday appearance of the mighty city, and its wonder and awe, the "quick dance of colours, lights and forms," all the multitude of hurrying men, with every character of form and face, so that he could say, the face of every one

> That passes by me is a mystery;

the sight of the great men who moved mankind; the orator, Burke, as he thundered against abstract rights; the peace of the London night, when all was still, and the business of the coming day was yet unborn; these were the things which, in this "theatre and burial-place of passions," moved him to the heart with that passion of the poet which answers the appeal of mankind for his interest and his love.

Daily and hourly, knowledge of Man poured in upon him from a multitude of scenes, and he found (to his delight in the strength and glory of his youth) that he had power to grasp the whole. It was less knowledge of particular phases of human nature, than the impression of a vast spirit of humanity diffused through time and space, which he gained. It was the sense of all that had been done and suffered, was doing and suffering now in the great city and in the world, which brooded over him like a vast shadow and filled his soul with thought. A solemn, awful ideal of the majesty and power of humanity now began to replace the vague ideal of his boyhood, the shattered ideal of his youth. To him London now was thronged; and the comparison is one of those sublime flights of imagination of which Wordsworth alone among modern poets has been capable:

> With impregnations like the Wilds
> In which my early feelings had been nursed—
> Bare hills and valleys, full of caverns, rocks,
> And audible seclusions, dashing lakes,
> Echoes and waterfalls, and pointed crags
> That into music touch the passing wind.

And the analogy which he felt is not obscure, for Nature, like mankind, bears the traces of a suffering past. Every rock-strewn valley tells of centuries of endurance and agony from storm and frost and lightning, in the rent channels of its streams and in the shivered peaks above it. And if in the past Nature has suffered, there is no moment of the present which does not tell of its intense activity; we cannot linger by the sea or in the woods without an impression, almost irritating, of unmitigated work and waste and reproduction. The same feelings as these were Wordsworth's in the city, when he passed through the forest, and wandered by the ocean, of humanity.

And as he had received higher ideas of God in spite of Nature " red in tooth and claw," and seen love underneath its awful forces and the apparent ruin that they worked; so in the city, owing to this early training, he was able, in spite of misery and guilt, to grasp the higher view of mankind, and to love mankind. He dwelt upon the real, but it led him to a new ideal. He saw what Man was, went down into the depths of his vice and guilt, and yet his trust in that which mankind might become was not overthrown. And when he turned from the darker to the lighter side, he saw that the Divine in Man was still Divine, nay, more beautiful even from the gloom through which it flashed to speak of Heaven in the hearts of men.

One more sublime idea came upon him and exalted the thought of Man. It was the idea of his unity. There was one Brotherhood held in one Father,—

> One Spirit, over ignorance and vice
> Predominant, in good and evil hearts:

one conscience shared by all alike, " as one eye for the sun's light." In this idea, among all the confusion of men, and whirl of good and ill, Wordsworth found rest, and in the rest and the blessedness of it he found God, and saw Him as the Master of mankind. He had reached the third stage in our thought of Man of which I spoke, when the disappointment we suffer from the overthrow of our youthful ideal of Man is accepted and corrected.

Thus from his boyhood, his thoughts—

> by slow gradations had been drawn
> To human-kind and to the good and ill
> Of human life—.

Nature had led him on; through her he had found the love of his race. But still, though the love of Man was growing day by day, it had not as yet reached that point at which it became predominant. He still was able to fly from humanity to her, to find refuge in her mighty calm from the guilt and anarchy of men.

> The world of human-kind outweighed not hers
> In my habitual thoughts; the scale of love
> Though filling daily, still was light, compared
> With that in which *her* mighty objects lay.

And for a short period in this year, 1791, he went to Wales and revived and sanctified his soul by communion with the hills. But the enthusiasm of Humanity, once awakened, is not a passion that goes to sleep again, and now the songs of liberty and the glory of the efforts France was making rang with a more alluring murmur in his ear. He was irresistibly drawn to the theatre of the Revolution, where the great questions which most deeply move the race and all their passions were playing the first act in that mighty drama in whose development we are now involved. To this, and the questions it involves, I shall devote my next lecture.

# LECTURE IX

At the beginning of these lectures we traced that which is called the Poetry of Man from Pope to the close of the life of Cowper. We found in his poetry a number of new ideas on the subject of mankind, the main characteristic of which was, that they all rested on the thought of an universal mankind, which in itself supposed the equality of all men in certain realms of thought and act. The ideas were new and revolutionary, but in Cowper they took no clear form. They floated in solution, they were not crystallised; they were the product of insensible not recognised influences of the time; mere green shoots of things which were to become mighty trees; the substance in faith of things hoped for, the evidence of things not seen; sparks of a kindling fire scattered only here and there, but full of a life whose first property was the will and the power to devour things too old and too corrupt to live. No one suspected then that they would burst into flame with such accumulating rapidity; but a few years only had passed by when they rose into a conflagration which, in the French Revolution, ran over the European world. In England the fire did not fall upon the State, but its inspiration, and the passionate emotion which attended it, fell upon the poets; and out of the hearts of Coleridge and Wordsworth the poetry of universal Man, of freedom, of equal rights, of infinite promise, of the overthrow of tyranny, leaped full-grown into a manhood which has never endured decay. It is the history of its influence on Wordsworth's mind which we have now to trace and to explain.

We have seen that this development of the poetry of Man in Wordsworth was preceded by that of the poetry of

Nature. I have worked out that in the previous lectures, and an astonishing growth it is—so astonishing in comparison with the work on the same subject done by Cowper, Crabbe, and Burns, that it seems, at first sight, inexplicable. But the first explanation of its rapidity is one already alluded to in the history of the growth of the poetry of natural description. It was in reality no swift creation, but the flowering of a plant that had already clothed itself with leaves and had nothing more to do but flower. It is true that the whole plant was covered almost in an instant with a mass of flowers, and their extraordinary richness of flowerage needs a further explanation. It is supplied when we realise that the long European movement which so suddenly took form in the French Revolution had reached in Wordsworth's early life that point of expansion which only needs a touch to cause the outburst. For at such a time there is that profound but latent excitement in which the minds of the poets, who are the first to feel excitements, become swiftly creative on all subjects within their range; when the work of a century is often done in a year. Supply a new and quickening element to the soil of the poet's thought, let the air which it breathes become nipping and eager, and things which have only been in leaf within him will cover their every spray with flowers.

One more explanation of this apparent rapidity is that the revolutionary movement contained within it a particular excitement on the subject of Nature. It took form in France in Rousseau's love of wild nature, in his thought that Nature was wiser, simpler, and greater than Man; but in him it was mixed with the ugliest imposition of his own diseased feelings on Nature. It took form in Germany in the songs of the young poets who stormed and raged in verse till Goethe, who had himself in his youthful time out-thundered the others, raised his tranquillising head above the waves. It had been growing into form for the last hundred years in England; and we find that, partly influenced by Rousseau, it preferred, shortly before Cowper, the wild and lonely landscape in which men could feel sentimental; next, it preferred the wilder and lonelier scenes for their own sake, and having felt them profoundly, it then became connected with the poetry of Man. The poets transferred their love of this wild nature to the men who lived in it, and looked on them as certain to be nobler and more independent than they could be in cities and the artificial world. It was there we ought to seek for the primæval and pure feelings of men: and Wordsworth, in the love which he bore to the shepherds, and the honour he paid to his own dalesmen, was following up to its legitimate conclusion that excitement on the subject of wild nature which was now one of the elements of the European disturbance.

We have thus been led, in thinking of the revolutionary movement as it bore on the idea of Nature, to the very point at which we left Wordsworth in the last lecture, when he had been led by the love of Nature to the love of Man. He had arrived, in solitude, and following his natural individuality, at the same point to which the world was being led by its new impulse, but the impulse had of course its insensible influence upon him. He was now fitted to become a part of it, and to consciously join in it. He had been led by the love of Nature to the love of the simple men among whom he lived. Passing into the world and mingling with men, he carried with him the teaching of Nature, and applied it to his conception of mankind. The self-investigation that Nature had forced upon him; the sense of the pre-eminent dignity of the human soul that he had learnt from her; and the previous conception he had formed of Nature as One, led him to investigate human nature, to recognise then its pre-eminent dignity, and finally to see mankind as One Being whose life and rights and powers and place in the world, whose origin and whose destiny he was above all bound to study. The revolutionary idea of one universal humanity began to germinate in his mind. A multitude of vague, formless thoughts on this subject were floating in the air. He breathed them, but as yet neither he nor any one had been able to realise them, for they were not made clear by being arranged under a few leading thoughts.

It was this which the French Revolution did for him and for the world. It gave sudden, clear, and terrible form to the long-prepared ideas of Europe; it placed the movement in which all had been sharing on lines on which it could run along to a known end. It did the work of the Prophet for the world; it gave voice to the voiceless passion of a million hearts. It said, Man is one and indivisible, and it attempted to carry out that idea and all its resulting thoughts in politics and society. How far it had anything to do with Christianity, and how it influenced Wordsworth, is the subject of my lecture.

It did not, as I have hinted, come on Wordsworth unprepared. He was himself a natural republican. He had been born in a poor district, in a primitive homely corner of English ground, and he had rarely seen, during his schoolday time, the "face of one vested with respect through claims of wealth or blood;" and when he passed to the university it was, he says, one of its benefits that it held up to his view something of a republic. All stood there on equal ground, men were brothers there in honour; distinction lay open to all alike, and wealth and title were less than industry and genius. Moreover, he had learnt obedience to the presence of God's power in the sovereignty of Nature; and again, fellowship with venerable books had sanctioned—

> the proud workings of the soul
> And mountain liberty.

It could not be, he says—

> But that one tutored thus should look with awe
> Upon the faculties of man, receive
> Gladly the highest promises, and hail
> As best, the government of equal rights
> And individual worth.

And to this natural republicanism he traces his first indifference on the outbreak of the Revolution. It did not seem so wonderful to him as the rest; for he had breathed unconsciously its air from the beginning. He was scarcely dipped at first, he says, into the turmoil, and the result was that he then possessed a sounder judgment than those who lived in the full rush of the excitement. Even afterwards when, having fully shared in the excitement, his mind subsided, he recovered quickly the cooler judgment he had possessed; and for a long time, when other men in England despaired, retained his faith in freedom in spite of the Terror. He had never been swept upwards on the shore so violently as others; he never was swept back to far as others in the reflux of the wave.

At the same time, and this is important for the comprehension of Wordsworth, there was a distant conservatism in his nature, that which belongs to the artist and poet who love the past for its romance, or for the nobleness it once possessed. In the very midst of earnest dialogues with Beaupuis in the forests of the Loire, his imagination carried him away from the turbulent present; and he saw the woods full of the forms of old Romance, that Romance the Revolution was destroying. Nor could he be unmoved when things, which had sacred or chivalrous associations growing round them like ivy round a ruin, were desecrated by the destroying element in the Revolution. Hence arose a conflict in his mind between delight in new-born freedom and its overthrow of corrupt states, and his sorrow for the many things which, once the origin of high emotions, went down in the same shipwreck. But the conflict itself was productive of that mental and imaginative excitement in which fine poetic work is done; and the slight tinge of conservatism acted as a kind of sobering restraint on the imagination, so that his sanity as a poet of Man was preserved in a time of furious excitement. And again, the imaginative work his poetic temper wrought around the old things of the past—a convent, a *château*, a hermitage—served also to balance the revolutionary passion.

> Imagination, potent to inflame
> At times with virtuous wrath and noble scorn,
> Did also often mitigate the force
> Of civic prejudice, the bigotry,
> So call it, of a youthful patriot's mind;
> And on these spots with many gleams I looked
> Of chivalrous delight.

But these feelings were only slight weights in the opposite scale. His hatred of absolute rule, and of the barren pride and oppression of the *noblesse,* and his longing for the redemption of the people at almost any cost, grew till they outweighed everything else, and in the first half of his artist-life his republican ideas were always predominant. Living in these ideas, and in the excitement of that contest in his own mind which I have pointed out, his work was marked by a wonderful freshness and life. In the second half the contest ceased—he was shocked back into conservatism; the little germ of it in him grew into an overshadowing tree under whose shade ideas died. Maxims and formulas replaced them, and, being essentially unpoetical, they all but killed his poetic nature. With the passing away of his revolutionary ideas, passed away the divine spirit of song, the strength of his thought, the majesty of his style, the emotion which thrilled through his verse and gave the kindling impulse to his style. He became pedestrian and contemplative, and we can no longer say of him, that he spoke *non verba, sed tonitrua.*

Nor is it difficult to account for this. The poet who is now to say great things of Nature or of Man, who is to be more than the mere describer of Nature, or the mere analyser of human nature, produces nothing worthy if he be not at heart influenced by the larger republican ideas.

To one holding no longer the great ideas, and feeling no longer the passions embodied in the words, Liberty, Equality, Fraternity, Nature could not speak as she did of old. For she is, to her core, republican. It is by the consent of all, and by its full value being given to the work of each, that her great community exists and moves and grows. Each thing, bird, and brook, and tree, sings and flows and clothes itself with its own beauty, by its own divine vitality, and at its own sweet will; all have equal rights in sun and earth, in rain and dew; all choose freely the dwelling-place most fitted for their self-development, and no one says them nay; and the seeming violations of this are nothing as against the rule, and indeed belong to the rule. All are brothers one of another and live and die for one another, and those things which have the mastery, like the sun, have it because they give away their life to others. They rule because they are the best givers.

And she deals with us with the same republicanism. We turn from the oppression of the world, from the selfishness of caste and the exclusiveness of wealth, to the blessed equalities of Nature; and find comfort in the knowledge that sunlight and rain fall as richly on the poor as on the wealthy, that her beauty is poured out on all, that she does not reserve the glory of the sunrise for the cultivated classes, nor the freshness of the dew for the nobility. It was this spirit of freedom, of the brotherhood of universal love, of unlimited life and beauty bestowed on all, contradicting by silent and hourly act the theories of the Tory, which strove in vain in later years to recover its early power over Wordsworth. He could not receive its teaching, and his poetry of Nature decayed as his life decayed.

As to the poetry of Man, it suffered still more. For in what high vein can he write in whom the spirit of prophecy is replaced by the spirit of mere teaching, infinite hope for Man by melancholy moaning over his fate, belief in the future by belief in the past? These are not the things which kindle the life of song, but depress it; they throw no consecrating light, but gloom, upon the landscape of Man; the sorrow born of them does not humanise the soul, but shuts it up within itself—and Wordsworth's verse suffered from their presence in his mind. He ceased to give voice to the deepest longings and hopes of men who cared for Man; and the poet loses the very breath and impulse of song when men, listening to his words, no longer send back to him a wave of sympathy and joy.

It is most pitiful when the poet, whose highest business is to hope and prophesy for Man, gives himself up to the melancholy pipe, and hymns only his own sorrow and the sorrow of the race by the riverside of time, as some of our modern poets do. There is no enduring life in such

poetry, and so far as Wordsworth fell into despair of the
Present and regret of the Past, his poetry lost its power
and its life. He was saved from the worst form of
this evil by that calmer judgment of which I spoke,
which enabled him to resist the full force of the shock he
received; but he was chiefly saved by his Christianity,
for in the belief in a redeeming God and in a divine
future he could still abide in hope, and live in faith of
a diviner freedom, for the race. But he was only partly
saved, for in rejecting the primary thoughts of the
Revolution he rejected half the ideas of Christianity. If
Christianity has any politics, they are democratic. It is
very well to say that it has been the servant of tyrants
over the body and the soul, because it has been made such
by priests and kings. But the reason is not far to seek.
They saw that it was the most dangerous element in the
world for them and their power, and their one effort has
been to prove that it was upon their side. But they
could not do this without denying or travestying its
primal ideas, and this they set themselves to do. They
took out of it its universality, its love, its socialism; its
proclamation of spiritual equality and of equal rights and
duties before God; its contempt for wealth, its hatred
of oppressors; its love for the poor, the ignorant, and
the low-born. And they made an aristocratic, exclusive,
oppressing phantom of it, and said to the world, believe
in this, or you are lost for ever. And men not only
believed in it, but believed that it was Christianity. It
followed that when the thoughts of the Revolution swept
away the political and ecclesiastical Christianity, men
cried out that Christianity itself was dead and buried
for ever. But it was not so. It rose again into a new
life; it found its true home among the new ideas; it
showed, as it grew, that it was not that thing which
men had long believed it to be; but the supporter of
freedom, of equality, of brotherhood, the most real force
in this world against tyranny and superstition, the asserter,
nay, the creator of the idea of an universal humanity,
and of all the thoughts which are the children of that
idea and of that of an universal Father. It is one of

the most distinctive marks of Christianity that it has never failed to commend itself—not as a dogmatic system, but as a spirit which influences by great thoughts and stirs deep emotions—to free states. It is equally characteristic of it when it has been degraded by despots into a political engine, and treated by the people as such, to rise out of its degradation and overcome the popular hatred, and re-assert itself, undecayed, and with fresh hopes in its eyes, as the religion of Democracy. Even in France this was the case; in proportion as the political work of the Revolution grew firm, its irreligious work decayed. The Christian Church found its life renewed in republicanism; and if France is now un-Christian, that is not due to republicanism, but to the ceaseless despotism which, prevailing under various forms to the present hour in France, has again undone the religious work of the Revolution, and again travestied Christianity, so that men must hate it as an enemy.

If there is one thing which above all we need now, it is that there should be some who should boldly say that a Christianity which denies the root thoughts of the Revolution is not Christianity at all, but an odious idol which takes its name. Only we must also say that Christianity is more than these thoughts; that it takes in, for example, not only the rights of men, but as Mazzini said, hitting fairly the great omission of the Revolution, the duties of men as the masters and the limits of their rights. With this addition—it being understood that I speak here of Christianity in its relation to the whole of mankind as a social being, not in its relation to personal feelings and wants, which forms a separate study—the leading ideas of Christianity are the same as the leading ideas of the Revolution, only in the one case they are applied in the religious, in the other in the political sphere: or, to express it otherwise, the revolutionary ideas are the Christian ideas applied to the relation of men to one another, and to the state.

But we must look further into this thought, for it enables us at once to show the theology that naturally belongs to Wordsworth's poetry of Man. " The Revolution," says De Tocqueville, " had no peculiar territory, it was not made for France alone, but for the world, and its result was in some sort to blot out of the map all the ancient frontiers. In spite of laws, traditions, character, and language, it brought men together on a common ground, changed enemies into compatriots, and formed above national peculiarities an intellectual country common to all, of which all men of all nations could become citizens." That is as true of Christianity as of the Revolution, if we change the word intellectual into spiritual; because both started from the one idea of a common humanity which made all men brothers, and therefore claimed for all men equal rights to freedom, to self-development, and to the enjoyment of the common gifts of the earth and sky. Both Christianity and the Revolution built their foundation on human nature itself.

"It brought together," De Tocqueville continues, " nations which scarcely knew one another, and united them by interests common to the race. It was disengaged from every special bond to a people or a form of government, or a society, or an epoch, or a race; it had no particular national end, no special French aim: its end was the general rights and duties of all men in political and social matters." That also was as true of Christianity as of the Revolution, if we leave out political matters with which Christianity did not directly meddle; and it is true of both, because they started alike from the one great thought, that there was only one nation, the nation of mankind, and that all its citizens were bound to sacrifice themselves for one another. In Christ, there is neither Jew nor Greek, German, French, or Englishman, but the one universal humanity which is all, and in all, and in which all men are one, equal, free, and brothers.

The ideas are the same in both, and whether politically, socially, or spiritually applied, they are Christian ideas. The difference lies in this, that the ideas of the Revolution were applied only to Man as Man, the Christian ideas sought for a higher unity than the mere basis of a common humanity. They found it in the common Fatherhood of

God and in the union of all men in the humanity of
Christ; and until the ideas of the Revolution, as they
have sometimes done, complete themselves in those two
higher thoughts, they will fail to do their work. They
cannot conquer of themselves that selfishness in man
which supports exclusiveness, ensures oppression, and
hates the freedom which equalises men. They cannot
prevent revolution from ending in despotism.

Naturally, along with these great thoughts of an uni-
versal mankind, of natural equality, of the brotherhood
of the race, were two other lines of thought—one which
went forward with passion to overthrow all institutions
which repressed the growth of Man or kept him in any
slavery; another which went forward with equal passion
to prophesy a glorious future for mankind—and in both
these lines of thought, Christianity and the Revolution
were at one. They were both the work of God in the
hearts of men, and they both became leading poetical
ideas in the new poetry of Man in England.

These were the principles of the Revolution, and the
great religious English poet took them up and supple-
mented them at once with their analogous Christian
ideas. Wordsworth could not help it; he did it almost
unconsciously. He found the doctrine of an universal
Man and an universal brotherhood in the doctrine of an
universal Father. He saw in God the source of the
rights of men to equality and liberty. It was God who
was the avenger of slavery, the vindicator of Man against
the evils of caste, of enforced ignorance, poverty, and
despotism over the bodies or souls of men; and he looked
forward through God, because He was eternal Justice
and Love watching over Man, to a glorious time of
universal joy and mutual love, when the race should be
regenerated. It was he who made the poetry of Man in
England not only revolutionary but theological.

It was thus the Revolution came on the hearts of
young and imaginative and religious men in England.
But we, who live upon the broad river of its thought, can
scarcely realise what it was to men when first it broke,
a living fount of streams, from its rock in the desert,

to quench the thirst of those who longed, but knew not, till it came, for what they longed. We who live in times which, though not dull, are sad coloured, can scarcely imagine the glory of that awaking, the stream of new thoughts that transfigured life, the passionate emotion, the love and hatred, the horror and the rapture, the visionary glories, the unutterable hopes, the sense of deliverance, the new heavens and the new earth, brimful of promise, which dawned on men:

> Before them shone a glorious world
> Fresh as a banner bright, unfurled
> To music suddenly.

In that early morning of hope, the love of liberty seized on men with a power, almost a violence, which prophesied a reaction, and forced itself forth in the young in violent poetry. I have already spoken of the uncontrolled and tempestuous verse of Coleridge on this subject. In his view also it was God who had awakened liberty. Freedom in France

> From the Almighty's bosom leapt
> With whirlwind arm, fierce minister of love.

Southey and Lloyd felt the same; vague expectations, wild schemes, flitted through their minds; they projected a socialist communion on the Susquehanna to which they gave the name of Pantisocracy, where all things were to be in common, and the " cluster of families, bound together by congenial tastes and uniform forms rather than in self-depending and insulated households," were to solicit their food from daily toil, a thing which De Quincey says might have been fortunate for Coleridge. But none felt the enthusiasm of the time more intensely, nor expressed it more nobly than Wordsworth. He was the true human poet of the time. He felt every pulse of the movement in his own heart, and responding to that he felt—

> From hour to hour the antiquated earth
> Beat like the heart of man.

He describes its effect in the *Excursion* on a sorrow-stricken, lonely man. He was roused from his grief by the crash of the Bastille, and from the wreck rose a golden palace, as it seemed, of equitable law and mild paternal sway.

> The potent shock
> I felt: the transformation I perceived,
> As marvellously seized as in that moment
> When, from the blind mist issuing, I beheld
> Glory—beyond all glory ever seen,
> Confusion infinite of heaven and earth,
> Dazzling the soul. Meanwhile, prophetic harps
> In every grove were ringing, " War shall cease;
> Did ye not hear that conquest is abjured?
> Bring garlands, bring forth choicest flowers, to deck
> The tree of Liberty."—My heart rebounded;
> My melancholy voice the chorus joined;
> —" Be joyful all ye nations; in all lands,
> Ye that are capable of joy be glad!
> Henceforth whate'er is wanting to yourselves
> In others ye shall promptly find—and all
> Enriched by mutual and reflected wealth
> Shall with one heart, honour their common kind."

He was reconverted to the world in the general joy. He haunted all assemblies where busy men, inspired with universal hope, met to unite nations. In the victory of mankind over wrong he found his faith in God again. He returned to public worship, and felt a new meaning in the Hebrew Prophets when they thundered against oppression, when they foretold a reign of peace.

Nor when Wordsworth describes its effect upon himself is he less enthusiastic—

> O pleasant exercise of hope and joy!
> For mighty were the auxiliars that then stood
> Upon our side, we who were strong in love!
> Bliss was it in that dawn to be alive,
> But to be young was very heaven!—Oh! times
> In which the meagre, stale, forbidding ways
> Of custom, law, and statute, took at once
> The attraction of a country in romance!
> When Reason seemed the most to assert her rights,

When most intent on making of herself
A prime Enchantress—to assist the work
Which then was going forward in her name!
Not favoured spots alone, but the whole earth,
The beauty wore of promise, that which sets
(As at some moment might not be unfelt
Among the bowers of paradise itself)
The budding rose above the rose full blown.
What temper at the prospect did not wake
To happiness unthought of? The inert
Were roused, and lively natures rapt away!
They who had fed their childhood upon dreams,
The playfellows of fancy, who had made
All powers of swiftness, subtlety, and strength
Their ministers,—who in lordly wise had stirred
Among the grandest objects of the sense,
And dealt with whatsoever they found there
As if they had within some lurking right
To wield it;—they, too, who, of gentle mood
Had watched all gentle motions, and to these
Had fitted their own thoughts, schemers more mild,
And in the region of their peaceful selves;—
Now was it that both found, the meek and lofty
Did both find, helpers to their heart's desire,
And stuff at hand, plastic as they could wish:
Were called upon to exercise their skill,
Not in Utopia, subterranean fields,
Or some secreted island, Heaven knows where!
But in the very world which is the world
Of all of us,—the place where in the end
We find our happiness, or not at all!

That was written in 1805 as he looked back on all he
had felt, and the enthusiasm of the time is not dead in
its noble verse. It was a dream, but it is a dream which
hour by hour is fulfilling itself; and dream or not, it
did a mighty work on Wordsworth. It built him into a
man; it added the enthusiasm of Man to the enthusiasm
of Nature; it took him away from contemplation of his
own soul to live in the hopes, to proclaim the faith, to
seek the love of mankind; it gave him the impulse to
write some work which should give form to the faith he
now possessed in the glory of the future, and in the
majesty of the powers, of Man. It led him all his life

long—even when his Conservatism got the upper hand—
to be the champion of liberty, the hater of oppression
in the present—however in his imaginative Toryism he
might glorify the past. It made him the singer of simple
life, of honest manners, of poverty and its sorrows, of
the honour of humanity in all ranks—it taught him to
see the face of God in every man.

It gave, De Quincey say, " to the whole system of his
own thoughts and feelings a firmer tone, and a sense of
the awful *realities* which surround the mind," of the
awful sorrows and guilt and the still more awful goodness
which belong to Man in times of profound emotion, and
underlie his nature always. And in this new and lurid
but absorbing light, the passion for Nature was quenched.
It reawoke afterwards, and how, we shall hereafter see;
but at present, the destiny of Man, his origin, his duties,
his rights, his possibilities, the agony of his battle, and
the God with him—these were all in all to Wordsworth.
He saw through a glass darkly, he only knew in part,
but he had put away childish things for ever. He had
entered on the dignity and sincere thinking of matured
manhood. He was now trained not only to be the
revealer of Nature, but also the Poet of Man.

THE Revolution with which Wordsworth came into contact in France made a revolution in his mind. It carried him forward from a life with Nature to a life with Man. I discussed last Sunday some of the ideas that seized on him, and I traced their relation to theology, and their effect on Wordsworth. I propose to-day to continue the subject, and to connect what is to be said, partly with Wordsworth's life in France during 1791-92, and partly with his poetry.

We have seen that in 1789 the influence of Nature was predominant; but after his stay in London, where he was brought into closer contact with mankind in mass, the revolutionary movement sucked him into its whirlpool with amazing force, and shortly after Louis XVI. had taken the oath of fidelity to the new Constitution, he went to France to find the whole nation mad with joy. At first his ardour for freedom was more a sentiment than one of those profound convictions which create an enduring passion. In the guise of an enthusiast, he made a relic of a stone picked up where the Bastille had stood; but things of this kind seemed to touch him less than the sentimental paintings in the Louvre. He was not as yet conscious of the power which had begun to move within him. But, passing on to live in Orleans, the passion of the time soon developed it. On his arrival, he haunted society where politics were tabooed; but he was soon wearied, and withdrew to a noisier world.

At first he associated chiefly with the officers stationed in the city, who were bent on restoring the old régime, their only wish being to undo that which had been done. One among them, however, who became his special friend, was of a different type, and his case is important as illustrating how the awful temper of the time mastered men who would otherwise have been frivolous. He had been a noted gallant, but now—in the conflict which raged within him between old feelings, traditions of caste and honour, and the new ideas and the revelation of the wrongs of mankind—his person, spirit, and character changed. He was like a man ravaged by inward pain. With every post from Paris—

> the fever came,
> A punctual visitant, to shake this man,
> Disarmed his voice and fanned his yellow cheek
> Into a thousand colours; while he read,
> Or mused, his sword was haunted by his touch
> Continually, like an uneasy place
> In his own body.

Such agitation in others soon awoke the same in Wordsworth. Indeed none could long remain at peace, for

> The soil of common life was, at that time
> Too hot to tread upon . . .
> The land all swarmed with passion, like a plain
> Devoured by locusts.

Small men, unheard of now, became, for the time, powers; the fire ran from Paris to the provincial towns, and from them to the remotest nook and village of the land; and Wordsworth, resisting the arguments of those who supported the past, threw himself into the arms of the republicans.

> Became a patriot, and my heart was all
> Given to the people, and my love was theirs.

He and his friend Beaupuis, who was rejected with hatred by his brother officers, lived almost together. Both were enthusiastic, both were full of hope, and the description which Wordsworth gives of him is in itself so beautiful, and illustrates so well the best type of the men of the earliest times of the Revolution, that I cannot refrain from quoting it,—

                                        A meeker man
Than this lived never, nor a more benign,
Meek though enthusiastic.   Injuries
Made *him* more gracious, and his nature then
Did breathe its sweetness out most sensibly,
As aromatic flowers on Alpine turf,
When foot hath crushed them.   He through the events
Of that great change wandered in perfect faith,
As through a book, an old romance, or tale
Of Faery, or some dream of actions wrought
Behind the summer clouds.   By birth he ranked
With the most noble, but unto the poor
Among mankind he was in service bound,
As by some tie invisible, oaths professed
To a religious order.   Man he loved
As man;  and, to the mean and the obscure,
And all the homely in their homely works,
Tansferred a courtesy which had no air
Of condescension;  but did rather seem
A passion and a gallantry, like that
Which he, a soldier, in his idler day
Had paid to woman:  somewhat vain he was,
Or seemed so, yet it was not vanity,
But fondness, and a kind of radiant joy
Diffused around him, while he was intent
On works of love or freedom, or revolved
Complacently the progress of a cause
Whereof he was a part:  yet this was meek
And placid, and took nothing from the man
That was delightful.

They talked together, while France stood on the brink of
its great trial, of Man and his noble nature, as it was in
itself; of the abstract political theories founded on the
conception of an universal mankind; and of the oppres-
sion and tyranny that had for centuries hindered Man's
development.  On these three lines of thought I shall
build what I have to say in this lecture and the following
one.

   I. And first with regard to Man, Wordsworth ap-
proached, he tells us, the shield

        Of human nature from the golden side,

and would have fought even to the death to attest that it

was gold. And charmed with the golden view, he was led to ponder, first on the individual man, on what was best in him—

> Wise in passion and sublime in power,
> Benevolent in small societies
> And great in large ones.

And he did this, stripping him of all adventitious ornaments, of rank and wealth, and traditional honours—looking at him as he was in himself, not as he was by that which he possessed. This habit which had grown upon him among the hills, but which he did not then consciously possess, became now the conscious habit of his life, and to express its results one of the principal objects of his poetry.

It was rooted in him by that which he saw at this time in France, when the whole nation sprang, as it were, into new being. He and Beaupuis rejoiced together, when, after long conversations on " the honourable deeds and noble spirits of ancient story," on the rise of sects and nations, and the natural union of men under the influence of forming ideas, they turned to the movement going on around them, and beheld, responding to the aspirations of their own minds—

> A living confirmation of the whole
> Before us, in a people from the depth
> Of shameful imbecility uprisen,
> Fresh as the morning star. Elate we looked
> Upon their virtues; saw, in rudest men,
> Self-sacrifice the firmest; generous love,
> And continence of mind, and sense of right,
> Uppermost in the midst of fiercest strife.

It was this that he carried back to England with him and wrought into his poetry. He moved among men, he says, with genial feelings; when erring, erring in the better part, and in the kinder spirit; indulgent to their weakness, rejoicing in their goodness; as much a child of Nature as before, only now giving to Man a stronger affection than he gave to Nature.

> Diffusing only those affections wider
> That from the cradle had grown up with me,
> And losing, in no other way than light
> Is lost in light, the weak in the more strong.

Trusting in the grandeur of the one human heart that he had learnt in France belonged to all, he made it his main subject, but he turned from it as seen in cities to its more natural aspects among the poor. He was the first in England—not excepting Crabbe, whose sternness, even whose cynicism of portraiture, leaves too little of that tenderness and pity, or of that reverence for the men which is necessary for poetic treatment of the poor—he was the first who threw around the lives of ordinary men the glory and sweetness of song. He was the first who poured around the dalesmen's cottages, and the wandering life of the pedlar, and the unheard struggles of the country and the mountain folk, the consecration and the poet's dream. He was the first who isolated life after life in tender and homely narrative, and made us feel that God was with simple men and women; that in their lives were profound lessons; that the same equal heart beat in the palace and the hamlet hidden in the hills; that all men were brothers in the charities which soothe and bless, in the moral duties which God demands, in the feelings which nature awakens in their hearts; that a spirit of independence and stern liberty is the birthright and the passion of the poorest shepherd, as well as of the patriots who fill the pages of history.

One of the best examples of this is the way in which he sympathised with the love of the *statesmen* for their land. In his *Repentance*, a pastoral ballad, he describes the misery, the consuming dullness of the small farmer's life who has parted with his estate, and lost with it the tie that bound him to his ancestors. In *Michael*, when misfortune comes on the shepherd, Wordsworth describes, and in lines that show how deep his sympathy was with the humble feeling, how strong it was—

> Isabel, said he,
> I have been toiling more than seventy years,
> And in the open sunshine of God's love

> Have we all lived; yet if these fields of ours
> Should pass into a stranger's hands, I think
> That I could not lie quiet in my grave.
>                                    The land
> Shall not go from us, and it shall be free;
> He shall possess it, free as is the wind
> That passes over it.

Nor did he in after-life lose this close sympathy with the independence of the individual. The last book of the *Excursion* is full of passages that maintain the rights of men to individual development, to freedom from the oppression of unremitting toil, to all the means of education that the State can give. The worst fate that could befall a poor as well as a rich man, was to be turned into a mere instrument,—

> Our life is turned
> Out of her course, wherever man is made
> An offering, or a sacrifice, a tool
> Or implement, a passive thing employed
> As a brute mean, without acknowledgment
> Of common right or interest in the end;
> Used or abused as selfishness may prompt.

Lines which might be taken as a motto by the Trades' Unions.

This was the practical way in which he carried out the revolutionary idea that each man was to have the freest room for self-development, to be considered separate from the rest, not lost in a class. And he embodied these views in his poems. The first book of the *Excursion* will never let us forget the power, the simple dignity, the capacity for refined feeling which may be in the poorest whom we meet. Two neglected poems, the *Brothers*, and *Michael*, are exquisite from the sense they leave in us of the human reality and passionate tenderness which are to be found in the humblest lives. It was indeed republican to gather round the sorrows of children and their innocent talk, round names like " Matthew, " and " Lucy Fell, " and the " Idiot Boy," the interests and the feelings of England. His very theory of poetic diction—that it should be that which men commonly use when in rustic life they express themselves simply, and in accordance with which the *Lyrical Ballads* were written—was itself due to his republican opinions. Both the theory and the poems astonished men at first; but they made their way, till a truer sentiment of equality and fraternity knit together the rich and the poor. He felt, and truly felt, that his writings of this kind " would co-operate with the benign tendencies in human nature and society; that they delineated not merely such feelings as all men sympathise with, but revealed such feelings as men may sympathise with, and such as there is reason to believe they would be better and more moral beings if they did sympathise with; " he wrote with " a view to show that men who do not wear fine clothes may feel deeply; that the spirit of resolution and independence was rooted in many parts of the country, and that the State should endeavour to support and not eradicate it; " with the design to " recover for the poor the rights of the human family, and the franchise of universal brotherhood, of which they had been robbed by the wealthy and the noble; to impress the world with a sense of their dignity in suffering, and the moral grandeur of their honest poverty."

Love had he found in huts where poor men lie.

Connected with the whole of this love for the lives of common men was his love for the lowlier flowers. We see the influence of this element of his republicanism in the thoughtful and tender poems that he wrote about the common people of the fields and hedgerows—the daisy, the celandine, the daffodils, the primrose, and the snow-drop. These also he exalted by the influence of his imagination as much as the poor who loved them, and it was his delight to make them and their ways the image of mankind.

Nor did he neglect the lower ranges of mankind. None was so low as to be scorned without a sin, none without offence to God cast out of view. The old beggars who wandered uselessly about Cumberland awoke his poetic pity. In describing one of them, Wordsworth saw in him a man who, though he perhaps did no good himself, was yet the cause of good in others, and to whom at least Nature was always kind.

> Then let him pass, a blessing on his head!
> And while in that vast solitude to which
> The tide of things has borne him, he appears
> To breathe and live but for himself alone,
> Unblamed, uninjured, let him bear about
> The good which the benignant law of Heaven
> Has hung around him: and, while life is his,
> Still let him prompt the unlettered villagers
> To tender offices and pensive thoughts,
> —Then let him pass, a blessing on his head!
> And, long as he can wander, let him breathe
> The freshness of the valleys; let his blood
> Struggle with frosty air and winter snows;
> And let the chartered wind that sweeps the heath
> Beat his grey locks against his withered face.
> .    .    .    .    .    .    .
> Be his the natural silence of old age!
> Let him be free of mountain solitudes;
> And have around him, whether heard or not,
> The pleasant melody of woodland birds.

He saw in the idiots who roved about the villages those whose life was hidden in God. He had compassion on the immoral; the gipsies who idly went through the country were the children of free Nature: the farmer of Tilbury Vale who had run away from his debts was one in whose frank ease of heart, and in whose simple affection for Nature, good lay hidden. And with an exquisite touch of loving-kindness he brings around those whom society had cast aside the gentleness and love of Nature, till, learning from her, we feel pity and kindness for the outcast. Every one knows the *Reverie of Poor Susan*, but the description of the old farmer in London and of the love of Nature for him, is not so well known, and is characteristic of Wordsworth's tenderness to the erring.

> In the throng of the town like a stranger is he,
> Like one whose own country's far over the sea;
> And Nature, while through the great city he hies,
> Full ten times a day takes his heart by surprise.

This gives him the fancy of one that is young,
More of soul in his face than of words on his tongue;
Like a maiden of twenty he trembles and sighs,
And tears of fifteen will come into his eyes.

'Mid coaches and chariots, a waggon of straw,
Like a magnet, the heart of old Adam can draw;
With a thousand soft pictures his memory will teem,
And his hearing is touched with the sounds of a dream.

Now farewell, old Adam! when low thou art laid,
May one blade of grass spring up over thy head;
And I hope that thy grave, wheresoever it be,
Will hear the wind sigh through the leaves of a tree.

Nor did this reverence for " the power he served, the
sacred power, the Spirit of Humanity;" nor his love of
the simple poor, and his sense that Nature loved them
though man might not, cease to abide with him as he
grew old. There is a sonnet, written in 1831, which
embodies this continuous interest. It ought to be read
along with another written nearly thirty years before
on the same kind of subject, not only for the interest of
comparing the same thought in different expressions, but
for the interest of comparing the change of style—the
earlier one being in his best manner.[1]  Even later, in

---

[1] I place these Sonnets opposite one another:—

| ADMONITION. | HIGHLAND HUT. |
|---|---|
| Well may'st thou halt—and gaze with brightening eye! | See what gay wild flowers deck this earth-built Cot, |
| The lovely Cottage in the guardian nook | Whose smoke, forth-issuing whence and how it may, |
| Hath stirred thee deeply: with its own dear brook, | Shines in the greeting of the sun's first ray |
| Its own small pasture, almost its own sky! | Like wreaths of vapour without stain or blot. |
| But covet not the Abode:—forbear to sigh, | The limpid mountain rill avoids it not; |
| As many do, repining while they look; | And why should'st thou?—If rightly trained and bred, |
| Intruders—who would tear from Nature's book | Humanity is humble, finds no spot |
| This precious leaf with harsh impiety. | Which her Heaven-guided feet refuse to tread. |
| Think what the Home must be if it were thine, | The walls are cracked, sunk is the flowery roof, |

1842, when he is mourning over the state of England, he feels himself the apostle of humanity. He describes his poems as coming from one whose voice

> —Devoted to the love whose seeds
> Are sown in every human breast, to beauty,
>   Lodged within compass of the humblest sight,
> To cheerful intercourse with wood and field,
> And sympathy with man's substantial griefs—

he hopes will not be heard in vain.

These were the results of the reverence for human nature which he had learnt from the Revolution, and to which he had added the strong religious element I have sufficiently indicated. I quote, in conclusion of this first part of my subject, and as resuming and confirming much that has been said, a passage from the preface to the *Lyrical Ballads* :—

" The principal object, then, proposed in these poems was to choose incidents and situations from common life, and to relate or describe them, throughout, as far as was possible, in a selection of language really used by men, and, at the same time, to throw over them a certain colouring of imagination whereby ordinary things should be presented to the mind in an unusual aspect; and, further, and above all, to make these incidents and situations interesting by tracing in them, truly though not ostentatiously, the primary laws of our nature: chiefly as far as regards the manner in which we associate ideas in a state of excitement. Humble and rustic life was generally chosen, because, in that condition, the essential

|  |  |
|---|---|
| ADMONITION. | HIGHLAND HUT. |
| Even thine, though few thy wants! — Roof, window, door, | Undressed the pathway leading to the door; |
| The very flowers are sacred to the Poor, | But love, as Nature loves, the lonely Poor; |
| The roses to the porch which they entwine: | Search, for their worth, some gentle heart wrong-proof, |
| Yea, all, that now enchants thee, from the day | Meek, patient, kind, and, were its trials fewer, |
| On which it should be touched, would melt away. | Belike less happy. — Stand no more aloof! |

passions of the heart find a better soil in which they can attain their maturity, are less under restraint, and speak a plainer and more emphatic language; because in that condition of life our elementary feelings co-exist in a state of greater simplicity, and, consequently, may be more accurately contemplated, and more forcibly communicated; because the manners of rural life germinate from those elementary feelings, and, from the necessary character of rural occupations, are more easily comprehended, and are more durable; and, lastly, because in that condition the passions of men are incorporated with the beautiful and permanent forms of nature. The language, too, of these men has been adopted (purified, indeed, from what appear to be its real defects, from all lasting and rational causes of dislike or disgust), because such men hourly communicate with the best objects from which the best part of language is originally derived; and because, from their rank in society and the sameness and narrow circle of their intercourse, being less under the influence of social vanity, they convey their feelings and notions in simple and unelaborated expressions. Accordingly, such a language, arising out of repeated experience and regular feelings, is a more permanent, and a far more philosophical language than that which is frequently substituted for it by poets, who think that they are conferring honour upon themselves and their art, in proportion as they separate themselves from the sympathies of men, and indulge in arbitrary and capricious habits of expression, in order to furnish food for fickle tastes, and fickle appetites, of their own creation."

II. With regard to the second point, Wordsworth found France steeped in the abstract political theories which her literary men had poured out upon her for half a century. They were not politicians in the sense of mingling in political action, but they occupied themselves almost altogether in writing about government, the origin of society, the natural rights of man, the limits of authority, the true principles of laws, the relations of man to man.

Every man had a different theory, but one general idea lay beneath them all—" the substitution of some simple and elementary rules of government in accordance with reason and the law of nature, for the complicated and worn-out traditions which directed their present society." That was the political philosophy of the eighteenth century, as De Tocqueville reads it.

These writings spread everywhere. All France read and thought, and by-and-by there grew up in the imagination of the people an imaginary society, in which all laws were simple, conformed to reason and nature; in which all men were equal, were brothers, and were free. It was a dream that seized on the hearts and minds of all men. They lived in an ideal city, the palaces of which were built by theory; and when what they dreamt was realised, as they thought, in America, the Revolution took substance. And Wordsworth with his friend took up these theories, and discussed with the ardour of youth the government of nations, what it ought to be, and how far the weal or woe of a people depends " upon their laws and fashion of the State." In long talks with Beaupuis he argued

> about the end
> Of civil government, and its wisest forms;
> Of ancient loyalty, and chartered rights,
> Custom and habit, novelty and change;
> Of self-respect, and virtue in the few
> For patrimonial honour set apart;
> And ignorance in the labouring multitude.

The noble passage I read last Sunday, in which he describes the romantic ardour with which all men were rapt away into schemes that did not then seem Utopian for the regeneration of mankind, is a picture of his own impassioned hopes at a time when the " senselessness of joy was sublime." He looked forward and saw Liberty building her palace upon strong foundations, and sending from her council-chamber laws which should make

> Social life,
> Through knowledge spreading and imperishable,
> As just in regulation, and as pure
> As individual in the wise and good.

How far these political theories and hopes entered into and formed part of Wordsworth's mind is now our subject. They made him ever afterwards interested in men, not only as persons, but as citizens of a State. They made him take the greatest interest, far greater than any other English poet of the time, in all political and national movements in England and Europe. Living apart from the world, retired as a noontide grove in the solitudes of Grasmere, he yet threw himself, and that with the passion of a poet, into the fate of France, of Switzerland, of Spain, of St. Domingo, of the war on the Continent. He wrote a long pamphlet on the Convention of Cintra, and cast the main thoughts of the pamphlet into poetic form in his sonnets. The internal government of England and the duties of the State to English citizens were continually before his mind. Every one remembers the dreary discussion in the *Excursion* upon Education; few have read his long essay on the Poor Law, in which he treats of the state of the paupers, of the workmen congregated in manufactories, of joint-stock companies, of the relation of capital and labour, and of the Church and Dissent. They were strange subjects for a poet, and he threw many of them into poetical form; and at least they prove that the seed sown in his mind on the banks of the Loire when wandering with his friend Beaupuis had grown into a tree. But the whole of its growth was modified by Wordsworth's individuality. After a gloomy passage in his life, when disappointed in France, he gave himself wholly up for a time to mere social theories—an experience of his that I shall speak of in another lecture—the theoretical element was cast aside, and the practical English sense of the man brought his early dreams to the test of fact. Nothing can better illustrate the difference between the two nations than the experience of Wordsworth. For a short time he was wholly French, indulging in those theories which, applied without political knowledge, make violent revolutions; returning to this country he became, though still re-publican, practical. Wishing for the overthrow of the monarchy and the aristocracy, believing that " hereditary

distinctions and privileged orders of every species counter-
acted the progress of human improvement," he yet spoke
strongly against the hasty destruction of them, and
" recoiled from the very idea of a revolution." In 1814
his theory of equality, as we see from the last book of
the *Excursion*, was based, not on the vague phrase of
the rights of Man, but on the facts that God has given
the same gifts to all alike—love of natural beauty, reason,
imagination, freedom in the will, conscience, death, im-
mortality, the primal duties, the common charities of
life. He who works from this ground will come to a
very different conclusion from that which landed the
French Revolution in a new and enthralling despotism.
For it is the ground of common duties making common
rights among men, and the common duties are founded
on the common Fatherhood of God and the Brotherhood
and Equality of men in Him. This is exactly the
principle which, in my last lecture, I said needed to be
added to those of the Revolution to secure their perma-
nence; and it is a theological idea which Wordsworth
added to the poetry of Man.

As to the right to political liberty which was then
contended for in France, and based on the theory of the
rights of Man without any distinct reference to God,
indeed, afterwards with a distinct repudiation of God; it
was supported by Wordsworth, as we have seen, with all
his heart, but it was supported as the will and work of
God. In the *Descriptive Sketches*, written in October
as he was wandering on the banks of the Loire, all
Nature is made more beautiful to him by his dreams of
the advent of perfect liberty; a milder light fell from the
skies, the river rolled with more majestic course, the
foliage shone with richer gold. But as he wrote he
heard the gathering of the enemies of freedom, he fore-
saw that the land would soon be wrapt in fire, and that
all the promise in his heart could not be fulfilled. Yet,
undespondent, he appealed to God as the source and
protector of the work that France was doing against
the oppressing kings of Europe.

> Great God! by whom the strifes of men are weighed
> In an impartial balance, give thine aid
> To the just cause; and, oh! do thou preside
> Over the mighty stream now spreading wide:
> So shall its waters, from the heavens supplied
> In copious showers, from earth by wholesome springs,
> Brood o'er the long-parched lands with Nile-like wings!
> And grant that every sceptred child of clay
> Who cries presumptuous, " Here the flood shall stay,"
> May in its progress see thy guiding hand,
> And cease the acknowledged purpose to withstand;
> Or, swept in anger from the insulted shore,
> Sink with his servile bands, to rise no more!

As to the various theories of government of which he heard, we do not find that they had much influence on him. He did not care for indulging in Utopias upon paper; and the only place where we meet cut and dry systems of government is when he began, in and after 1832, to put forward a kind of strong Conservative programme in opposition to Reform, in such pieces as the *Evening Voluntaries*, and the *Sonnets dedicated to Order*, and the *Warning to England*. In the early times, however, from 1801 to 1813, he put forward no political theories at all, either of government or of liberty. He turned from them to ask more practical questions, as he thought; to discover by what inward forces a nation was free, by what moral powers a state grew into the best organisation. The complete breakdown of theory in France, when the whole nation without a word gave itself into the power of one man, " of men the meanest too," forced him into this inquiry; and no wiser or nobler answer exists on the subjects than in that magnificent series of sonnets dedicated to national independence and liberty. They begin with 1802, when he was again in France, and found the nation bending before Napoleon as First Consul. He looked on the people and found them wanting in all that could establish true political greatness or true liberty, and the lines in which he characterises France have only too much meaning now. Speaking of A. Sidney, Marvel, Harrington, and Vane,

as those " who knew how genuine glory was put on,"
he adds—

> France, 'tis strange
> Hath brought forth no such souls as we had then.
> Perpetual emptiness! unceasing change!
> No single volume paramount, no code,
> No master spirit, no determined road;
> But equally a want of books and men.

Their master spirit was himself a slave (and nothing is
finer in Wordsworth than his consistent scorn of Napoleon),
and the nation that obeyed him must be without the true
elements of political liberty. They could not exist where
power was worshipped as mere power. Unless it was
applied for ends useful and kindly to men, it was not
great, but an idol whose service debased and enslaved
a people. It was even worse when it was founded on
warlike glory or force.

> 'Tis not in battles that from youth we train
> The governors who must be wise and good,
> And temper with the sternness of the brain
> Thoughts motherly and meek as womanhood.
> Wisdom doth live with children round her knees:
> Books, leisure, perfect freedom, and the talk
> Man holds with week-day man in the hourly walk
> Of the mind's business; these are the degrees
> By which true sway doth mount; this is the stalk
> True Power doth grow on; and her rights are these.

For under a power founded on mere glory in war, a nation
lost its own liberty and combined to take liberty from
others. This was the sight he saw in France, and he
turned within himself and to history to find the contrast.
The liberty and greatness of a nation, he answered, were
in its harmony with the laws of God, such moral laws as
the prophets of Israel laid down; the ground of its
existence and success was a moral ground, the test of its
liberty was in the virtue and unselfishness of its citizens.
By the soul only, by patience and temperance, by

> Honour that knows the path, and will not swerve;
> Affections which, if put to proof, are kind,
> And piety towards God;

by lives given to labour, prayer, to nature, and to heaven, by virtuous homes, and political wisdom founded on moral law, are nations great and free. It was not riches, which were akin, " to fear, to change, to cowardice, and sloth," for did not ennobling thoughts depart " when men changed swords for ledgers and the student's bower for gold? "— but " plain living and high thinking " that were the vital power in a people against oppression. It was not in warlike force, but in the patience, temperance, hope, and fortitude of men who loved liberty for the sake of men and not of themselves, that a people found power to win their freedom against oppresson. Not from

> fleets and armies and external wealth,
> But from within proceeds a nation's strength—

Nor is it intellectual power, or scientific research which in evil days does most for the cause of Man, but simple moral force and the strength of natural human feeling towards things loved by all.

> A few strong instincts and a few plain rules,
> Among the herdsmen of the Alps, have wrought
> More for mankind, at this unhappy day
> Than all the pride of intellect and thought.

He sought for these in England, and in 1802 he could not find them. One knows the sonnet in which, deploring the evils of his country, he asserts the necessity of the opposite qualities for the greatness of a people.

WRITTEN IN LONDON, SEPTEMBER 1802.

> O Friend! I know not which way I must look
> For comfort, being, as I am, opprest,
> To think that now our life is only drest
> For show; mean handy-work of craftsmen, cook,
> Or groom!—We must run glittering like a brook
> In the open sunshine, or we are unblest:
> The wealthiest man among us is the best:
> No grandeur now in nature or in book
> Delights us. Rapine, avarice, expense,
> This is idolatry: and these we adore:
> Plain living and high thinking are no more:
> The homely beauty of the good old cause
> Is gone; our peace, our fearful innocence,
> And pure religion breathing household laws.

Equally fine is the sonnet written in the same year to Milton, and those which follow calling on his countrymen to remember the great men of the past who taught us how rightfully a nation shone in splendour; to be worthy to speak the tongue

> That Shakespeare spake, the faith and morals hold
> Which Milton held.

But the despairing view soon passed away, and when the country went to war with the despot, he became ashamed of his " unfilial fears " and found in her the " bulwark for the cause of men; " one, at least, who held that it was

> an accursèd thing to gaze
> On prosperous tyrants with a dazzled eye.

Shall the Godhead, he asks, who dwells in Nature and the affections and the soul of Man, pour his bounty on city and on field, and yet have no thought of the awful contest for the liberties of Man; is it to be our doom, to have no hope, to have faith in no promise of God?

> Nay, forbid it Heaven!
> We know the arduous strife, the eternal laws
> To which the triumph of all good is given,
> High sacrifice, and labour without pause,
> Even to the death—else wherefore should the eye
> Of man converse with immortality?

He followed the whole continental struggle of the nations against Napoleon, step by step; and as year by year the ambition of Napoleon declared itself as the will of France, as the nation which had preached liberty laid itself at the feet of one man, and went forth to enslave; as year by year the nation which had declared the equal right of man, fought to take away those rights; as year by year the nation which had said that there was but one nation, the nation of mankind, laboured to prove by violence that there was only one nation—the nation of France—that mankind was created for France and not France for mankind; as year by year every principle of the Revolution was reversed—Wordsworth felt more and more strongly the uselessness of mere political theories to give birth to permanent liberty, and he put them out of his mind.

But it was a somewhat perilous thing for a poet of Man to lose his interest in theories of Man. For it is on theory and the ideas it presupposes that the poet who would speak of mankind exists. They are his nectar and ambrosia, and when he can delight in them and assimilate them no longer, he sinks out of the ideal life and world, where art abides, into the common and the commonplace. But if he have once lived therein, he brings with him and retains for a time the celestial light, and he may manage, as Wordsworth did, to find poetry in life's familiar face for many years. Yet, as time goes on—never soaring into the impossible or towards it, never lost in an idea—he wins no Promethean fire, breathes none of that diviner air which would enable him to glorify the common, to see the infinite hope in the mean reality. Then the light he has had lingers, but it slowly dies away, and the prose of life overcomes his human poetry in the end. It was very well for Wordsworth to give up theories about the future of Man, but he did so too completely, and the end thereof was Prose.

# LECTURE XI

## WORDSWORTH—*continued*

IN speaking last Sunday afternoon of the three great lines of thought on which Wordsworth's interest ran, when in France he was brought into contact with the Revolution, I omitted the last, for which there was no time. It was the moral aspect of the Revolution as the avenger of oppression, and the general hatred of the oppression of nations by tyrannous rule. It was a hatred which he learnt from what he saw in France, and it lasted almost his whole life, though it changed its form. And it was accompanied—though he had put aside theories of liberty and the rights of Man—by a steady ardour for liberty, which diminished but never altogether died. These are the points on which I shall enlarge in this lecture.

The Revolution which began in a dream of the Golden Age ended in the Reign of Terror. Arising as the saviour, it became the inveterate destroyer. And this was the reason of the change—that the theories which the literary class had conceived the ignorant and brutalised lower classes carried out, and the natural result was the fury and blood of the Terror. The lower classes were ignorant and slaves; at every point of daily life they were met by the greed of the nobles, and by the irresponsible action of the law; tax after tax wrung from them the fruits of all their labour; and the taxes, being exacted not so much by government as by the class of the *noblesse,* fixed their hatred on a class with whom they had now neither political nor social ties. The government itself educated them for the revolutionary work they did in the Reign of Terror. It seized on property at its own arbitrary will. All the land was by right the king's, and whenever the State wished to make a road, it drove it right through one small property after another, generally without paying a penny. Every poor proprietor, so damaged, learnt the doctrine that private property must give way, without any claim, to public interests. It was a root idea of the Revolution. Again, in the case of crimes against the State, there were exceptional tribunals; the villages were visited by night, men were carried off without a warrant and never seen again, their condemnation was done in half an hour under a mere form of trial. No man's liberty was safe from the caprice of those who had power or interest with those in power.

In this way, a taste for this sort of work was actually taught to the people—they were educated for the revolutionary tribunals. The forms of these things were given by the old *régime ;* the Revolution added to them, says De Tocqueville, the atrocities of its genius.

With all this and its results Wordsworth was brought into contact. He touches on all the points I have mentioned in the *Prelude ;* he and his friend discussed them with fiery indignation, till at last, " hatred of absolute rule where the will of one is the law of all," and where the nobles were on the side of absolute dominion as against the people, seized on them, mingled with pity and with love for the miserable multitude. They met a hunger-bitten girl, driving her heifer through the lane in despairing solitude—" 'Tis against *that* that we are fighting," said Beaupuis in agitation; they heard a dreadful and pathetic story of two lovers, Vaudracour and Julia, where, by the monstrous law that enabled a father's tyranny to imprison a son, the man was driven to fatal crime, and both man and woman to hopeless misery. Seeing these things the two friends were thrown into passionate opposition, and into as passionate hopes that at least the time was come when

> Captivity by mandate without law
> Should cease; and open accusation lead
> To sentence in the hearing of the world,
> And open punishment, if not the air
> Be free to breathe in, and the heart of man
> Dread nothing.

More even than this negative hope they dreamed—

> I with him believed
> That a benignant spirit was abroad
> Which might not be withstood, that poverty
> Abject as this would in a little time
> Be found no more, that we should see the earth
> Unthwarted in her wish to recompense
> The meek, the lowly, patient child of toil:
> All institutes for ever blotted out
> That legalised exclusion, empty pomp
> Abolished, sensual state and cruel power,
> Whether by edict of the one or few;
> And finally, as sum and crown of all,
> Should see the people having a strong hand
> In framing their own laws; whence better days
> To all mankind.

When Beaupuis left him and afterwards " perished in supreme command" in the war against La Vendée, Wordsworth went to Paris at the end of 1792. The September massacres were just over, the King in prison, and the quarrel between the Girondists and the Mountain in full swing. It was a time well calculated to excite to a higher level the mind of Wordsworth, and the passage in which he describes the intensity with which he felt the passion of the whole city is one of the finest in the *Prelude*.

> But that night
> I felt most deeply in what world I was,
> What ground I trod on, and what air I breathed.
> High was my room and lonely, near the roof
> Of a large mansion or hotel, a lodge
> That would have pleased me in more quiet times;
> Nor was it wholly without pleasure then.
> With unextinguished taper I kept watch,
> Reading at intervals; the fear gone by
> Pressed on me almost like a fear to come.
> I thought of those September massacres,
> Divided from me by one little month,
> Saw them and touched: the rest was conjured up
> From tragic fictions or true history,
> Remembrances and dim admonishments.
> The horse is taught his manage, and no star
> Of wildest course but treads back his own steps;

For the spent hurricane the air provides
As fierce a successor; the tide retreats
But to return out of its hiding-place
In the great deep; all things have second birth;
The earthquake is not satisfied at once;
And in this way I wrought upon myself,
Until I seemed to hear a voice that cried,
To the whole city, " Sleep no more." The trance
Fled with the voice to which it had given birth;
But vainly comments of a calmer mind
Promised soft peace and sweet forgetfulness.
The place, all hushed and silent as it was,
Appeared unfit for the repose of night,
Defenceless as a wood where tigers roam.

His very inmost soul was agitated, but not for a moment against the principles of the Revolution. He took the side against Robespierre, but felt that Robespierre was the strongest; and a hundred hopes and desires went rushing through his mind, as he thought how the earlier form of the movement might be preserved. Would not all nations come and help France to carry out her first great resolutions? Will not some one man, trusting in ideas and strong in such trust, self-restrained, nobly trained for rule, arise and dominate the struggle, even though he met with death? Would not death be nothing to such a man, for he would gladly obey the sovereign law that calls for sacrifice? For one thing was only to be sought for—the overthrow of tyrants. One thing was sure— for he had no doubt of the end—freedom must win the day as against oppression. He threw himself into the party of the Brissotins, and it was only " by the gracious providence of Heaven," or, as it seemed then to him, " dragged by a chain of harsh necessity," that, compelled to leave France, he escaped the fate of his friends. From thence he watched the growth of the Reign of Terror in France, but though he hated its excesses, he was not shocked by it into any retreat from his opinions. He saw in it all, though he confessed its enormity, the neces- sary work of vengeance—the vengeance of God Himself upon the guilty. However done, these long cruelties had to be expiated, and the abuses which caused them crushed, and if there were men who still supported them, so much the worse for the men. They must die who innocently or guiltily subserve oppression; nor should war be avoided with those who from without hindered the march of freedom, even though his own country took part in such a war. Therefore it was that when he returned to England, and war, after the execution of the king in 1793, was declared by England against France, he received a blow which shocked his whole moral nature. Was it possible that his country was on the side of oppression against the destroyers of oppression; and so deep was the feeling that he, than whom none was a truer patriot, but who yet was more a prophet of humanity than a patriot, wished and prayed that the arms of England might fall lifeless in the battle, and her hosts be scattered by the young Republic? He exulted in the victories of the Republic, he followed them with as great delight as was the sorrow with which he groaned over the insults heaped on liberty by the crew of Robespierre. But even the Reign of Terror at its worst did not make him lose hope; when the tyrant fell, he prophesied a new deliverance for France.

But when the career of Napoleon began, though his ardour for liberty did not alter, it changed its form. Oppressed France became the oppressor, and the work of Napoleon stirred into a warmer flame the hatred of oppression which the Revolution had awakened in Wordsworth. In wrath and pity he threw himself into the cause of distressed nationalities; he remembered the starving people —the cruelty which came of irresponsible will and greed, and he saw in Napoleon the concentration into one man of all the elements of the evil which had darkened the old *régime*. All men, all people who fought against him, were on the side of God, even though they had been on the side of the devil for years before. An indignant sonnet recorded his horror at the attack upon the Swiss, another mourned for the fate of Venice, once the eldest child of liberty; another poured its pity upon Toussaint, imprisoned by Napoleon, and in a noble outburst bid him

live and take comfort, for the worlds of Nature and of
Man fought upon his side.

> Thou hast left behind
> Powers that will work for thee: air, earth, and skies,
> There's not a breathing of the common wind
> That will forget thee; thou hast great allies;
> Thy friends are exultations, agonies,
> And love, and man's unconquerable mind.

A whole series followed with eager hope and encourage-
ment the struggle of Hofer and the Tyrolese; another
series records his passionate interest in the efforts of Spain
against the oppression of France. One of these I quote,
partly because it was a favourite of Wordsworth's, but
chiefly because it hits sharply the vile falsehood by which
Napoleon most defamed the Revolution when he declared
that he came as the apostle of freedom to the nations over
whom, the moment they were lured into his hands, he set
up an exhausting tyranny. It is entitled *The Indigna-
tion of a High-minded Spaniard.*

### 1810.

> We can endure that He should waste our lands,
> Despoil our temples, and by sword and flame
> Return us to the dust from which we came;
> Such food a Tyrant's appetite demands:
> And we can brook the thought that by his hands
> Spain may be overpowered, and he possess,
> For his delight, a solemn wilderness
> Where all the brave lie dead. But, when of bands
> Which he will break for us he dares to speak,
> Of benefits, and of a future day
> When our enlightened minds shall bless his sway;
> *Then*, the strained heart of fortitude proves weak;
> Our groans, our blushes, our pale cheeks declare
> That he has power to inflict what we lack strength to bear.

At last, the year after the *Excursion* was published, the
long contest closed at Waterloo, and the oppressor was
overthrown. Two *Thanksgiving Odes* show how greatly
he was moved, and both bear that deep religious stamp
which marked his work; both prove how closely he knit

together the fate of nations with the government of God;
both are full of genuine enthusiasm for his country and of
joy at her success, but it is an enthusiasm and a joy which
are gathered together in humble gratitude to God, in faith
that it is He who has done the work of liberty against
tyranny by the hands of England.

Our greatest poet since Milton was as religious as
Milton, and in both I cannot but think the element of
grandeur of style which belongs so pre-eminently to
them flowed largely from the solemn simplicity and the
strength which a dignified and unbigoted faith in great
realities beyond this world gave to the order of their
thoughts.　Coleridge was flying from one speculation to
another all his life.　Scott had no vital joy in his belief,
and it did not interpenetrate his poetry.　Byron believed
in Fate more than in God.　Shelley floated in an ideal
world, which had not the advantage of being generalised
from any realities—and not one of them possesses, though
Byron comes near it now and then, the grand style.
Wordsworth alone, combining fine artistic power with
profound religion, walks when he chooses, though he
limps wretchealy at times, with nearly as stately a step
as Milton.　He had the two qualities which always go
with the grand style in poetry—he lived intensely in the
present, and he had the roots of his being fixed in a great
centre of power—faith in the eternal righteousness and
love of God.

And he had this, I believe, more than any other poet
of the time—more practically far than Shelley—because
the cause of Man was so dear to him, and because he saw
that the cause of Man was the cause of God.　That truth,
the profoundest truth of Christianity, he had grasped
with his greatest strength.　His poetic work did not
enthral him—did not in itself alone possess its own desire;
he bent it to larger ends than those of giving transient
pleasure.　He not only reflected faithfully the feelings of
human nature, he went further.　A great poet, he says,
ought to do more than this; he ought " to rectify men's
feelings, to give them new compositions of feeling, to
render their feelings more sane, pure, and permanent; in

short, more consonant to Nature, that is, to eternal
Nature and the great moving spirit of things." And he
has proved by his work that the great poet ought to do
more than even this; he ought to expand men's sym-
pathies over the great interests and movements of nations,
to beautify the great truths on which the moral and
political progress of nations rest, to add emotion to the
ideas of liberty and brotherhood, to bid men look forward
and labour for not only their own country's highest good,
but for the restoration of all things, to keep the hope and
faith of a millennium ever before our eyes, to be the
prophet of mankind. And this was something of Words-
worth's work, only it was not done by vague prophecies
like Shelley's; it was done by taking up the events of the
day and applying to them principles which led him to give
as much interest and emotion to the struggles of distressed
Europe with an overwhelming imperialism as he gave to
the struggles of the dalesmen of Grasmere with the over-
mastering forces of Nature.

The pity of it is, that this power did not last till the
very close. After Napoleon's overthrow he grew some-
what sick of the present, and for the first time turned to
the past for his subjects. It was then that such poems
as *Laodamia* and *Dion* were written. As time wore on,
he became less widely human and more Wordsworthian:
the intense one-sidedness with which he always treated
his subjects grew more conscious of itself, and at last
pleased with itself; the want of living in the world,
among men and movements, the want of being himself
moved by any great impulse such as had transported
him in youth, fixed him down into illiberal opinions at
last. He still maintained his hatred of oppression, his
love of liberty, but in practice both the hatred and the
love broke down. The moral, temperate element in him,
the abhorrence of violence and disorder, the love of the
old—which in the first part of his life had formed a useful
check upon his revolutionary enthusiasm, so that he
always kept his head, grew—now that the Revolution
and the Empire itself had horrified him—into devouring
prominence, and he lost in his old age that balance of

opinions which mark sanity of mind.   It is not strange to find him opposing the bill for admitting Nonconformists to the Universities without any subscription or declaration of conformity to the Church, but it is strange that he should think that this would endanger the monarchy and social order.   It is strange to find him maintaining that civil disabilities ought to be removed from every class, and yet that they ought not to be removed from the Roman Catholics, because to give liberty to them promoted the cause of spiritual tyranny.   It is curious liberality which in order to promote liberty violates liberty.   It is stranger still, when we look back to the enthusiast of the Revolution, to find him saying in 1832 that the Constitution of England would be destroyed by the Reform Bill, and writing letters on the subject which are even duller than such poems as the *Warning,* and the *Sonnets to Order,* and that is saying a great deal.   What a change from the earlier dignity of his poetry, how curiously infelicitous the phrases, how meagre the style —a kind of poor extemporary prayer in verse—are the following lines:—

> O for a bridle bitted with remorse
> To stop your Leaders in their headlong course!
> Oh may the Almighty scatter with his grace
> These mists, and lead you to a safer place,
> By paths no human wisdom can foretrace—
> May He pour round you, from worlds far above
> Man's feverish passions, His pure light of love!

Nevertheless it is but right to say that Wordsworth's dislike to the liberal movements in 1832 and afterwards was in his own mind founded on love of constitutional liberty.   It is the statement of the Conservative, but still it would be unfair to call him a bigoted Conservative. He wished, for example, that representation could be thrown more fairly into the hands of the property of the country, and less into the hands of the great proprietors. It was a change from the time when he thought it degrading to human nature to set up property in preference to person as a title to legislative power, but it was not a bigoted change. He could speak plainly even in 1844 as to the duties of the great landowners and manufacturers to the poor. " One would wish," he writes, " to see the rich mingle with the poor as much as may be on a footing of fraternal equality. The old feudal dependencies and relations are almost gone from England, and nothing has yet come adequately to supply their place. Why should not great landowners look for a substitute for what is lost of feudal paternity in the higher principles of Christianised humanity and humble-minded brotherhood? " It was on these principles that the old man himself lived among the poor that surrounded him, when young and old met at Rydal to keep his birthday.

Nor was it change he disliked, but reckless sweeping change; and the changes wrought by the Reform Bill seemed such to him. We must remember that he was then sixty-two years old, and had lived too much apart from men. Much may be pardoned to old age that one does not pardon to youth, and Wordsworth himself says that he had lost " *courage* in the sense the word bears when applied by Chaucer to the animation of birds in spring time." He had seen a Revolution in a foreign country, and he had not courage now to face another in his own. He expected that something of the same violence which had made him recoil from France, would prevail in England after the Reform Bill, and he advocated, if change was necessary, a slower, wiser change. The following sonnet, not so poor poetically as others of the same period, is interesting as embodying his views and referring to the French Revolution.

Long-favoured England! be not thou misled
By monstrous theories of alien growth,
Lest alien frenzy seize thee, waxing wroth,
Self-smitten till thy garments reek dyed red
With thy own blood, which tears in torrents shed
Fail to wash out, tears flowing ere thy troth
Be plighted, not to ease but sullen sloth,
Or wan despair—the ghost of false hope fled
Into a shameful grave. Among thy youth,
My Country! if such warning be held dear,

> Then shall a Veteran's heart be thrilled with joy,
> One who would gather from eternal truth,
> For time and season, rules that work to cheer—
> Not scourge, to save the People—not destroy.

When things, however, were not so close to him, when he came into contact with the struggle of liberty in a foreign country, his sympathy with the oppressed seems to have been nearly as strong as ever. One would scarcely conceive Wordsworth, when almost seventy, as a supporter of the Carbonari, but such was the case, and those who love Italy and Wordsworth cannot but be pleased to bring them together. In 1842 he mourned over the decay of Italy, and saw in the Lago Morto its emblem. " Be its depths quickened," he cries out with some return of his ancient energy—

> What thou dost inherit
> Of the world's hopes, dare to fulfil:  awake,
> Mother of Heroes, from thy death-like sleep!

And in another sonnet, the last part of which I quote, he breaks into a prophecy which God has fulfilled in our own time—

> Fallen Power!
> Thy fortunes, twice exalted, might provoke
> Me to glad notes prophetic of the hour
> When thou, uprisen, shalt break thy double yoke,
> And enter, with prompt aid from the Most High,
> On the third stage of thy great destiny.

But in the case of Italy also, taught, as he held, by the fate of France, he was against all rash schemes and popular passion. Writing about the insurrections in Bologna in 1837, he declares that by no mere fit of sudden passion is freedom won, and urges gradual progress, noiseless pains, and moderation. And the advice he gives is noble enough and characteristic of him, nor is it one which the Italians would despise. It was at the root of all Mazzini's later teaching to his people. " O, great Italian nation," Wordsworth writes,—

> Let thy scope
> Be one fixed mind for all: thy rights approve
> To thy own conscience gradually renewed;
> Learn to make Time the father of wise Hope;
> Then trust thy cause to the arm of Fortitude,
> The light of Knowledge, and the warmth of Love.

It has seemed to me worth while, though at some length, to look into the question of Wordsworth's later Conservatism, and to show that he did not merit the violent expressions used about his change. Apostate, renegade, were terms equally unjust and unworthy to be applied to one who had done so much for Man. Still he suffered from the change. I have already said that with the decay of his natural republicanism, and with the loss of the ideas of republicanism as the leading thoughts of life, decayed his poetical power when he spoke of Man, even to a certain degree when he spoke of Nature. With their overthrow decayed also that larger Christianity in him, which is not personal, but human; but at the same time his personal Christianity grew deeper. Nor must we blame him much for this. 'Twould have been better had he been as before, the prophet of liberty and right, the declarer that the cause of Man is the cause of God; but it is but natural that, as age grows on, our thoughts should centre more round the relation of God to our own soul than our relation to the world of men, that the *Evening Voluntaries* should succeed the *Sonnets dedicated to Liberty and Independence.*

# LECTURE XII

## WORDSWORTH—*continued*

In my last lecture, I was carried far forward to the close of Wordsworth's life by my wish to bring under one theme his earlier and later feelings with regard to the Revolution. It is necessary now to return to his personal history, as it touches on the poetry of Man and of Nature. In doing so there will be some unavoidable repetition, but that which is repeated will be used in a different connection and for a different purpose. I have in this lecture to trace how the failure of his hopes for Man impaired his love of Nature and his love of Man; how they were restored, and, finally, how that marriage of his human mind and Nature, to which we have been looking forward for so long, was at last fulfilled.

I must, therefore, in order to arrive at the causes which impaired his love of Nature and Man, return to his personal history. We left him when he was driven by stress of circumstances from France to England in 1793. He had nearly been involved in the fate of his friends the Brissotins, and he followed with intense eagerness the progress of affairs in France. He refused to seek the country, and remained in London. It is characteristic of him at this time, that he took but little interest in the movement for Negro Emancipation, for he felt that if France prospered, slavery must perish. The principles there fought for, if established, would strike at the root of all oppression, and with the destruction of the root, all the branches of the tree of human slavery would be destroyed, negro slavery among the rest.

But as he watched in passionate desire, two things deprived his watch of all delight and threw him into almost despair. The first was the union of England with the confederate powers against France; the second

was the Reign of Terror. He never heard the sunset
cannon from the English fleet, as he watched it riding in
the Solent, ere it went to war,

> Without a spirit overcast by dark
> Imaginations, sense of woes to come,
> Sorrow for humankind, and pain of heart.
>
> *Prelude*, Bk. x.

It was this first threw him out of his love of Man and
soured his heart. It was misery to him to sit among the
worshippers who gave praise for his country's victories,
" like an uninvited guest whom no one owned, to sit
silent, and to brood on the day of vengeance yet to come."
It was still worse to be tossed between love of England,
and delight that she was beaten by her enemies because
she was false to liberty: a woeful time which those
who afterwards attacked Wordsworth had never gone
through.

Nor did he ever cast his eyes on France without
misery: misery because God seemed to have forgotten
Man, because liberty seemed to have forgotten herself
and to wear the robes of tyranny, because the deeds
then done would be brought in charge against her name.
For years his dreams were haunted with the ghastly
visions of that time; he saw the dungeons, the execu-
tions, the unjust tribunals, and in sleep he seemed to
plead in long orations before their judges,

> With a voice
> Labouring, a brain confounded, and a sense,
> Death-like, of treacherous desertion, felt
> In the last place of refuge—my own soul—

Moved in this way to the very centre of his being with
the passion of humanity, troubled, even tortured, with
conflicting emotions, he compared this new love of Man
with his early love of Nature, and both in their relation
to God.

His love of Nature, whose veins were filled from the
fountain of the grace of God,

N

Was service paid to things which lie
Guarded within the bosom of God's will.
Therefore to serve was high beatitude;
Tumult was therefore gladness, and the fear
Ennobling, venerable; sleep secure,
And waking thoughts more rich than happiest dreams.

*Prelude*, Bk. x.

But this new love of Man, how unspeakably unlike! With what a different ritual did one serve, through it, the Power Supreme who made Man divine! Faith and calmness seemed to leave his heart when he felt how full of doubt, dismay, and sleepless trouble, how sorrowful the tumult, how dreadful were the dreams, which belonged to this new service of mankind.

Yet, as he looked deeper—and that he could do this marks the temperate courage of Wordsworth as a thinker, and the mastery of his intellectual will over mere emotion —he saw no reason to despair of Man. As the prophets, who in their highest inspiration worked with a human heart troubled for the woes of man, wanted not consolation in that they saw God in the punishment of evil, and the triumph of moral law, so Wordsworth saw beneath the misery of France God in moral retribution, and God educating the nation. That was one theological aspect in which he viewed events.

He looked again, and saw another star of hope for Man in the self-sacrifice and virtues of those who suffered. He saw in a hundred instances that God had not forsaken human nature. Green spots appeared in the desert, bright islands of "fortitude, and energy, and love," of honour, faith, and sanctity,

And human nature faithful to herself,

amid the dark and stormy seas of the time. For a time he was thus kept true to his belief of God in Man, in spite of repeated shocks: his worship and his love, though dark, were touched with breaks of sunlight.

Then came to support this hope the news that Robespierre was dead. He heard it as he crossed the estuary of the Leven, and hope revived within him, more than hope—enthusiasm.

> Great was my transport, deep my gratitude
> To everlasting Justice, by this fiat
> Made manifest. " Come now, ye golden times,"
> Said I, forthpouring on those open sands
> A hymn of triumph; " as the morning comes
> From out the bosom of the night, come ye—
> Thus far our trust is verified."
>
> *Prelude*, Bk. x.

The world would now, he thought, go forward to righteousness and peace and liberty.

But he was still doomed to disappointment. Preserving amid the weakness of the new government his trust in the people, he found it slowly ebb away; and when Frenchmen changed " the war of self-defence for one of conquest, and lost sight of all they struggled for; " when, finally, to close her gains, a Pope

> Was summoned in to crown an Emperor;

when he saw a people, that once looked to Heaven for manna,

> take a lesson from the dog
> Returning to his vomit,

then the crash was too great; he lost faith for a time in God, in moral right; the old miseries returned to add their weight to the new; the hopes that had risen again against the shocks he had received, died now finally; and he lost his true love of Nature, his true love of Man, or rather he lost the true foundations on which they were based. It will be my business to trace how these two affections were impaired, and how they were restored, and how, after passing through this trial, they mingled into one.

In the account given of this mental crisis in the *Prelude*, in books xi., xii., and xiii., the two subjects of the Love of Man and Nature are mingled up together as poetic emotion led him to speak of each. For the purposes of the lecture we must isolate them from each other, but it must be always remembered that they went on together, *pari passu*, in his mind.  With regard to the love of Nature, it lost its natural, intuitive quality; it became a business of the intellect as stimulated by sensible images, more than of the heart as impressed by the same.  The first step towards this impairing of his love of Nature—and it shows how the two things were mingled up in his mind—was made when he lost hope for and love of Man in the present and began to look beyond it, in a merely critical spirit, for a coming race.  He became absorbed in the picture of an ideal mankind in the future, wholly different, he hoped, from the wretched creature he knew in the present. He looked back also to the sages, patriots, and heroes of the past, and it seemed to him, so dark his mind, that their " best virtues were not free from taint."  He went to the poets to find purer creatures, but if " Reason be nobility in Man," can anything, he asked, be more ignoble than the creature they delight to picture,

> the miserable slave
> Of low ambition and distempered love.

This was the wretched carping condition into which he fell; he judged mankind by the intellect alone, and shut out the heart as co-assessor with the intellect.  It was by the understanding alone that he tried to solve those mysteries of being that make of the human race one brotherhood, and in so doing he cut himself off from his poetic nature, and

> From all the sources of his former strength.

He even, by the exercise of his critical faculty on Man, lost the power of conceiving Man as a whole, for it is only in belief in things not subject to the critical faculty working alone, such things as the universal sense of right and wrong, of truth, of common and natural emotions, of a God, that we have any absolute grounds for holding the doctrine of an universal humanity.

The slave then of this critical faculty, he could not help applying it to Nature.  Long ago he had believed in a soul in Nature, and looked beneath her outward forms in order

to feel this soul and its " impassioned life," with heart
and intellect at one in the work, and the Soul of Nature
answered to his love and told to him her secrets.[1]  But
now he had abandoned the thought of a soul within the
world, and love could no longer rule his life with her.  He
criticised its surface beauty like an art critic, " even in
pleasure pleased unworthily."  He liked here and disliked
there as artistic rules led him, applying rules of art " to
things above all art."  He compared landscape with
landscape, to the disadvantage of one—

> Bent overmuch on superficial things,
> Pampering myself with meagre novelties
> Of colour and proportion—to the moods
> Of time and season, to the moral power,
> The affections, and the spirit of the place
> Insensible.
>
> *Prelude*, Bk. xii.

In this way that spiritual imagination was impaired
which penetrates to the living heart of Nature, and feels
it beating against the human heart.

Another phase of the same thing also beset him.  The
eye took despotism over the rest of his senses and powers,
and held his mind in slavery to its special pleasure.  It
had vivid but not profound pleasure in roving from one
landscape to another, and in craving new combinations

---

[1] I place the passage here in order that it may be read in connection
with the lecture in which I have maintained that Wordsworth gave
a life to Nature different from ours.

> O Soul of Nature! excellent and fair!
> That didst rejoice with me, with whom I, too,
> Rejoiced through early youth, before the winds
> And roaring waters, and in lights and shades
> That marched and countermarched about the hills
> In glorious apparition, Powers on whom
> I daily waited, now all eye and now
> All ear; but never long without the heart
> Employed, and man's unfolding intellect:
> O Soul of Nature! that, by laws divine
> Sustained and governed, still dost overflow
> With an impassioned life, what feeble ones
> Walk on this earth! how feeble I have been
> When thou wert in thy strength.
>
> *Prelude*, Bk. xii.

of beauty. Still worse, it took pride in this power, and began to think it nobler than the power of feeling, so that, at last, it grew so important to him that it laid the inner faculties asleep.

It is an experience which we see repeated at the present day, and its lesson should not be lost on us. A more complex worldly life creates often, and is creating now among us, a worldliness of the eye. It lusts after mere outward beauty, harmonies of colour, picturesqueness, exquisiteness of form. And in its insatiable pursuit of these, which only touch the senses, the influence of Nature on the heart is lost. It cannot rest quiet and content with any beauty; nor assimilate the teaching Nature gives to the heart and conscience: for it has no true love of Nature, and without that it only looks long enough to satisfy the eye. It is only love which enables us to dwell on a thing without weariness. And this delight in mere outside beauty soon finds satiety, and flies to something else, and, flying thus incessantly, it never remains long enough by anything to be able to comprehend it. For a time this was Wordsworth's failing, and the cause of it lay not only in that of which I have spoken, but also that the troubles of human life in which he was now involved overrode the silent influences of Nature, and made his life with Nature share in the excited life he was leading with Man. He contrasts this " thraldom of the sense "—this feverish worldliness of the eye—with the life which his sister lived with Nature. In her—

The eye was not the mistress of the heart;
Far less did rules prescribed by passive taste,
Or barren intermeddling subtleties,
Perplex her mind: but wise as women are
When genial circumstance hath favoured them,
She welcomed what was given, and craved no more;
Whate'er the scene presented to her view
That was the best, to that she was attuned
By her benign simplicity of life,
And through a perfect happiness of soul,
Whose variegated feelings were in this
Sisters, that they were each some new delight.
Birds in the bower, and lambs in the green field

Could they have known her, would have loved; methought
Her very presence such a sweetness breathed,
That flowers, and trees, and even the silent hills,
And everything she looked on, should have had
An intimation how she bore herself
Towards them and to all creatures.   God delights
In such a being; for, her common thoughts
Are piety, her life is gratitude—.

*Prelude*, Bk. xii.

So it was with him of old, when he " worshipped among
the depth of things," without criticising overmuch; but
now it was different.   Yet the evil did not last long; the
poet was too strong in him and Nature herself too close.
She fought, he held, against the tyranny of any one sense
over the others—

Summons all the senses each
To counteract the other, and themselves,
And makes them all, and the objects with which all
Are conversant, subservient in their turn
To the great ends of Liberty and Power.

Bk. xii.

There is an exact analogy to this in Christianity.   It
employs all the virtues, and by insisting on a harmony
of them all in the character, endeavours to thwart the
tyranny of any one virtue, which dwelt on exclusively
passes into a vice.   But the harmony of all, each doing its
own work in mutual service, makes action free, and gives
to the will power towards righteousness.

But what redeemed him chiefly were the recollections of
early impressions which he had received from certain
scenes in Nature.   He had known, in youth, too forcibly,

Visitings of imaginative power,

for this evil habit to endure their remembrance.   Youth
and its powers return to the true heart, however troubled
it has been; the memory of passionate feeling waked by
the influences of grandeur or beauty in Nature, inspires
such joy that we cannot but return to win from her
again the same passionate feeling as of old.   For there
are certain spots of time, and I analyse here a long

passage, the recollection of which possesses a renovating virtue; there are passages of life which give

> Profoundest knowledge to what point, and how,
> The mind is lord and master—outward sense
> The obedient servant of her will.   Such moments
> Are scattered everywhere, taking their date
> From our first childhood.

*Prelude*, Bk. xii.

In these moments Nature impresses herself as a living force of passion on the soul.   The impressions are deepest when we are alone and Nature is dreary.   For when we are alone the soul is most receptive, and when she is dreary there arises in us, aroused by her touch, a wild, involuntary, apparently causeless sorrow.   It is, in Wordsworth's thought, the spirit mourning in itself for that imperial palace whence it came, the recollection of a time of disembodied joy and purity, before it came to earth. These are the intimations of our immortality in childhood.   Nature, working on us from without, sends a kindling touch that awakens the slumbering powers of the soul.   We are lifted beyond our life of thoughtlessness, and feel, half unconsciously, the greatness of the soul.   To these hours we look back, and there is in them, all sorrowful and vague as they are, virtue to recall us— when they are refashioned by association and added to by experience—to higher thoughts, to nourish and repair imagination when it has been dulled by the wear and stress of life; to lead us, through their memories, to find beauty again in the commonplace, the ideal in the dull reality of life, and the presence of the soul and the passion of the heart in communion with the life of Nature.   Such regenerating memories were Wordsworth's, and they wrought in him that "working of the spirit," those "inward agitations," which carry us beyond ourselves into that region of the spiritual which we always touch but so seldom enter, into that region of the heart which lies so close to us, but which too often we despise for the region of the understanding.

Influenced by them, the poet escaped at last from the

critical, analysing spirit with which he had for a time confronted the soul of Nature. I shook the habit off, he says—

> Entirely and for ever, and again
> In Nature's presence stood, as now I stand
> A sensitive being, a *creative* soul—

with power as of old to receive sensitively all impressions from Nature, with power to create, by the working of imagination on the impressions, new images of thought. So was it with his love of Nature.

The trial through which his love of Man went ran on much the same lines. As in the love of Nature so in the love of Man, he slipt out of the region of intuition in which the poet most keenly lives, into the region of speculative opinion. It is not difficult to understand how he got into that region; for it is characteristic of human nature in youth, when enthusiastic opinions which have been loved have received a shock from the contradiction of events, to fight against that contradiction, even though the heart is failing under the blow it has received. This was the case with Wordsworth. Events seemed to prove that the principles he would have laid down his life for were null and void, and a vague despair began to move in his heart. Along with this was combined the sneer of men who had hated the Revolution from the beginning. They turned on Wordsworth with ridicule and mocked his opinions. And he replied indignantly: he fought for his views, clung to them as a man clings to religious opinions of which he has an inner doubt, saying to himself, " If I am wrong, then all is lost " But having this inner doubt, his heart and conscience were forced to cease to take part in his battle against the world, and his intellect alone was engaged. And then, in the heat of contest, opinions became all he cared for, till round his mind

> They clung, as if *they* were its life, nay more,
> The very being of the immortal soul.

He threw himself into speculative schemes of socialism, formed an ideal of Man, exalted his reason as the sole

lord of his acts, and strove to conceive a community in
which, like Robert Owen's, social liberty should be built
on personal, laws should be wholly directed by circum-
stances, man live by his intellect alone, and, shaking off
all degrading pursuits, be absolutely free,

> Lord of Himself in undisturbed delight.

But before realising this scheme it was necessary to make
an accurate study of society, and he did this by the help
of the understanding alone.  He brought all systems,
creeds, and laws before the bar of the reasoning faculty
and asked them to prove their rightness.  He demanded
that the soul should give formal proof of its powers.
How did it know that it could distinguish between right
and wrong, how did it know it was immortal?  Had
morality or religion any ground in fact?

What was the result?  It was, that looking into these
things without love, and leaving out of the investigation
the imagination and the spirit as means of judging, he
saw not life but death in the world; he lost all certainty.
As one piece of evidence was strong he believed in the
greatness of the soul, as one piece was weak he disbelieved
in it.  He found himself endlessly perplexed with questions
about impulses and motives, whether what seemed wrong
was not sometimes right, and what seemed right, wrong.
He could not decide whether there was any eternal rule
of duty, whether it had any ground in the nature of
things, whether what seemed its sanctions were sanctions,
or whence the sanctions came; till at last he became a
sceptic, and yielded up all moral questions in despair.
Man was either—

> The dupe of folly or the slave of crime.
>
> Bk. xii.

This was the lowest depth he reached, and from this he
was saved, first, by the common sense so characteristic of
him among the poets.  It led him to employ his puzzled
reason on some subject whose elements were not disturbed
by human passion.  He took to the study of abstract
science, and in realising its calm realities his mind grew

calm. He was saved, secondly, by the influence of human love, which restored to him that reverence for the heart which he had lost. It was through his sister's influence that this sacred work was also wrought. She who lived from the heart, moved ever by his side; she believed for him when he disbelieved; she saw that his scepticism was more the flight of clouds across his mind than any vital change in his mind itself; she went with her own eager sympathy through all his trouble,—

> Then it was—
> Thanks to the bounteous Giver of all good—
> That the beloved Sister in whose sight
> Those days were passed, now speaking in a voice
> Of sudden admonition—like a brook
> That did but *cross* a lonely road, and now
> Is seen, heard, felt, and caught at every turn,
> Companion never lost through many a league—
> Maintained for me a saving intercourse
> With my true self——
>
> *Prelude*, Bk. xi.

she "whispered still that brightness would return," and herself, loving Nature intensely, as her delightful Diary proves, not only restored to him his ancient love of Nature, but also opened to his heart again the fountains of human love and bade him drink them and be whole; brought him back to his real work,—

> preserved him still
> A Poet, made him seek beneath that name,
> And that alone, his office upon earth.

It was thus he began to find his love of Man again.

But another power now joined in his sister's work. He had refound, as we have seen, his love of Nature, and Nature led him now again, as she had done of old, to the love of Man. In his youth he had seen in her Beauty and Sublimity; he now, influenced by his study of Science on the one side, and by desire to be freed from confused opinions on the other, saw in her not only Beauty and Sublimity but divine and quiet Order. She seemed to him the image of right reason, the witness to calm obedi-

ence to eternal Law; she held before his eyes no disturb-
ing passion, but a " temperate show of objects which
endure." It was a view which sank deep into his troubled
human heart; he took it with him to the world of Man,
and it taught him to seek in it, beneath the wild disturb-
ance of the surface sea of life,—

> Whate'er there is desirable and good
> Of kindred permanence, unchanged in form
> And function, or, through strict vicissitude
> Of Life and Death, revolving.
>
> *Prelude*, Bk. xiii.

And having found these things in human life, he turned
again to Nature, and in feeling his brotherhood with
Man, felt his brotherhood with her complete. Those
" watchful thoughts " were re-established which had
early tutored him—

> To look with feelings of fraternal love
> Upon the unassuming things that hold
> A silent station in this beauteous world.

Both had been fully regained—the love of Man, the love
of Nature.

Freed thus from unregulated emotion, he sought with
quiet judgment to find the great truths which underlie
human life, and the permanent feelings of human nature,
and to rest on these amid the storm of passions and
opinions, for there, among much evil, was the abiding
good in Man, the dwelling-place of God.

> Thus moderated, thus composed, I found
> Once more in Man an object of delight,
> Of pure imagination and of love——

but it was now a wiser love; it had given up theories of
Man, it only sought now a humbler object—to find out
what Man was when unspoilt, through the power of a
sympathising human heart. And seeking thus, he re-
covered his clear belief in right, his clear sight of wrong,
his faith in the eternity of pure feelings and the divine
nature in the human. Sanguine schemes, ambitious
projects for the regeneration of mankind, pleased him

less; the wild dream of promise which had flown before him in the Revolution, "retired into its due proportion." "I sought," he says,—

> For present good in life's familiar face
> And built thereon my hopes of good to come.

Where now was he to seek this present good, where find the divine wealth of pure feeling and honest life of which he was now convinced? Where, he answered, but among the natural abodes of simple men, the men among whom my life was passed; thither I turn from national interests to individual, and perhaps in finding there personal lives true to duty, the heart, and conscience, I may best learn what makes the true worth and dignity of Man, and why this glorious creature should not be counted by thousands, not by one only in ten thousand. I will "inspect the basis of the social pile, and ask how much of mental power and genuine virtue they possess who live by bodily toil,"—

> therefore did I turn
> To you, ye pathways and ye lonely roads;
> Sought you enriched with everything I prized,
> With human kindnesses and simple joys.

There he learnt the wisdom of the poet, the wisdom to feel deeply and to know things and men through love; healing and repose came to his wounded heart as he wandered over the moors, or sat on the cottage bench, or by the well-spring, and talked with all he met. This was his school, it was here he read the passions of mankind, and the depths of the human heart, and heard

> From mouths of men obscure and lowly, truths
> Replete with honour.

He sketches such a life in the character of the Pedlar, in the first book of the *Excursion*, and he drew it from himself. It was the life he would have chosen, and no words can describe better than the following—a few lines being excepted—the character of Wordsworth at this time:—

> He wandered far; much did he see of men,
> Their manners, their enjoyments, and pursuits,

Their passions and their feelings; chiefly those
Essential and eternal in the heart,
That, 'mid the simpler forms of rural life,
Exist more simple in their elements,
And speak a plainer language.    In the woods,
A lone Enthusiast, and among the fields,
Itinerant in this labour, he had passed
The better portion of his time; and there
Spontaneously had his affections thriven
Amid the bounties of the year, the peace
And liberty of nature;  there he kept
In solitude and solitary thought
His mind in a just equipoise of love.
Serene it was, unclouded by the cares
Of ordinary life; unvexed, unwarped
By partial bondage.    In his steady course,
No piteous revolutions had he felt,
No wild varieties of joy and grief.
Unoccupied by sorrow of its own,
His heart lay open; and, by nature tuned
And constant disposition of his thoughts
To sympathy with man, he was alive
To all that was enjoyed where'er he went,
And all that was endured; for, in himself
Happy, and quiet in his cheerfulness,
He had no painful pressure from without
That made him turn aside from wretchedness
With coward fears.  He could *afford* to suffer
With those whom he saw suffer.   Hence it came
That in our best experience he was rich
And in the wisdom of our daily life.

It was thus for a time he lived, till at last, inspired by such
communion with " men as they are men within them-
selves," he resolved, seeing what holy worship was offered
unto God in the wayside chapels of humble and loving
hearts among poor and simple men, to make his song of
these.   This, then, was his work, this the aim he had at
last found for his poetic life; to

> Deal boldly with substantial things; in truth
> And sanctity of passion, speak of these,
> That justice may be done, obeisance paid
> Where it is due: thus haply shall I teach,
> Inspire, through unadulterated ears

Pour rapture, tenderness, and hope,—my theme
No other than the very heart of man,
As found among the best of those that live,
Not unexalted by religious faith,
Nor uninformed by books, good books, though few,
In Nature's presence: thence may I select
Sorrow, that is not sorrow, but delight;
And miserable love, that is not pain
To hear of, for the glory that redounds
Therefrom to humankind, and what we are.

*Prelude*, Bk. xiii.

It was a work to which men " accomplished for communion with the world, most active when they most are eloquent," but needing admiration to develop them, might not care to listen. But there were others who would; men who uphold themselves, and by their own solitary might and joy create—others, too, and those chiefly found among the walks of homely life—

men for contemplation framed
Shy and unpractised in the strife of phrase;

who cannot speak, nor tell their secret heart, but whose

is the language of the heavens, the power,
The thought, the image and the silent joy:
Words are but under-agents in their souls;
When they are grasping with their greatest strength
They do not breathe among them—this I speak
In gratitude to God, who feeds our hearts
For His own service; knoweth us, loveth us,
When we are unregarded by the world.

Bk. xiii.

This was his work, to make unworldly men listen to the beating of the heart of natural humanity.

And now having taken the world of humanity into himself, the world of Nature, which he had received and loved before, united itself to the world of humanity within him, and the marriage of the Mind to the Universe, of which we spoke so much, was complete in Wordsworth. He saw how Nature consecrated and made grand the human life which was lived among her beauty and sublimity. He felt also that the visible world and all its

forms gave teaching and pleasure to the mind in pro-
portion as human passion worked upon them, and that, in
turn, the forms

> Of Nature have a passion in themselves,
> That intermingles with those works of man
> To which she summons him; although the works
> Be mean, have nothing lofty of their own;
> And that the Genius of the Poet hence
> May boldly take his way among mankind
> Wherever Nature leads; that he hath stood
> By Nature's side among the men of old,
> And so shall stand for ever.

And he dares to hope

> That unto him hath also been vouchsafed
> An insight that in some sort he possesses,
> A privilege whereby a work of his,
> Proceeding from a source of untaught things,
> Creative and enduring, may become
> A power like one of Nature's.

Bk. xiii.

Feeling, hoping thus, he looked into the world of Nature,
and felt within it a living spirit, moving unseen, but
making all its life.   He looked again, and below the sur-
face of the world of Man he gained sight of a new and
living world also, a world ruled by those fixed laws

> Whence spiritual dignity originates,
> Which do both give it being and maintain
> A balance, an ennobling interchange
> Of action from without and from within;
> The excellence, pure function and best power
> Both of the object seen and eye that sees.

Hence, when these two spiritual worlds were bound
together in holy wedlock in the poet's heart, he could speak
from both of them alike, and reveal the mutual action on
each other of Nature and the human mind, and his work,
issuing from such origins, not only be a creation of the
human mind, but also a power like one of Nature's,
speak to men, as the winds and ocean speak; move them
as the beauty of the evening moves them; and make them
thrill, as does the thunder in the tempest, with a sense of

grandeur; soften, soothe, and bless, as the quiet of the stars or the ripple of the water. For the poet is the living voice of Nature as he is the expressing voice of Man.

Profoundly, then, impressed with Man, he did not desert his first love, Nature. He threw on her the light and emotion he had won from knowledge of the sorrows, passions, battles, and destiny of Man, till she trembled not only with her own emotion but with his. He saw in her— thus infinitely sympathetic to those who loved her, and brought the power of humanity to her—the teacher, the guide, and yet the servant of Man. And in this light, the intercourse he had with her was not as in boyhood a wild passion, nor a solitary one—it had now a softer, gentler, more enduring feeling, as if felt to a lover or a friend. She was no longer apart from Man, but thrilled through all her veins with sympathy for Man in good: no longer apart from God, but a life whose life was that of God; and as such the external master, guide, and anchor of his being.

This new position of Wordsworth's mind is, perhaps, worth illustrating at some length from his poetry, and I will sketch some of its phases. It appeared in the very first poems he published after his return from France, in the *Descriptive Sketches* in 1793. In them the natural landscape and those who lived in it were knit together, so that Nature was conceived of as inspiriting Man, and Man as making Nature more sublime and fair. In 1795 he illustrates in the lines written near the yew-tree on Esthwaithe Lake the opposite state of mind—in the case of a man so absorbed in himself as to lose the good of the influences of Nature and to be separated from mankind. In 1798, in the lines written when visiting Tintern Abbey, the union of Man and Nature in his mind is complete. The beginning of it is a condensation of all that we have gone through with him in the *Prelude* as to the education and influences of Nature on his life. There he looks back on what he was five years before when Nature was all in all to him, and her forms were " a feeling and a love "

> That had no need of a remoter charm
> By thought supplied, nor any interest
> Unborrowed from the eye.

Now it is different, he loves not Nature less; but mankind and its vast interest is wedded to her; and beyond both and yet in both, in the universe without and the mind within himself, there is an all-pervading divine spirit. Well-known as they are the lines must be quoted:—

> For I have learned
> To look on nature, not as in the hour
> Of thoughtless youth; but hearing oftentimes
> The still, sad music of humanity,
> Nor harsh nor grating, though of ample power
> To chasten and subdue. And I have felt
> A presence that disturbs me with the joy
> Of elevated thoughts; a sense sublime
> Of something far more deeply interfused,
> Whose dwelling is the light of setting suns,
> And the round ocean and the living air,
> And the blue sky, and in the mind of man:
> A motion and a spirit, that impels
> All thinking things, all objects of all thought,
> And rolls through all things. Therefore am I still
> A lover of the meadows and the woods,
> And mountains; and of all that we behold
> From this green earth; of all the mighty world
> Of eye, and ear,—both what they half create,
> And what perceive; well pleased to recognise
> In nature and the language of the sense,
> The anchor of my purest thoughts, the nurse,
> The guide, the guardian of my heart, and soul
> Of all my moral being.

The same position of mind, only marked with less of joy and more of sober sadness is expressed in the latter part of the *Ode on the Intimations of Immortality*.

Of the poetic result of this marriage in himself of Nature and his human mind I have already given an instance in speaking of the stanzas on the picture of Peele Castle, and explained how the imaginative creation of the poem was not the result only of an impression received from Nature, or of his own thought, but of the blended might of both embracing to produce a child different from both, but having something of the nature of both. I give another instance now in the most imaginative of his poems, *Yew Trees*. He walks in the shade of the yews of Borrowdale, those " fraternal Four, joined in one solemn and capacious grove," and there flows into his passive mind from Nature a vivid impression of gloom, of darkness and silence. Then his mind springs into activity, fastens on the impression, knits round it thoughts that are similar but different, thoughts of the sacred groves such as that where the Eumenides were worshipped, of groves where ancient powers were seen by wandering men, of death, of all those solemn moral powers that brood silently over Man. At last, out of both these working together, is born the imaginative Creation, and there rises before his eyes an ideal grove in which the ghostly masters of mankind meet, and sleep, and offer worship to the Destiny that abides above them; while the mountain flood, far, far away, as if from another world, makes music to which they dimly listen. Nothing can be more intense in imagination, nor is there anything more unique in English poetry:—

> But worthier still of note
> Are those fraternal Four of Borrowdale,
> Joined in one solemn and capacious grove;
> Huge trunks! and each particular trunk a growth
> Of intertwisted fibres serpentine
> Up-coiling, and inveterately convolved;
> Nor uninformed with Phantasy, and looks
> That threaten the profane;—a pillared shade,
> Upon whose grassless floor of red-brown hue,
> By sheddings from the pining umbrage tinged
> Perennially—beneath whose sable roof
> Of boughs, as if for festal purpose, decked
> With unrejoicing berries—ghostly Shapes
> May meet at noontide; Fear and trembling Hope,
> Silence and Foresight; Death the Skeleton
> And Time the Shadow;—there to celebrate,
> As in a natural temple scattered o'er
> With altars undisturbed of mossy stone,
> United worship; or in mute repose
> To lie, and listen to the mountain flood
> Murmuring from Glaramara's inmost caves.

In this case it was chiefly thought alone which acted on

the images received, but for the most part in Wordsworth the natural impressions are met by thoughts connected with human love, and the creation which ensues in the poem is one which is obedient to the sympathies of Man, and yet not forgetful of gratitude to Nature, so that both are honoured and exalted. There is a little sonnet written in later life, and one of his best, which illustrates the whole method of work, and yet marks how unconsciously —as it was bound to be—it was followed.

XLVIII.

Most sweet it is with unuplifted eyes
To pace the ground, if path be there or none,
While a fair region round the traveller lies
Which he forbears again to look upon;
Pleased rather with some soft ideal scene,
The work of Fancy, or some happy tone
Of meditation, slipping in between
The beauty coming and the beauty gone.
If Thought and Love desert us, from that day
Let us break off all commerce with the Muse:
With Thought and Love companions of our way,
Whate'er the senses take or may refuse,
The mind's internal heaven shall shed her dews
Of inspiration on the humblest lay.

Finally, the last book of the *Prelude* has this same position of mind towards Nature as its under-thought. It begins by a magnificent description of the ascent of Snowdon by night, at first in mist, and then as a light fell upon the turf, he looked up, and lo! [1]

[1] I insert this passage, not that I want it particularly, but because it is one of the finest specimens of Wordsworth's *grand style*. It is as sustained and stately as Milton, and here and there one catches the note of Milton as in the two lines beginning, "Not so the ethereal vault," but it is different from Milton's style in the greater simplicity of diction, in the more feminine and gliding motion of the verse, and in the want, therefore, of the solemn chords of mingled sound and thought with which Milton clashes in again and again in a long passage, making the reader halt to breathe. It differs, also, considered as an illustration, from Milton's manner in this, that Milton uses his illustrations for the purpose of making the thing illustrated more real to the sight, whereas in this one feels beforehand in reading it, that it is being prepared to serve a moral or intellectual purpose. It is a feeling which somewhat spoils the passage from the artistic point of view.

The Moon hung naked in a firmament
Of azure without cloud, and at my feet
Rested a silent sea of hoary mist.
A hundred hills their dusky backs upheaved
All over this still ocean; and beyond,
Far, far beyond, the solid vapours stretched,
In headlands, tongues, and promontory shapes,
Into the main Atlantic, that appeared
To dwindle, and give up his majesty,
Usurped upon far as the sight could reach.
Not so the ethereal vault; encroachment none
Was there, nor loss; only the inferior stars
Had disappeared, or shed a fainter light
In the clear presence of the full-orbed Moon,
Who, from her sovereign elevation, gazed
Upon the billowy ocean, as it lay
All meek and silent, save that through a rift—
Not distant from the shore whereon we stood,
A fixed, abysmal, gloomy, breathing-place—
Mounted the roar of waters, torrents, streams
Innumerable, roaring with one voice!
Heard over earth and sea, and, in that hour,
For so it seemed, felt by the starry heavens.

*Prelude,* bk. xiv.

Out of this vision of the night, when it was wedded to Thought, he creates the image of a majestic intellect, "what in itself it is and would become." Nature had shadowed forth in the whole scene the emblem of such a mind, with all its functions; and he saw, through the power of his own soul, the ideal substance the shadow of which lay before him. But the possibility of this inter-action lay in the original harmony which he believed had been established by God between the Mind of man and the outward Universe, whereby things in the one were certain to resemble things in the other.

On these resemblances he dwells, always working, observe, on the same large idea. And the analogy which he makes illustrates another part of his theory—the distinct and active personality of Nature. She is said to exercise a power over the face of outward things, so that moulded, joined, abstracted, and endowed,

With interchangeable supremacy

they make men feel the life that is behind them.

The power that the highest minds bear with them is " the express resemblance " of this power that Nature exhibits. Their mind works as if it were Nature herself, and in a like manner. They also send forth power from themselves which changes, moulds, abstracts, and endows with life the objects of sense, and the thoughts of others; which creates new existence out of the impressions and thoughts it receives; the least suggestion enables them to build up great things in Thought and Act; they are equally willing to receive passively impressions, or to work on them; and often when God sends to them from Nature a new idea—something, as Wordsworth thinks, created for them—they catch it, or are caught by its " inevitable mastery." It is a ceaseless play, a ceaseless interaction between the world of their mind and that of the universe, and both the worlds are living. The imagination of lower minds—for of course this power of which he speaks is imagination, imagination

> Which, in truth
> Is but another name for absolute power
> And clearest insight, amplitude of mind,
> And Reason in her most exalted mood—

is enthralled by the sensible impressions, and therefore their mind is not wedded to the universe; but in the loftier souls, the imagination seizes like a master on the sensible impressions and feels through them the vivid spiritual life in Nature; and this life united to their own inward life quickens them.

> To hold fit converse with the spiritual world
> And with the generations of mankind.

They pass, that is, beyond the bounds of their own mind, and of the outward universe, into a higher world than either, a world which is, as it were, the child of these two parents, but a child greater than either of its parents.

And the result of having attained this higher region is a noble moral life, a life of liberty and blessedness.

> Such minds are truly from the Deity,
> For they are Powers; and hence the highest bliss

That flesh can know is theirs—the consciousness
Of Whom they are, habitually infused
Through every image and through every thought,
And all affections by communion raised
From earth to heaven, from human to divine;
Hence endless occupation for the Soul,
Whether discursive or intuitive;
Hence cheerfulness for acts of daily life,
Emotions which best foresight need not fear,
Most worthy then of trust when most intense.
Hence, amid ills that vex, and wrongs that crush
Our hearts—if here the words of Holy Writ
May with fit reverence be applied—that peace
Which passeth understanding, that repose
In moral judgments which from this pure source
Must come, or will by man be sought in vain.

Bk. xiv.

But the result is not only a noble moral life, but also
a deep religious one. Wordsworth brings out this by
returning a little on his past, and asking in reference to
the passage just quoted, whether he has in his own life
gained this moral freedom. It is a humbler destiny, he
answers, that he has pictured. He has had his visitations
in the solemn temples of the mountains, from careless
youth to conscious manhood; he had been a suffering man
and suffered with mankind, but he has never tampered
with conscience, never yielded in any public hope to
selfish passions, never been enslaved by worldliness, never
allowed the tendency

Of use and custom to bow down the soul
Under a growing weight of vulgar sense,
And substitute a universe of death,
For that which moves with light and life informed,
Actual, divine, and true.

It was fear and love that had done this—and here he is
referring to his boyish time—but only love at last, in
which fear was drowned; love by which "subsists all
lasting grandeur, without which we are dust;" love such
as in early spring all things feel for one another; love such
as the lover feels for her who is "his choice of all the
world;" love which soars beyond all earthly love, but

which contains it, the spiritual love that adoring finds its
end in God. Here, where the medieval Platonists ended,
Wordsworth ends. The life he had found in his own
mind, the life he has found in the outward universe,
mingling together " in love and holy passion," have led
him finally to the source of the life of both in God. The
delight of earthly passion is pitiable:—

> Unless this love by a still higher love
> Be hallowed, love that breathes not without awe;
> Love that adores, but on the knees of prayer,
> By heaven inspired; that frees from chains the soul,
> Lifted, in union with the purest, best,
> Of earth-born passions, on the wings of praise
> Bearing a tribute to the Almighty's Throne.

And then he resumes the whole of this history of his
mind. The organ of this spiritual Love is Imagination,
and it has been the " feeding source " of his long labour:—

> We have traced the stream
> From the blind cavern whence is faintly heard
> Its natal murmur; followed it to light
> And open day; accompanied its course
> Among the ways of Nature, for a time
> Lost sight of it bewildered and engulphed;
> Then given it greeting as it rose once more
> In strength, reflecting from its placid breast
> The works of man and face of human life;
> And lastly, from its progress have we drawn
> Faith in life endless, the sustaining thought
> Of human Being, Eternity, and God.

And he who has reached this point, and has the express-
ing power of the poet, is to be the prophet of Nature and
of men, to tell them of the Manhood that is greater than
Nature;—and the revealer in his own life through the
power of God whom he adores within him, of a more
beautiful and unworldly time, of a world where the heart
of Man may become more free and full of purer thought.
This is the duty of the poet—this ought to be the poet's
life. Two passages contain it, one at the end of the
*Prelude*; the other at the end of the preface to the

*Excursion.* I throw them both together, and close my lecture with them:—

> Prophets of Nature, we to them will speak
> A lasting inspiration, sanctified
> By reason, blest by faith: what we have loved,
> Others will love, and we will teach them how;
> Instruct them how the mind of man becomes
> A thousand times more beautiful than the earth
> On which he dwells, above this frame of things
> (Which 'mid all revolution in the hopes
> And fears of men, doth still remain unchanged)
> In beauty exalted, as it is itself
> Of quality and fabric more divine.

> And if with this
> I mix more lowly matter; with the thing
> Contemplated, describe the Mind and Man
> Contemplating; and who, and what he was,
> The transitory Being that beheld
> This Vision; when and where, and how he lived;—
> Be not this labour useless. If such theme
> May sort with highest objects, then—dread Power!
> Whose gracious favour is the primal source
> Of all illumination—may my Life
> Express the image of a better time,
> More wise desires, and simpler manners:—nurse
> My Heart in genuine freedom:—all pure thoughts
> Be with me;—so shall thy unfailing love
> Guide, and support, and cheer me to the end! "

# LECTURE XIII

## WORDSWORTH—*continued*

It was natural to Wordsworth, self-removed, as he was, from the crowd of men and from the more everyday interest of the world, that much of his religion should cluster round two things; one of which was the larger interest and vocation of the whole of mankind, and the ideas which push forward or backward the growth of Man; and the other, the interests and affections and duties that belong to the natural relations of parents and children, brothers and sisters, friend and friend, wife and husband. The former I have already treated of, showing how this secluded man threw himself with ardour into the general struggle of Man for liberty and right, and even in his later conservatism, preserved his vivid interest in human doings. The latter, however, I did not touch on, and my subject this afternoon is the religious thoughts which Wordsworth collected round the days and life of childhood, and, in connection with this, his view of Immortality.

And first, whatever may have been his stated creed, he laid aside as poet the severer doctrines of Original Sin, which stains the child with evil from its birth, and brings it into the world as the child of the devil. He compares his infant daughter who makes her "sinless progress," through a world

> By sorrow darkened and by care disturbed,

to the moon "that through gathered clouds moves untouched in silver purity,"

> Fair are ye both, and both are free from stain.

And instead of being far away from God, the child is

nearer to Him than the man; its first faint smiles, of
which we cannot tell the cause, are to Wordsworth—

> Tranquil assurances that Heaven supports
> The feeble motions of thy life, and cheers
> Thy loneliness.

And this is supported by the well-known ode in which
we find the isolated Platonic doctrine of reminiscence,
which Wordsworth partly modified by Christianity. To
understand that ode, to understand hundreds of allusions
in Wordsworth's poems, it is necessary to have some
clear idea of this doctrine, a doctrine seriously held by
Plato throughout a great part, if not the whole, of his
philosophic life. Its proof rested on the truth of his
doctrine of abstract ideas. These had an eternal exist-
ence; justice, temperance, knowledge, love, truth, and
the other things of God are real existences, and are the
glorious and blessed sights of Heaven, and the divine
life of the gods is in beholding them; they visit them
day by day, and draw life and power from their con-
templation. Now the soul of each man before it comes
on earth has lived in the train of the gods, and gone up
with them to look upon the vision of absolute truth, gazing
with the gods on that divine landscape of abstract ideas
which make up Eternal Being. But it has only looked
on it imperfectly; glancing at it, as it were, over the hill;
seeing it for a moment, and then departing. At some
time or other then it comes to earth in human shape, and
there its nature is threefold. It is rational, sensual, and
moral or spiritual. Then comes in the doctrine of reminis-
cence. For the whole of after existence is spent in
regaining by a series of recollections, and through a
continual struggle, the glorious vision which has been
lost—the vision of absolute ideas; and the regaining of it
will be entrance into true being. Of these ideas, the only
one that has any visible form on earth is Beauty. Now,
whenever we see earthly beauty, the memory of the
heavenly comes back, faintly, but enough to excite the soul;
and the germ of the wings the soul once possessed and lost
begins at the sight to push itself forth. It is then that

the struggle begins. The sensual soul, which Plato images as a large, misshapen horse, of a dark colour, beholding beauty, rushes blindly to enjoy it, and sees only and desires only the earthliness of beauty. But the spiritual soul, imaged as a white and immortal steed, looks beyond the earthly beauty to the heavenly that it images—and the intense struggle between the two is only settled with difficulty, in those who truly aspire, by the continued dragging back and subduing of the black horse by the rational soul, who sides with the white horse and is the charioteer. At last, after many efforts, the sensual soul is wholly brought under sway, and the vision of true beauty is reached, and with it the vision of the other noble ideas of wisdom, temperance, justice, and the rest. It takes ten thousand years, Plato thinks, before the soul can regain the imperial palace whence it came.

But it is not only the inward sensual desires that dim the light, and hold back the true soul from attaining ideas, but the world of the senses also, the material world, hampers its efforts and confines it. The only world in which the soul can truly live is the world of ideas; and the immortal steed is depressed and languishes in a sensible unreal world which has no harmony with it. But the effort ends at last. Again and again the vision of the eternal world, of the ancient glory, flashes before the soul, and recalls the pre-existent life: at each time the soul either falls away from it or draws nearer to it; and finally in those who do not continue falling, the wings the soul had once are entirely reformed, and it rises to abide among the gods, and daily to see the divine land-scape of ideas, and to live by the sight of it. The soul re-enters eternal life.

Hence, the doctrine of pre-existence, and that of remi-niscence, are in Plato connected with the doctrine of immortality as a necessary fulfilment of the two former. We have been once in union with absolute life; we recall in many lives here on earth that past, and grow gradually into union with it; and at last having recalled it all through effort and conquest of the animal nature, we resume it again for ever.

This is the philosophic doctrine a portion of which Wordsworth modified after his own fashion in the *Ode on the Intimations of Imortality from Recollections of Early Childhood.* He draws from it the conclusion, a conclusion Plato would not have drawn, that the child is nearer to God and to the vision of glory and loveliness than the man. Plato, on the contrary, would have made the grown philosopher more conscious of it than the child. But Wordsworth was really nothing of a Platonist; he only liked these ideas of pre-existence and reminiscence, and made his own thought out of them. Coming in childhood fresh from God, all the world seemed to his soul—since the heavenly light still lingered in it—

> Apparelled in celestial light,
> The glory and the brightness of a dream.

But now, as man he can see this glory no longer; yet in the season of May, when the heavens laugh and the earth adorns herself with joy, he recovers something of the recollections of childhood, he remembers at least that there was a visionary gleam, a glory and a dream that now are fled. And he explains it thus by the main ideas of the Platonic opinion:

> Our birth is but a sleep and a forgetting:
> The Soul that rises with us, our life's Star,
> Hath had elsewhere its setting,
> And cometh from afar:
> Not in entire forgetfulness,
> And not in utter nakedness,
> But trailing clouds of glory do we come
> From God, who is our home:
> Heaven lies about us in our infancy!

But soon the sensible world begins to do its work and drags us away from the vision of beauty and life. The growing boy feels the shades of the prison-house closing round him—the youth travels further from it, but is still attended by it:

> At length the Man perceives it die away,
> And fade into the light of common day.

Even Earth herself, the kindly mother, bringing her
natural pleasures of sense and affection, of human ties,
and with no unworthy aim, lures the child away from,
and makes the man forget

> the glories he had known
> And that imperial Palace whence he came.

This, you will see, may be called modified Platonism. The
next remarkable passage, however, is not Platonism, and
indeed, as expressed, it runs close to nonsense. We can
only catch the main idea among expressions of the child
as the best philosopher, the eye among the blind, that
deaf and silent reads the eternal deep, and is haunted for
ever by the eternal mind, the mighty prophet, the seer
blest—over whom his immortality broods like the day, a
master o'er a slave—expressions which, taken separately,
have scarcely any recognisable meaning. By taking them
altogether, we feel rather than see that Wordsworth in-
tended to say, that the child, having lately come from a
perfect existence, in which he saw truth directly, and was
at home with God, retains, unknown to us, that vision—
and because he does, is the best philosopher, since he sees
at once that which we through philosophy are endeavour-
ing to reach; is the mighty prophet, because in his actions
and speech he tells unconsciously the truths he sees, but
the sight of which we have lost; is more closely haunted
by God, more near to the immortal life, more purely and
brightly free, because he half shares in the pre-existent
life and glory out of which he has come.

The child is not conscious of this vision. He does not
know that he sees God; that he is, as he speaks, revealing
the truths of the world in which he half lives; that his
common thoughts and feelings have their beauty from his
directer sight of the glory he has left: that the glory and
beauty which he sees in the world of Nature is the reflec-
tion of the glory and beauty he saw in another life—that
he himself carries with him some of that celestial light.
He knows nothing of it. But we, looking back on our
childhood, or looking at childhood itself, from an age out
which has faded the light we had, remember the light of

this vision in our own childhood, and recognise its results
and quality in children. We know that what we then
felt and now see in children was and is divine, know it
from the bitter contrast, for

> The things which we have seen we now can see no more.

We are conscious that they were, because we have lost
them.

Many of the slighter poems of Wordsworth have this
thought as their root. He is thinking of it when he
describes the characteristics of a child of three years old,
and dwells upon her utter gladness, her self-sufficingness,
on the unexpectedness of her words and actions. For she
has companions, he would say, that we wot not of. She
is living in a world that we cannot see, and acts from
impulses derived from it of which we know nothing.
Here are the lines:

> Even so, this happy Creature of herself
> Is all-sufficient; solitude to her
> Is blithe society—who fills the air
> With gladness and involuntary songs.
> Light are her sallies as the tripping fawn's
> Forth-startled from the fern where she lay couched,
> Unthought of, unexpected, as the stir
> Of the soft breeze ruffling the meadow-flowers;
> Or from before it chasing wantonly
> The many-coloured images imprest
> Upon the bosom of a placid lake.

His sister is thinking of the same, when she speaks of
the child who is unconscious of the limits of our thoughts
of time and space:

> Who, worn out with the mystery
> Of time and distance, night and day,
> The bonds of our humanity.

Wordsworth is thinking of the same in his little poems
of *We are Seven*, and in the *Anecdote for Fathers*. The
child in the first has no idea of any severance between
earth and heaven; her dead brother and sister are still a
part of the family; death is nothing to her knowledge;

and she speaks, in saying, We are seven, one of those " truths which we are toiling all our lives to find," and the recollection of which, as felt by us when a child, is an intimation of our immortality. In the second poem, Wordsworth questions his little sons, as to the reason he should like one place more than another, and drives the boy at last into finding a reason in the existence of a weather-cock in one place and not in the other. The boy had no real reason to give, and the father felt that he had forced the child to say what was untrue. But in the saying of it, he, unconsciously, made Wordsworth conscious of the wrong he had done. He felt that he was reproved, as it were, by the God in the child; and the poem, which is a poor one, and only interesting from our being able to refer it to the same thought that prompted the great ode, closes thus:

> O dearest, dearest boy, my heart
> For better love would seldom yearn,
> Could I but teach the hundredth part
> Of what from thee I learn.

No lovelier expression of that thought exists than in the last lines of the sonnet composed by the seaside:

> Dear child! dear girl! that walkest with me here,
> If thou appear untouched by solemn thought,
> Thy nature is not therefore less divine:
> Thou liest in Abraham's bosom all the year,
> And worship'st at the Temple's inner shrine,
> God being with thee when we know it not.

Still more strongly does the same thought appear in the little poem to Hartley Coleridge, then six years old. The first ten lines are steeped in the philosophy of the ode:

> O thou! whose fancies from afar are brought,
> Who of thy words dost make a mock apparel,
> And fittest to unutterable thought
> The breeze-like motion and the self-born carol;
> Thou faery voyager! that dost float
> In such clear water that thy boat
> May rather seem
> To brood on air than on an earthly stream;

Suspended in a stream as clear as sky,
Where earth and heaven do make one imagery;
O blessed vision! happy child!
Thou art so exquisitely wild,
I think of thee with many fears
For what may be thy lot in future years.

And once more, in speaking of presentiments, he falls back also on this thought, and says:

The tear whose source I could not guess,
The deep sigh that seemed fatherless,
Were mine in early days.

As the boy grows, this innocent unconscious life in the eternal is more and more invaded by the outward life of which he becomes directly conscious. His games, his father's love, the outward scenery of nature and of human life, all enthral him, and the vision grows dim and dimmer. The conscious life of earth replaces the unconscious life of heaven.

But he is not left without visitations. Nature takes up the work, or rather the divine life in Nature makes itself felt again and again, and thrills the boy who has forgotten his immortal life with a vague sense of it. In the midst of his eager earthly life, he is suddenly checked, the beauty, or the terror, or the mystery of Nature touching him for a moment. It is a sudden recalling—a shadowy recollection of the childish glory; only it is now often linked with fear, since it has become unknown. For an instant he feels as if the outward world had no reality, and is forced to make things real to him by touching them; it misgives him that things are as they seem; mysterious feelings of fear beset him in solitude, as if a Presence that he could not put by were there; he has dreams, instincts of things greater than he can grasp, that break suddenly in upon him in the midst of wild enjoyment, and which make him thrill with excitement, surprise, and dread. They come to him, he knows not how, brought by

A rainbow, a sunbeam,
A subtle smell that Spring unbinds;
Dead pause abrupt of midnight winds,
An echo, or a dream.

P

Their origin from Nature, we have already traced in speaking of the *Prelude*.[1] Certain natural impressions caused in his brain the sense of unknown modes of being. Certain motions of the sense made him conscious through their ministration of a world beyond this world, of something in him which he had lost and suddenly remembered. They were, he says, "gleams like the flashing of a shield," that lit for an instant the mind with memory of the ancient glory, and brought with them a touch of subdued sadness and surprise.

Such is the thought at the root of the lines on the boy of Winander; such is the thought which gives its special quality to the poem on the *Cuckoo*, where the far-off wandering voice of the bird made it the image of a mystery, and woke a dim sense of mystery; to the poem of *Nutting*, when in the midst of the exulting destruction that a boy delights in, a dim reproach creeps in as if he had done harm to living things. It belongs to many other poems, where Nature is represented as touching into momentary consciousness of life the sleeping forms of the ancient life of the soul before it came on earth, as sometimes in our more common life some slight event will bring back during the day a dream we had dreamt, but had wholly forgotten.

These are the things which, whether coming unannounced to the soul itself, or led to it by Nature, are, when remembered in after years, powerful to put the mind into a world different from this; to reprove, exalt, and give light by bringing to our mind our immortal birth; to support us in hours of obscure distress by the high thought that we belong to God, and are born to regain the truths that once we had—and they come again and again till even in manhood we get back through the memories of childhood to the imperial palace whence we came.[2]

---

[1] See Lectures vi., vii.

[2] In my last lecture I touched on this subject, and the passage in the *Prelude*, Book xii., which I analysed there, ought to be read along with the ode. I insert one passage here for comparison:

> Oh! mystery of man, from what a depth
> Proceed thy honours. I am lost, but see

There is the noblest expression of all this in the ode:

> Not for these I raise
> The Song of thanks and praise,
>     But for those obstinate questionings
>     Of sense and outward things,
>     Fallings from us, vanishings;
>     Blank misgivings of a Creature
> Moving about in worlds not realised,
> High instincts before which our mortal Nature
> Did tremble like a guilty Thing surprised:
>     But for those first affections,
>     Those shadowy recollections,
>         Which, be they what they may,
> Are yet the fountain light of all our day,
> Are yet a master light of all our seeing;
>         Uphold us, cherish, and have power to make
> Our noisy years seem moments in the being
> Of the eternal Silence; truths that wake,
>         To perish never;
> Which neither listlessness, nor mad endeavour,
>         Nor Man nor Boy,
> Nor all that is at enmity with joy,
> Can utterly abolish or destroy!
>         Hence in a season of calm weather
>         Though inland far we be,
> Our Souls have sight of that immortal sea
>         Which brought us hither,
>         Can in a moment travel thither,
> And see the Children sport upon the shore,
> And hear the mighty waters rolling evermore.

Such things grow less and less as years go on; as middle age touches us, it is only the memory that we

> In simple childhood something of the base
> On which thy greatness stands; but this I feel,
> That from thyself it comes, that thou must give,
> Else never canst receive.   The days gone by
> Return upon me almost from the dawn
> Of life: the hiding-places of man's power
> Open; I would approach them, but they close.
> I see by glimpses now; when age comes on,
> May scarcely see at all; and I would give,
> While yet we may, as far as words can give,
> Substance and life to what I feel, enshrining,
> Such is my hope, the spirit of the Past
> For future restoration.

have had such visions that keeps us true to our immortal
destiny; as to the visions themselves, they leave us
altogether, and the light is only the light of common day.
Still, now and then the vision does arise, and it came to
Wordsworth in 1818, on an "evening of extraordinary
splendour and beauty." He sees the wonderful effulgence
of the sun setting over hills, the silent spectacle of glory
and radiance on the earth below; and he is swept beyond
the earthly beauty to aspire to the heavenly—nay, half of
the beauty is itself of heaven, out of the heart of the
perfect life.

> Thine is the tranquil hour, purpureal Eve!
> But long as godlike wish, or hope divine,
> Informs my spirit: ne'er can I believe
> That this magnificence is wholly thine;
> From worlds not quickened by the Sun
> A portion of the gift is won.

The mountain ridges seem a golden ladder, on which one
might ascend to heaven; "wings at my shoulders seem to
play"—the very Platonic expression—he calls on droop-
ing old men to come forth, and see to what fair countries
they are bound; he bids the genii wake the traveller that
he may meet the dower God gives him in such beauty.
Then comes this passage:

> Such hues from their celestial Urn
> Were wont to stream before mine eye,
> Where'er it wandered in the morn
> Of blissful infancy.
> This glimpse of glory, why renewed?
> Nay, rather speak with gratitude;
> For, if a vestige of those gleams
> Survived, 'twas only in my dreams.
> Dread Power! whom peace and calmness serve
> No less than Nature's threatening voice,
> If aught unworthy be my choice,
> From Thee if I would swerve;
> Oh, let thy grace remind me of the light
> Full early lost, and fruitlessly deplored;
> Which, at this moment, on my waking sight,
> Appears to shine by miracle restored;
> My soul, though yet confined to earth,
> Rejoices in a second birth!

Thus, felt in childhood, often recollected, sometimes renewed in middle age, he prays in another place that his old age may keep to its latest breath these visions of the soul, these dreams of an immortal life; that he may rejoice, with quickened spirit, in the admonitions of God's voice given in the quiet of the heart, or suddenly flashing on him from Nature—till he feel secure of life in God, and pray the prayer of one whose immortality is sure.

> Breathe through my soul the blessing of Thy grace:
> Glad through a perfect love, a faith sincere,
> Drawn from the wisdom that begins with fear,
> Glad to expand, and for a season, free
> From finite cares, to rest absorbed in Thee.

This is the growth of the faith in immortality. Direct vision of the eternal world and life in it, during infancy—recollection of the glories of that vision when the world has hidden it from our eyes; frequently repeated recollections, all leading us back to the heavenly life and accustoming us to trust in it—sudden outbursts of actual vision such as childhood possessed, when moved by some splendid sight or inspired act; rarely coming, but when assisted by the recollections intensely convincing—quiet philosophic faith in the intuitions of the soul that tell of eternal life, so that

> though nothing can bring back the hour
> Of splendour in the grass, of glory in the flower;
> We will grieve not, rather find
> Strength in what remains behind;
> In the primal sympathy
> Which having been must ever be;
> In the soothing thoughts that spring
> Out of human suffering;
> In the faith that looks through death,
> In years that bring the philosophic mind.

Then, as the old man looks back, he sees that his wish has been fulfilled; the same divine remembrance of beauty that made his heart leap up when he beheld a rainbow in the sky is with him still. That which was his as boy, has been his as man, is his, now that he is old. The child has been Father of the man, his days have been " knit each to each in natural piety." The piety is the piety of immortal hopes; the old man's vision of the future life is co-incident with the child's vision of the pre-existent life. Age is not desolate then. The unutterable dewy light of joy is gone, it rests no longer on Man or Nature. But the love which has come of suffering, the long union with the human heart, the sad but hope-lit experience, do not make him love Nature less than when he tripped as lightly as the brooks that fret their channels, but more; he can still enjoy the innocent brightness of a new-born day; the beauty of all things is not less, but more, because touched with the sentiment of mortal sorrow and mortal victory; they take a sober, but not less lively colouring; and the meanest flower that blows, to a heart so trained, leads him beyond itself to live in the eternal, in the land where men weep not for either joy or sorrow, for the thoughts that are there are too deep for tears.

Abiding then in old age we look back to our childhood. We were nearer then to the divine life, and there the soul recognises most clearly its immortal features:

> Ah! why in age
> Do we revert so fondly to the walks
> Of childhood—but that there the Soul discerns
> The dear memorial footsteps unimpaired
> Of her own native vigour; thence can hear
> Reverberations; and a choral song,
> Commingling with the incense that ascends,
> Undaunted, toward the imperishable heavens,
> From her own lonely altar?

We look forward also, that we may see the life to come, the resurrection of that we once possessed; we have not really lost, but gained, by age, if we have been true to the divine gleams that we could not wholly lose. Old age is then great—raised above the thraldom of the passions that beset guilt, the ambitious worldliness which made the light such common day, the very world of sense that made us forget our ancient spiritual home.

> Rightly it is said
> That Man descends into the Vale of years;

Yet have I thought that we might also speak,
And not presumptuously, I trust, of Age,
As of a final Eminence; though bare
In aspect and forbidding, yet a point
On which 'tis not impossible to sit
In awful sovereignty; a place of power,
A throne, that may be likened unto his,
Who, in some placid day of summer, looks
Down from a mountain-top,—say one of those
High peaks that bound the vale where now we are.
Faint, and diminished to the gazing eye,
Forest and field, and hill and dale appear,
With all the shapes over their surface spread:
But, while the gross and visible frame of things
Relinquishes its hold upon the sense,
Yea almost on the Mind herself, and seems
All unsubstantialised—how loud the voice
Of waters, with invigorated peal
From the full river in the vale below,
Ascending? For on that superior height
Who sits, is disencumbered from the press
Of near obstructions, and is privileged
To breathe in solitude, above the host
Of ever-humming insects, 'mid thin air
That suits not them. The murmur of the leaves,
Many and idle, visits not his ear;
This he is freed from, and from thousand notes
(Not less unceasing, not less vain than these,)
By which the finer passages of sense
Are occupied; and the Soul, that would incline
To listen, is prevented or deterred.

    And may it not be hoped, that, placed by age
In like removal, tranquil though severe,
We are not so removed for utter loss;
But for some favour, suited to our need?
What more than that the severing should confer
Fresh power to commune with the invisible world,
And hear the mighty stream of tendency
Uttering, for elevation of our thought,
A clear sonorous voice, inaudible
To the vast multitude, whose doom it is
To run the giddy round of vain delight,
Or fret and labour on the Plain below.

                              *Excursion*, Bk. ix.

It was in this faith that Wordsworth lived and died. It was in deep belief in God and Immortality, and in a Saviour from sin, that he passed his quiet days, and found peace far from the strifes of men. It was in the calm—alike removed from stormy passion, and from the disturbing lusts of the world—that this faith gave him, that he wrought out and lived, the high morality which he has given to us in the *Ode to Duty*, in the fine strain of the *Happy Warrior*, and in many noble passages in the *Excursion*. It was in this faith that he quietly reposed in his domestic life, and by it enhanced all the faithful affection for wife and sister, children and brother, that nowhere in English poetry burns with a lovelier or a purer light. As age grew on, his calm deepened, he had " the silent thoughts that search for steadfast light;" he wished, and realised the wish, to present to God his life as a " pure oblation of divine tranquillity." Nor was he without joy in the midst of calm; there was no stagnant water in the deep lake of his heart; such poems as the *Ode to Duty* and others are filled with a resolute and exalted joy; and there were times when, as the old man prayed, his delight was transfigured:

> I bent before Thy gracious throne,
> And asked for peace on suppliant knee,
> And peace was given—nor peace alone,
> But faith sublimed to ecstasy.

Nor can I better close these lectures upon him than by the sonnet in which he looks back and looks forward in a strain, where clear knowledge of what Man is in himself alone, is mingled with quiet faith in what he is in God.

### AFTER-THOUGHT

> I thought of Thee, my partner and my guide,
> As being past away.—Vain sympathies!
> For, backward, Duddon! as I cast my eyes,
> I see what was, and is, and will abide;
> Still glides the Stream, and shall for ever glide;
> The Form remains, the Function never dies;

While we, the brave, the mighty, and the wise,
We Men, who in our morn of youth defied
The elements, must vanish;—be it so!
Enough, if something from our hands have power
To live, and act, and serve the future hour;
And if, as toward the silent tomb we go,
Through love, through hope, and faith's transcendent dower,
We feel that we are greater than we know.

# LECTURE XIV

WHEN speaking at the beginning of these lectures of
theology in the earlier poets of the Natural School, in
Cowper and Crabbe who preceded the great outbreak of
song, I omitted Robert Burns. I now fill up that gap,
which was left for a sufficiently good reason—that though
the influences which came on England at that time did
have their result upon Burns, they had far less result
than on others, because he was essentially the creation
of his own land, and of another poetic descent than that
of England. With regard to the poetry of Nature, he
only carried on in a more vivid and tender way, and on
precisely the same lines, the same sort of natural descrip-
tion which had been worked by the Scottish poets from
the time they began to write. With regard to what I have
called, along with others, the poetry of Man, he was less
universal and more national than the English poets who
followed him. But when we look at his work on this
subject, and compare it with that of the English poets who
preceded him, or with that of his contemporaries, Cowper
and Crabbe, we find in him a peculiar quality which gives
him a distinct rank in the history of English poetry, of
which I may as well speak in this connection. He restored
passion to our poetry. It had not belonged to it since
the days of Elizabeth. No one would guess, who began
to read our poetic literature shortly after the death of
Shakespeare, how rich the veins of nature and emotion
had been in our country. He might read through the
whole of our poetry, with the exception of a few songs
and sonnets, down to Burns, and not find any poetry
which could truly be called passionate. So, when the
fire broke out again in Burns, it was like a new revelation;
men were swept back to the age of Elizabeth, and heard

again, though in different chords, the music which had then enchanted the world. And since his time, our poetry has not only been the poetry of Man and of Nature, but also of Passion. And it sprang clean and clear out of the natural soil of a wild heath, not out of a cultivated garden; it was underived from other poets, for Burns read nothing but a collection of English songs; it was unassisted by the general culture of a literary class, for it was born when he was reaping in the fields, and when he held the handles of the plough; it came direct out of a fresh stratum of popular life. It was as if the Muse had said, I am weary of philosophy and satire, weary of faded sentiment, of refined and classic verse, and of stern pictures of misery, and I will have something fresh at last; and had driven a shaft down through layer after layer of dry clay, till she touched, far below, a source of new and hidden waters, that, loosened from their prison, rushed upwards to the surface, and ran away a mountain torrent of clear bright verse, living and life-giving. Burns added passion to the poetry of Nature and Man.

But independent of the poetry that has to do with these two subjects, and the theology of which I shall speak of in this lecture and the following, there is in Burns a poetry of personality. On this, in its religious aspect, I shall speak in my third lecture.

Our subject to-day is the Poetry of Man from a theological point of view, as we find it represented in Burns. The poetry of Man began distinctly in England with the first coming to the light of the ideas of the Revolution. Before the great singers came we can trace these ideas in English poetry, and I have traced them in Cowper and Crabbe. They appear also in Burns, but in by no means so full a form. They influenced him insensibly; he does not recognise their power. But in one point he was consciously at one with them, in their claim that the poor should be thought of as men; in the placing of Man—apart from all consideration of caste and rank and wealth and race—foremost. How far he was touched by this, and how far it was specially modified in him, we have now to consider, and it is part of our subject, for it either flowed directly from a new and larger idea of God, or was creative of a larger view of Him.

He was born in 1759, and the first edition of his poems was in 1786. His first work and his youth preceded, then, the outbreak of the Revolution. We cannot therefore say that he was revolutionised, but he was a born revolutionist, in the sense of being ready, when he thought it needed, to take the part of his own class against selfish rank and wealth; and to appeal for his right to do this to the common duties and rights of man as man. Not in Cowper, not in Crabbe, not in any of the after poets, was the cry of the Revolution more clearly heard than in the whole of the fine song—

> Is there, for honest poverty,
>   That hangs his head, and a' that?
> The coward slave, we pass him by,
>   We dare be poor for a' that!
>     For a' that, and a' that,
>     Our toils obscure, and a' that;
>     The rank is but the guinea stamp,
>     The man's the gowd for a' that.

Being thus himself poor, "following his plough along the mountain side," and having in him, not discontent with his poverty, but a heart framed to enjoy and love all beauty, and to feel all that was human, and being insensibly influenced by the spirit of the time, he threw into tender and humorous song the sorrows and affections of his own class, their religion and their passions, their amusements and their toil, till all the world laughed and wept with Ayrshire ploughmen. As in England, so in Scotland, we now find something better than the distant sentimental view which we found the poets took of the poor. Burns did in 1786 the work which Crabbe began in England in 1783 and Cowper in 1785. Mark the dates, how they all run together. And I have often wondered in looking at these lines of Gray's, which Burns put as motto to the *Cottar's Saturday Night*—

> Let not ambition mock their useful toil,
> Their homely joys and destiny obscure;
> Nor grandeur hear with a disdainful smile
> The short but simple annals of the Poor—

whether he recognised in them the note of distance, and meant to make his own vivid, lifelike description of a poor man's home a contrast to the fine-gentleman sentiment of Gray.

One would think so from the preface and the after-dedication to his poems. The passages are interesting, and bear upon the present question.

" The following trifles are not the production of the poet who with all the advantages of learned art, and, perhaps, amid the elegances and idlenesses of upper life, looks down for a rural theme, with an eye to Theocritus or Virgil. To the author of this, these, and other celebrated names their countrymen are, at least in their original language, a fountain shut up and a book sealed. Unacquainted with the necessary requisites for commencing poet by rule, he sings the sentiments and manners he felt and saw in himself and his rustic compeers around him, in his and their native language."

And in the Dedication—

" The Poetic Genius of my country found me, as the prophetic bard Elijah did Elisha—at the Plough, and threw her inspiring Mantle over me. She bade me sing the loves, the joys, the rural scenes and rural pleasures of my native tongue: I tuned my wild, artless notes as she inspired."

At home, then, among the poor, he gave them his best work, and it was done, as all the highest work is done, with passion.

In the movement of thought and feeling towards the recognition of the poor and working men as sons of God, and as made of one blood with the rich and learned, there was as yet no natural passion. Cowper and Crabbe, though their sympathy with the lower class was deep, spoke for it and of it, not out of it; and naturally there was no personal passion in their work. They led men to feel with the poor, but it was as men feel with the sorrows and joys of a different race. But when Burns came, it was a different business. I have said that he restored passion to our poetry. He brought it now into this movement.

He added its fire to the work which Cowper and Crabbe had done, and threw around poor life and rural nature, for the first time for centuries, " the light that never was on sea or land." When he spoke, whether to ostlers at the inns, or to " jewelled duchesses," as Carlyle calls them, or to literary men in Edinburgh, they one and all felt his fire, and believed that rustic hind and milk-maid, field labourer and beggar, were of like passions with them-selves, were just as good and just as wicked, and in the same way, as they were themselves. They recognised the truth when it was told with a passion that was born directly out of the life of poverty and labour, and they said—These, then, are men and women, not shadows any longer: bone of our bone and flesh of our flesh.

The same passion ran through all he said and did. No one felt more keenly than Burns that tingling of. the heart which at its height produces poetry of word and deed. In that which men ordinarily call Love, we are told that his agitation exceeded anything his friend had ever seen; but of that I do not speak. His emotion was as great, though not so disturbing, in all the other spheres of emotion. Who has not felt the intense thrill of passion in the lines on *Mary in Heaven*, in *Mary Morison ?* and hearken to this, in which he describes that which most pleased him in the songs of Lapraik—

> There was ae song amang the rest;
> Aboon them a', it pleased me best,
> That some kind husband had addrest
>      To some sweet wife:
> It thrilled the heartstrings through the breast
>      A' to the life.

And his only wish was not to produce finespun emotion, or to write to please the critics, but to touch the heart.

> Gie me ae spark of Nature's fire,
> That's a' the learning I desire;
> Then though I drudge thro' dirt and mire,
>      At plough or cart;
> My Muse, though hamely in attire,
>      May touch the heart.

And so it has done. Even the wildest pieces of mad

humour like *Tam o' Shanter* or the *Jolly Beggars* have so much of intense humanity in them, that they move natural emotion, and reconcile us even to coarseness for the moment. We feel that men are kindly, even in their ill: though I must speak afterwards of the bad results of Burns' victory over the ascetic party in Scotland.

But whatever the ill results, this bright, tender, heart-felt representation of the life of the poor not only brought the rich and comfortable near to the poor and struggling, and placed both on the common platform of humanity, but it also made the poor themselves contented and in love with life, by bringing out the nobility and beauty of the simple human passions, and of the common working life of men. Even in the sharp contrast which he draws in the *Twa Dogs* between the lives of poor and rich, he himself prefers that of the poor, and gives clear reasons for it—reasons which had their root in no sentimental view of the question. He was then no mere wild revolutionist; he did not wish to level all. He preached a crusade against the selfishness of the rich, but he did not wish the poor to become as the rich. Keep to your own life, he said to them; learn to live it, to live truly and honestly in it—to recognise in it the dignity of Man, to rejoice in its hardy independence, in its simple but deep emotions.

Nor was all this without a religious basis. It was connected in the mind of Burns with the thought of God as the Father of the Poor, of God as even the universal Father before whom each man stood, stripped of wealth, of rank, of outward show—a character alone. And this God, in the poet's mind, was Love, and the source of all Love was in Him. It was impossible then for Burns to hold the strong Calvinistic view of the reprobation of the greater part of mankind. He was continually in antagonism with it, and many and shrewd were the blows he dealt it. To him, as well as to Shelley and Byron, we owe much of our freedom from this inconsiderate view of God, a view which only could have been born in a society that was rooted in an aristocratic view of the world, though strange to say, yet explicable enough if one

had time to go into the matter, it has been the favourite
religion of democracy.   As to Burns, his deep conception
of the universal power of God's love, led him to pity the
Devil and to hope for his redemption, a hope that many
who still believe in the Devil share with him.

> Ye aiblins might—I dinna ken,
> > Hae yet a stake.

On the other side, God's love for Man would make Him
indignant with those who oppressed the weak or injured
the poor.   And the poems of Burns are full of this indigna-
tion.   Not all the rage of winds and biting frost are more
unkind, he says, than the miseries

> That heaven-illumined man on brother man bestows.

All his religion, he says, came from the heart; and
it drove him, when he thought of his poor people and
their hard lives, and how beautiful they often were with
natural feeling; when he thought how much they suffered
and how much was due to them, to refer the origin of
their good to God, and to leave the righting of their
wrongs to God.

He went further, and threw over the lives of the poor
the light of God.   Every one knows the scene in the
*Cottar's Saturday Night;* every one has felt how solemn
and patriarchal it is, and how all the charming gossip
and pleasant human fun, and modest love which charm
us in it are dignified by the worship of God that follows.
But that poem must not be taken as representing the
religious feeling of Burns; it is purposely made religious;
and all we can truly say of Burns is, that whether as
regards his own art, or when he speaks of the lives and
love of the poor, he was one of those men who at the end
of last century claimed for men a universal Father in
God, and vindicated the poor as His children.   It is not
of course stated directly—that would not be the way of
a poet—but it is a spirit in his work, and it flows through
all his graver poems.   It affects also distantly all his
poetry, and owing to its influence, we find the grace and
tenderness of human feeling used to make beautiful that

which the world calls common, even that it calls unclean. This is, indeed, the most sacred work of poetry, and it has so strict an analogy with the means Christ chose to use in His teaching, that it forms another point of union between Christianity and poetry. I have often said that if we would understand Christ's words and works, we must approach them as we approach poetry. The parables that have to do with Man are poems, in which the common lives and sorrows of men are made divine by interpreting them as symbols of God's relation to men. The world can never forget the shepherd seeking his sheep, the father's joy over his son lost and found, the blessing given to the children, the life the Saviour lived among the outcasts and strayed of earth, the glory of love which was shed over the fisher's life, the way in which the whole of humble working life was linked to God, the proclamation of the care of the Highest for the shepherd on the hill, for the sower in the field.

And whatever one may have afterwards to say of Burns' religion, the practical result of much of his poetry in his age was to do similar work to that of Christ — to exalt and beautify the life of the poor, to make them feel that they were cared for and known of God.

It was then, in this way, by upholding Manhood as first, and by exalting the poor as men, and by preaching a common brotherhood, that Burns developed the poetry of Man, and was a child of the ideas of the Revolution. But there was another human element in his poetry which I must speak of now—his strong nationality. It was connected with theology, and it was unconnected with the Revolution. One of the main ideas of the Revolution was its rejection of all nationalities for the sake of mankind. It proclaimed one country of which all men were citizens, one nation of which all men were members, of which all men were patriots, to which all men were bound to offer up their lives. A man was not, in the first instance, an Englishman, Frenchman, or Italian, he was a man. Its tendency was then to repress any strong feeling of nationality, and to substitute for it a strong Humanity. And we have found that element in the poets in England who were

most influenced by the Revolution.  We do not find it in
Burns.  Nor is it likely that we should; for if love of
Nature is one of the distinguishing elements of all Scottish
poetry, love of Scotland is the other, and Burns is the
descendant of the one as well as of the other.

It seems to be doubted both by Burns and Carlyle
that Scotland was fond of herself till Burns arose—by
Burns in lines to W. Simpson which I shall quote after-
wards; by Carlyle when he speaks of the remarkable
increase of nationality in Scottish literature, and attributes
it chiefly to Burns.  Both of them seem to forget, or not
to know, that the poetry of Scotland has never failed to be
national, even after the union of the two crowns, the time
of which they speak.  The Lowland poetry began in
Scotland with James I., and took its first inspiration from
Chaucer, whom James had read while a prisoner in
England.  But the remarkable thing is, that while it
retained the manner of Chaucer, it kept none of his spirit.
It was not English, nor even medieval.  It became
entirely Scottish in spirit; it employed itself on Scottish
subjects; and whatever form it took up, ballad, or fable
or pastoral, or allegory, it gave them all a special Scottish
turn.  And one of its characteristics is a devotional
patriotism.  Ballad after ballad records it, and when we
come to the greater makers, it is intense.  Dunbar's
*Golden Terge* is one instance; Douglas brims over with it;
even Lyndsay, before he was carried away from purely
poetic work to political, gives himself to glorify his land.
Again, at a time when personification raged in Scottish
poetry, one of the most frequent personifications is that
of Scotland herself.  She appears as Warden of the Land,
in a noble song of Alexander Scott's, full of manly freedom
and patriotism; and it is patriotism whose main desire
is not for warlike glory, but for the glory which belongs
to a nobly-governed country whose citizens were free
from falsehood, flattery, and impurity.  Or, as in Dunbar's
*Thistle and Rose*, life is given to the Royal Arms, and the
animals and flowers sing of the glory of the land.  The
same strong feeling—and in this short sketch I can give
you no idea of its strength—is continued through Ramsay

and Ferguson and a number of minor poets, right down
to Burns, whose *Vision* and *Scots wha hae wi' Wallace bled*
are the legitimate children of this long patriotic passion.
A flood of Scottish prejudice, he says, has been poured
along my veins, and I feel it will boil there till the flood-
gates shut in eternal rest.

> The roughbur thistle spreading wide
> Amang the bearded bear,
> I turned the weeder clips aside
> An' spared the symbol dear.

In nearly all his poems we find this traditional nationality,
and it entirely prevented him from receiving the dena-
tionalising idea of the Revolution. All the characteristics
of the past poets belong to him. He keeps himself
throughout to Scottish subjects; his scenery is entirely
Scottish, his love of liberty concentrates itself round
Scottish struggles; his muse is wholly untravelled; and
while it gains a certain strength within its sphere from
this limitation, it loses that breadth of view and depth of
passion which belong to the greater poets. He may have,
as Carlyle says, a resonance in his bosom for every note
of human feeling—and he has—but all the human feeling
is Scottish. There is no need to account for this; the
reasons are plain in his position and his life. Nor have
we any need to regret it, for if Burns had been more
universal we should have lost him; he could not have
built a loftier rhyme than his own rustic national one,
and he knew that well. When the Muse of Scotland
appeared to him, she bade him sing his own people; her
mantle was adorned with rivers, hills, and boroughs of
Scotland, and in her face was the character of Scotland's
poets—

> A hair-brained, sentimental trace,
> Was strongly marked in her face;
> A wildly witty, rustic grace
>       Shone full upon her;
> Her eye, ev'n turned on empty space,
>       Beamed keen with Honour.

And the same " wildly witty, rustic grace " that shone

full upon her shines in all his work. For Scotland's glory and Scotland's beauty

> I kittle up my rustic reed
>      It gies me ease.

And nothing can be better or brighter than the lines in which he expresses this, written to W. Simpson,

> Ramsay an' famous Ferguson,
> Gied Forth an' Tay a lift aboon;
> Yarrow an' Tweed to monie a tune,
>      Owre Scotland rings,
> While Irwin, Lugar, Ayr an' Doon,
>      Naebody sings.

> The Ilissus, Tiber, Thames an' Seine,
> Glide sweet in monie a tunefu' line!
> But, Willie, set your fit to mine,
>      An' cock your crest:
> We'll gar our streams an' burnies shine
>      Up wi' the best.

> We'll sing auld Coila's plains and fells,
> Her moors red-brown wi' heather bells,
> Her banks an' braes, her dens an' dells,
>      Where glorious Wallace
> Aft bure the gree, as story tells,
>      Frae Southron billies.

> At Wallace' name, what Scottish blood
> But boils up in a spring-tide flood?
> Oft have our fearless fathers strode
>      By Wallace' side:
> Still pressing onwards, red-wat-shod,
>      Or glorious dy'd.

And this profound patriotism had, in that religious country, where religion lies deeper among the peasantry than anywhere else, where the strife of religion has been violent in proportion to the feeling that it was a matter of life and death, its root in God. God was claimed as the source of patriotism; it was He that made men love their country, he who inspired those who warred for its liberty. I might quote passage after passage from Douglas, from Dunbar, from Sir D. Lyndsay, from the others; but let Burns himself answer the call—Burns, whose "warmest wish to heaven was sent" for his dear, his native soil.

> O Thou! who poured the patriotic tide
> That streamed through Wallace's undaunted heart;
> Who dared to, nobly, stem tyrannic pride,
> Or nobly die, the second glorious part,—
> The patriot's God, peculiarly thou art,
> His friend, inspirer, guardian, and reward—
> O never, never, Scotia's realm desert;
> But still the patriot, and the patriot bard,
> In bright succession raise, her ornament and guard!

In these days, when we think less of a national and more of a universal God, it may strike us as limiting and dividing a great idea to speak of a patriot's God. And, when we consider well, there is a great disadvantage in thinking of a God whose peculiar care is England, or France, or Germany; indeed, if we do so, in war for example, our idea of God must become wholly confused. One or other side must be wrong in claiming God as specially theirs. God is the God of mankind; His equal love belongs to and falls on all, on the meanest as fully as on the most cultured races. That is the large conception which will free us from the national selfishness into which patriotism degenerates, and increase that international kindness and communion which are beginning to be a mark of our time; nay more, bring us slowly up to the thought which a century hence will, I hope, dominate politics — national self-sacrifice. The Christian thought of personal life is to surrender our personal life and its interests for those among whom we live. The Christian thought of social life is to surrender our personal interest for the sake of the well-being of society, not only of our own country's sake, but of human society. The Christian thought of national life, which has been prominently put forward by the Comtists, is that each nation, when the interests of the whole race are concerned in such sacrifice, should give up its national interests for those of all mankind. Till we attain that, and it will necessitate a general confederation of nations, we cannot be called Christian nations, for we are not regulating our national conduct by the Christian rule of life.

Keeping, however, this thought of God clear as the foundation of our life, we are then able—without ill or unreason following from it—to love God as the God of our country also, as the source of a noble patriotism. For we no longer think of God as the God of England in rivalry or contest with other nations, and claim Him as specially ours to the exclusion of others. We say to ourselves, on the contrary—" Our country has a special work to do in the progress of the whole race; work which is fitted to our national character, and which our special gifts enable us to do better than any other nation. It is God who in His education of the whole of mankind has given us that work. Within its sphere, then, and with this object before us, which is first universal, and afterwards national, God is the source of our patriotism." We love our country then in God, when we love it for a higher reason than its own glory—for the reason that it is the instrument of God to do a special work for Man. We support and cherish the peculiar characteristics of England, because these are needful for the growth of mankind. We love and cherish its scenery because that is one of the most formative elements of our national character, and that character is needed for the growth of Man. We are patriots because we are men who believe that the decay or death of England would damage the interests of the whole race, and delay its progress to the great goal whither God is driving it.

And nothing is lost in that idea of the old power and dearness of patriotism. The old conception is taken up into the new, only all the evil of national selfishness is taken out of it. We love our country none the less because we love man more.

In my last lecture I spoke of the poetry of Man as found in Burns, and I dwelt especially on the way in which he —in accordance with the new spirit which was stealing into the world—devoted his work to the interests of the poor among whom he lived, not of set purpose like a philanthropist, but because he could not help it like an artist.

It is his natural poetry of which I shall speak to-day, and we can connect it with the previous lecture by the thought that among the joys that God has given to the life of the poor one of the deepest is the beauty of Nature, and the heart to love it; such a heart as Burns himself possessed, who

> In his glory and his joy
> Followed the plough along the mountain side.

Things without money or without price, beauty not hid in galleries, but spread abroad a feast of delight on every mountain-side and stream-fed meadow—this was God's gift to the poor. And strange to say, Burns seems to think, and he should know something about it, that the poor were better able than the rich and cultured to enjoy the loveliness of the world. That certainly would not be true of England now; for there are few things we have so attentively cultivated as the love of Nature. But it may have been true in his days that

> The Laverock shuns the palace gay,
> And o'er the cottage sings;
> For Nature smiles as sweet, I ween,
> To shepherds as to Kings.

Wordsworth, too, takes up the same thought; he himself is formed by Nature, step by step; it never seems to occur to him that his companions—dalesmen, shepherds, pedlars, even the little children—can be otherwise than lovers of Nature, and able to enjoy its beauty; and we must take his witness as true, for he lived among them all his life. But this is certainly not the case further south, and the lower one goes in England, the less one finds of it, except in the upper classes, among whom it has now become almost instinctive.

We have, then, this curious problem at the very outset of our lecture—that the poor of the north-western part of England on the border, and of the west border of Scotland, are lovers of Nature, while the poor of Midland and Southern England are not. I do not say that I can solve that problem; I cannot—but I can make a few conjectures about it, and it will lead me to speak of the Nature poetry of Scotland, a poetry so distinct from that of England that it is necessary to say something about it before we touch on it in Burns.

The higher appreciation of Nature among the men of the west border may partly be owing to the grandeur or wildness of the scenery they live amongst. The imagination cannot help being awakened and impressed by desolation. Fear is easily stirred in boyhood by the storm on the moor, or the majesty of mountain loneliness, and fear awakes imagination. Afterwards, when with manhood comes courage, fear passes into a sense of the sublime, and terror has its beauty, since it stirs emotion. But when perception of the sublime exists, perception of the beautiful in the peace of nature soon follows: the one throws the perceiver into the arms of the other. That may be one explanation, but it is not a sufficient one. It does not account for this love of Nature among the dwellers in the quiet scenery of Ayr and Lanark.

Therefore I cannot help conjecturing that a great deal of the intense perception of Nature's beauty which we find in early Scottish poetry—especially the wild love of colour—the descriptions of Gawin Douglas blaze like an Oriental monarch—may be due to some far-off admixture of Celtic blood. All the Scottish poets of early date possess it, and it seems to spring out of nothing. There is no cause for it in the influence which Chaucer and his school had on poetry in Scotland, for it does not exist among them; nor in the French, for there it does not exist at this early time of which I speak, except, indeed, where one gets a touch of Celtic influence. In the absence of any real cause that I can absolutely point to, I am forced to conjecture that this love of nature was a legacy left by the Celtic blood among the English of the Lowlands. The old kingdom of Strathclyde ran up from our present Wales to the Clyde, taking in the half of the Lowlands and the more western parts of Northern England. The Celtic poets had this intimate desire to look at Nature, this passion for colour, this wish to glorify the woods and streams, which is so remarkable in Douglas and the rest. They take, as the Scottish poets do, isolated natural objects—a rock, a tree, a glade—fall in love with them, and bring them with one magical touch into the domain of Fairyland. Their early literature, their romances, their songs are full of this. There is nothing of it in early English poetry. A few distant echoes of it are heard in Shakespeare, but scarcely any true notes of it in England, till Keats and Shelley and Tennyson. In Scotland we find it at once, not at all in its perfection, but sufficiently distinct to sever Scottish poetry from all others of the time, and to make it of a different race from English.

Now my conjecture is, that this Celtic element of natural love of the beauty of the world, this special power of seeing Nature, and delight in observing her—which came so early to Scotland, and so late to England—crept in from Strathclyde, mingled in the blood of the English of the Lowlands, and left behind it, when the Celtic race died away, its peculiar note in the Lowland mind. Anyway, this is true, that Scotland has always been a land where poets loved Nature, and that she first sent that love down to England.

The original impulse of the Lowland poetry came, as we have seen, from Chaucer through James I. We might then expect that its natural description, with which we have now to do, would retain some of the pecu-

liarities of Chaucer's landscape. That is not the case.
The intense nationality of the Scots of which I have
already spoken seized on this element in poetry, and at
once and for ever put aside the conventional landscape
of Chaucer. The Scottish poets could not realise smooth
and soft meadows and fair gardens, and trees standing so
many feet apart. There was nothing of the kind in Scot-
land. Their own scenery forced itself on their notice,
and they loved it well. In all the poems, the trees, rocks,
rivers, and valleys are distinctly Scottish; the sun rises in
Scotland, the months and seasons as described by Douglas
have the character of his own country. We may say that
the law which bids a poet describe what lies before him,
and write with his eye on the object, in distinction from
that which insists on the landscape being always made
up of certain stock properties, is due to the Scottish poets.
In England it did not *prevail* till Cowper's time—in
Scotland it was carried out, owing to the love of her
people for their own country, before the seventeenth
century. It is a curious anticipation by many years of
the love of Nature for her own sake which was first
rooted in our literature by Wordsworth.

With regard to the description of Nature itself, it is
absolutely unique at the time. It is perfectly amazing
to find, in the sixteenth century, in Scotland, elaborate
natural description full of close touches of reality, over-
laden with colour, minute, enthusiastic, at a time when
nothing of the kind existed, or had existed in England.
Here and there it is touched by the convention of Chaucer,
as in the use of Latin names for the sun—a survival
which we find in Burns—but the feeling for Nature of
Douglas and Dunbar, and their natural description, are
not only unlike anything that had ever been in England,
they remain unlike anything which prevailed in England
down to the very end of the eighteenth century. The only
man in whom we miss this minute, observant, patient effort
to represent Nature as she is, is Drummond—and he was
not of the Scottish line—he was Elizabethanised. The
whole thing is a curious literary problem, and one of the
conclusions to be drawn from it is this—that we owe

our special natural poetry to an impulse received from Scotland. It is not too much to say that the first touches of love of Nature in Pope's time which we find in Gay were due to the influence on him of his friend Ramsay's poems. Neither is it strange to find that he who broke away from the tea-tray landscape of Pope, and was the first poet in England who painted Nature directly, was Thomson, a Scotsman, who came to London with the MS. of his *Winter* in his pocket. He started the impulse which ended in the natural poetry of Wordsworth, Shelley, Keats, and Tennyson, but he drew himself the impulse from a long line of Scottish ancestors who had loved and described Nature.

This is the ancestry of the natural poetry of Burns. If we except the extraordinary love of colour which is one of the characteristic marks of the early Scottish poets, he has the same intense love of Nature and accuracy of description that they possessed. In two things, however, he differs from a man like Douglas. First, his range is not so wide. There was nothing Douglas saw which he did not describe—I might even say catalogue, for the things are put down one after another without any power of artistic combination—but there are only certain things which strike Burns. In fact they come in so often and are so nearly always the same, that a certain amount of conventionality prevails in his natural descriptions. It is the ordinary Lowland scenery on the borders of the hills; milk-white thorns, corn-fields, running rivers under birchen shade, the singing of birds, sheep wandering on the hills, heather and its flowers, streams in spate, and certain conditions of the sea—with a special love for spring and winter—winter being always a favourite of the Scottish poets. He does not get far beyond this range, and it is, as I said, narrow. But within the range it is exquisitely true and tender, the sentiment of it is perfect, it is never exaggerated, nothing is forced or over-dwelt on; it is the natural and swift reproduction in words of the landscape, and all that is said sounds sweetly and smells sweetly to the sense.

Secondly, his natural description arises out of a deep

and natural love of Nature, but it is never alone as that of Douglas was, never without the element of humanity. In a delightful passage, when the genius of Scotland's muse speaks to him in vision, Burns expresses his early passion for natural beauty.

> I saw thee seek the soundng shore,
> Delighted with the dashing roar;
> Or when the North his fleecy store
>     Drove through the sky,
> I saw grim Nature's visage hoar
>     Strike thy young eye.
>
> Or when the deep green-mantled earth
> Warm cherished every flow'ret's birth,
> And joy and music pouring forth
>     In every grove,
> I saw thee eye the gen'ral mirth
>     With boundless love.

Nature, too, was bound up with his art: it was she who gave it half its fire, she who thrilled him often with so much emotion that he broke into poetry, she who was mingled up with all his love and sorrow in humanity.

> The Muse nae Poet ever found her,
> 'Till by himsel' he learned to wander
> Adown some trotting burn's meander
>     An' no think lang:
> O sweet to stray and pensive ponder
>     A heartfelt song—

and there is not a song of his which has not its background of tender landscape. But strong as this love of Nature was in Burns, it never wholly absorbed him. He could not, like Wordsworth or Shelley or Keats, sit down in a wood or on a hill-side and describe what he saw, for the love of it alone, without a thought of humanity, without a thought of self, absolutely lost in love of the world. His natural descriptions are always the background for human figures, for human love or sorrow or mirth. Man is always first in Burns; and he either wholly subordinates Nature to humanity, or he uses it as illustrative of human life. I take the lines to the *Lass of Ballochmyle.*

'Twas even, the dewy fields were green:
On every blade the pearlis hung,
The zephyrs wantoned round the bean
And bore its fragrant scents along.
In every glen the mavis sang,
All Nature listening seemed the while,
Except where greenwood echoes rang
Amang the braes of Ballochmyle—
With careless step I onward strayed,
My heart rejoiced in Nature's joy.

That is complete enough. Wordsworth would have left it there, Burns cannot—over the braes he brings a maiden—

Perfection whispered, passing by,
Behold the lass of Ballochmyle.

It is the same in the two well-known poems of *Mary in Heaven*, and the *Banks of Doon*—his landscape is always not for itself, but for the human feeling with which he links it; and where the feeling is most deep, the landscape is most lovely.

This humanisation of landscape is the transition step between a poetry like Pope's which has Man only as its subject and rejects Nature, and such poetry as much of Wordsworth's, in which Nature assumes the first place. It was made in England by such men as Gray and Collins, in whose work, if you remember, Nature is moralised for Man's sake, while it is described with a certain affection. Burns, who carefully read Gray, represents in Scotland such a standpoint, only that it is there not in progress to a future, but in retrogression from a past poetry of Nature; and also, the landscape is not moralised by Burns, but made passionate with love.

He mingled Man and Nature together, and in doing so he transfers the depth of his personal affections to natural objects, and speaks of them with often a sudden tenderness, an exquisite mournfulness of pity, or a quick sympathy with their joy. His address to the daisy makes one feel for it as if it were a beautiful child too rudely treated.

Wee, modest crimson-tipped flower,
Thou's met me in an evil hour,
For I maun crush amang the stoure
    Thy slender stem.
To spare thee now is past my power,
    Thou bonie gem.

But even here he cannot, as Wordsworth does, leave the daisy and its fate alone.   He is driven to compare it with helpless maid and luckless bard—and finally with himself—

Ev'n thou who mournst the Daisy's fate,
That fate is thine—no distant date;
Stern Ruin's ploughshare drives, elate,
    Full on thy bloom,
Till crushed beneath the furrow's weight
    Shall be thy doom.

The same quick, simple tenderness went to animals.   One sees how Burns loved birds in almost every song.   He was a hater of field sports; and even when in driving his plough he turned up the field-mouse's nest, he could not bear the sorrow he was causing; he enters into all the pain and wants of the little thing as if it were a child, till he feels that the mouse is his companion and that he has harmed a fellow-creature.

I'm truly sorry Man's dominion
Has broken Nature's social union,
An' justifies the ill opinion,
        Which makes thee startle,
At me, thy poor, earth-born companion,
        An' fellow mortal!

But here, again, he cannot help, like Gray, moralising, nor in the end getting back to himself.

But, Mousie, thou art no thy lane,
In proving foresight may be vain:
The best laid schemes o' mice an' men
        Gang aft a-gley,
An' lea'e us nought but grief an' pain,
        For promised joy.

> Still thou art blest, compared wi' me,
> The present only toucheth thee.
> But, Och! I backward cast my e'e
>                     On prospects drear!
> An' forward, tho' I can na see,
>                     I guess an' fear.

Take one more example, which combines this tenderness of pathos towards the animal creation with one or two of his vivid natural touches of storm.

> I thought me on the ourie cattle,
> Or silly sheep, wha bide this brattle
>                     Of wintry war,
> Or through the drift, deep-lairing sprattle,
>                     Beneath a scaur.
>
> Ilk happing bird, wee helpless thing,
> That in the merry months of spring
> Delighted me to hear thee sing,
>                     What comes o' thee?
> Where wilt thou cower thy chittering wing
>                     And close thy ee?

As to the theology in all this love of Nature, there is not much of it. Burns had no special philosophy any more than Keats about the relation of God to Nature. He adopted the old simple view of God as the Creator and sustainer of the universe that the stern religion of Scotland had taught his fathers. But the poet's love of all things was so strong in him that he added to that idea the thought of God as the lover of the universe he had made and supported. And the love that God had for the universe was reflected in the breast of Burns, and so wrought that when he was most full of it, he drew nearest to God. It was a love which had no wild tempest of passion in it, which did not strive or cry in his heart. In it he did not "feel his pulse's maddening play," nor was he hurled blindly into wrong. Therefore, all the depth of his nature found in it peace which had no fierce reaction; and an uplifting of heart which was freed from over-driven excitement, and pure. It was when Nature was most softly fair or when it was sublime that Burns drew nearest to God. He has recorded this himself in a kind of preface to one of his poems.

"There is scarcely any earthly object gives me more— I do not know if I should call it pleasure—but something which exalts me, something which raptures me—than to walk in the sheltered side of a wood or high plantation in a cloudy winter day, and hear the stormy wind howling among the trees, and raving over the plain. It is my best season for devotion: my mind is wrapt up in a kind of enthusiasm to Him, who in the pompous language of the Hebrew bard, 'walks on the wings of the wind.'"

In such a sentence we see Burns lifted for one moment into that imaginative but dark piety which the Covenanter had, and which was largely derived from the solemn and terrible aspects of the mountains and storms he often lived among. But such piety will often be as gloomy and cruel as the climate, and link to itself a superstition passionate and dark with fear in inferior men, stern and unrelenting in stronger men. From this Burns was freed by the tenderness of his heart, which made him, when he was devotional, love and not fear God; and the terror and gloom of Nature—never very great in the Lowlands— did not make him stern to others, nor alas! stern to himself. His love of Nature then did not lead him to that practical love of God which shows itself in doing for love's sake what is right.

It is the case of many: love of Nature often goes with a character gifted or sometimes cursed with an intense power of sympathy which shrinks from putting itself in action; with strong passions which are not controlled by will; with a joyousness and a power of sorrow which carry the man beyond himself into a region where neither piety nor morality exists, and where he becomes of the same temper as Ariel or Puck, so that if either a call of duty then comes, or a temptation, he will be likely to ignore the first, or fall into the latter. In such a state there is no conscience. We see and feel, and no more; we do not think of acting. This was especially the case with Burns.

Has then the love of Nature no religious power? Is it

better to be without it? I cannot think so. Those who do not feel it, who see and love no beauty, may be moral, but they will never reach the nobler enthusiasms of religion: their religion itself will be without the loveliness and tenderness which attract the soul, and their theology more intellectual than spiritual in its statements. Moreover Ruskin is quite right when he says, " that, supposing all circumstances otherwise the same with respect to two individuals, the one who loves Nature most will always be found to have more faith in God than the other." For far more fully than in erring Man are certain grand qualities of God revealed in Nature, righteousness, order, justice, peace, omnipotence, beneficence, judgment. It is strange, I think, how much this knowledge of God through His works, and its natural influence in producing faith, has been neglected in religious teaching, when one remembers that the whole of the Old Testament is full of it. All the Hebrew poets were profound lovers of Nature, but of Nature seen as the revelation of God's character. When God wishes to convince Job of His unalterable goodness and justice, He makes the whole of Nature and its wonders pass before him. He gives him no theological or pious teaching, but out of the whirlwind asks, Hast thou considered, etc., etc. Through the whole range of the poets who speak in the Psalms, the same spirit is felt. The hundred-and-fourth Psalm is almost a kosmos, but it begins with the source and power of all —with God. The angels are God's messengers to direct the forces of Nature. Nature herself is the image of God, His possession and His voice. A hundred texts occur to us. The sea is His and He made it, and the strength of the hills is His also. His righteousness is like the great mountains, His judgments as the deep. In wisdom did He make His manifold works, and He himself rejoices in them. The heavens declare His justice, and His glory; and listen to this, Ps. lxv. v. 5-13.

By terrible things in righteousness wilt thou answer us, O God of our salvation; who art the confidence of all the ends of the earth, and of them that are afar off upon the sea:

R

Which by his strength setteth fast the mountains; being girded with power:

Which stilleth the noise of the seas, the noise of their waves, and the tumult of the people.

They also that dwell in the uttermost parts are afraid at thy tokens: thou makest the outgoings of the morning and evening to rejoice.

Thou visitest the earth and watered it; thou greatly enrichest it with the river of God, which is full of water: thou preparest them corn, when thou hast so provided for it.

Thou waterest the ridges thereof abundantly: thou settlest the furrows thereof; thou makest it soft with showers; thou blessest the springing thereof.

Thou crownest the year with thy goodness; and thy paths drop fatness.

They drop upon the pastures of the wilderness; and the little hills rejoice on every side.

The pastures are clothed with flocks; the valleys also are covered over with corn; they shout for joy, they also sing.

No one wants to take away the work of Science, the result of which among cultivated men is by deepening the observation of Nature to increase the love of it; but we want to add to it this old Hebrew notion of a Divine life and character within it; and this ought to be the work of the poets, whose business it is to give vitality to things. For if we are left to contemplate a dead world, as much as modern science leaves us to do, the true love of Nature—that which exalts and makes tender—will slowly die away; we cannot long give affection to that which we conceive as lifeless. If we would love Nature well, we must find life in it: and when we find its life in finding God pervading it, then love of Nature leads to faith in God.

It is true little of this is found in the New Testament. The Apostles were so overwhelmed with their special practical work, and so overtaken with the multiplicity of it, that it is no wonder we find nothing of their life with Nature, or of Nature as revealing God. But that does not say that it did not exist in them; and it probably did, if they were influenced deeply by the teaching of Christ. For there alone in the New Testament is this love of Nature seen as leading to love of God, is Nature used as revealing God. He Himself, as I have often said, has made plain in His life how dear to Him was the beauty of the world. He loved to wander by the lake, among the corn, and on the grassy hills. He marked the aspects of the sky, the growth of trees, and the beauty of flowers. He loved animals, and drew some of his loveliest teaching from their ways. When weary, He sought the hill-top by night; when uplifted by strong communion, the higher ridges of Hermon; when exceeding sorrowful, the lonely olive grove.

And His teaching lays the whole of Nature under contribution. He makes Nature a parable of which God in His relations to Man is an interpretation. The ways of the sun and wind and rain, of the grass and flowers, of the corn-field, the fig-tree and the vine, were all taken up into the religion that He taught. He bid us seek the Heavenly Father, not only in the words and life in which He manifested God, but in the book of the common things of earth and air. And he who walks with Christ through the world may feel that the love of Nature is religious.

Still more connected with a moral life, and with one which prepares the soul for God, are the same tenderness and love when they are felt for animals. I have already said that no poet ever more deeply felt the sorrows of created things than Burns, nor stronger anger against their slaughter for sport. The *Wounded Hare* will live in men's memories when hares are no longer shot for sport. To him horses, dogs, birds, the dwellers on the moors and in the grass were friends. When Mailie died

> He lost a friend and neebor dear
> In Mailie dead.

That is the feeling which marks civilisation. The savage must slay for life and life's support; the half-civilised man carries out the practice of the savage without his excuse; and it is the characteristic of that class of ours, which one of our own day has called the barbarian class, to find amusement in slaying. It is of course a remnant of barbarism, and it is obliged to be kept up by laws which bear hard on the poor, for the sake of the sport of the rich. Before an advancing civilisation such laws as the game laws, and such barbarisms as keeping whole tracts of country desert for the sake of game, must perish.

There is no doubt in my mind, that however amusing and however manly such sports may be, they are hardening to the heart; and they set men apart from the nobler thoughts and tenderer feelings of life, not altogether, but up to a certain point. They are cruel, and the indulgence of cruelty, however it may be condoned by society, barbarises it. And so far as it is cruel and accustoms to cruelty, it separates men from God and from love; and that it is unconscious cruelty and is not felt as such by the conscience, does not make the matter better, but worse. One of the things then that our Christianity has to get rid of, is the destruction of life for the sake of sport; of all sports which bring with them needless suffering of animals and needless irritation of men. The whole thing is a part of that aristocratic element which lingers still among us, but is passing to its fall.

Every poet then, who, like Burns, increases that larger tenderness of the heart which not only loves men, but hates to give pain to the lower animals, is, so far at least, religious in his poetry. And nearly all our later poets have done this sacred work, and have made it a part of their theology. Their device has been the device of Coleridge—

> He prayeth well, who loveth well
> Both man and bird and beast.

# LECTURE XVI

### ROBERT BURNS — *continued*

I HAVE spent two Sunday afternoons in speaking of the poetry of Man and of Nature and of the theology in them, as represented in the work of Burns.  Our subject to-day is concerned with some aspects of his life so far as they bear on the personal religion that appears in his poetry, and with his relation as a poet to a special form of theology.

We have seen how well and manfully, when he was young, he accepted his place as a poor man, and how he honoured poverty by song.  But his poverty did not guard him against the temptations which beset his artist nature.  He had but little power of will when his passions were excited, and whether it was love, or fame, or the pleasures of the table, he was swept away by all alike. The natural result of this course of life, combined with want of will, was that he never set himself to any ordered music, never adopted or pursued any end with any perseverence.  These elements in his character were developed into unfortunate prominence by his visit to Edinburgh.  He was taken out of his natural atmosphere, and though he kept his independence, and retained his free nature, his life was spoilt by the change.  His frankness and audacious personality made him unwelcome to those who had lionised him at first, and he was gradually dropped.  And when he was put aside he did not like it, and he could never breathe easily again the air of humble life.  It was a severe trial.  A few weeks before he was flying from his country, an exile and in despair, and now he was at the summit of the wave of Society, his name in every mouth.  A few weeks later and the whole pageant had dissolved.  He was back again in a small country place, discharging the most unpoetical of offices.  He took the glory and the fall with equal good temper and manliness, though they both intensified his errors. He was not dazzled at Edinburgh into believing that his fortune was made. He knew that he was too bold and rough to win patronage, and he went home to fulfil his duties as an exciseman, the only place that Society could find to employ the genius of Burns. It was like Society; and yet, though we are indignant, it would be unfair to lay all the blame of the poet's life on the neglect of Society. If Burns had been a little nobler in character, with some self-restraint, some purposefulness in life, he might have been happy and written his poems as an exciseman. But he could not; passions, appetites, and irregular excitement, carried far beyond what he could bear, soon ruined his life. He had gained a taste for fame, and he was continually invaded by persons who led him away from his work. His fashionable life produced results which brought him to an early death. It stimulated the fatal qualities of his nature; it spoilt the unity of his life by fixing one end of its axis among the rich and another among the poor, and it threw him into the worst company—the company of the lionisers of genius, who seek it to be amused and then mock at the source of their amusement. It was, no doubt, his own fault that he perished; but it would have been well if the big people had let him alone, or at least, if they who flattered him had done something better for him than set him to catch smugglers. It is all well summed up in Carlyle's *Lectures on Heroes*, in a delightful passage, which I remember being told by one who heard it, was closed exactly as it is in the book—Carlyle pronouncing with inimitable meaning in his voice the last word " But "—and then rapidly passing behind the curtain of the platform.

" Richter says, in the island of Sumatra there is a kind of Light-chafers—large fireflies—which people stick on spits and illuminate the ways with at night. Persons of condition can thus travel with a pleasant radiance, which they much admire. Great honour to the fireflies! But——! "

I do not think I ever see fine and fashionable people " taking up " a poor artist, or making a show in their drawing-rooms of a struggling genius—and trying, in their blind, barbarian way, to help him on—especially when they demand that the artist should submit his individuality to their caprices—without a desire to say to him—For God's sake, bear any poverty rather than yield to this. They do not mean badly, but they have no intelligence to mean better; and their tender mercies will kill your powers. You may not be Samson, but it is bitter to make sport for the Philistines. It degrades the intellect and corrodes the heart.

There were two things, then, in his life which spoiled him. Want of aim was one; and unrestrained passion was the other; and both characterise one type of the artist, the second or rather the third-rate type. In the highest artist, the aim of his life is clear, and he never fails to see it and to labour for it. His passion also, which he must possess, is always in his power. He may choose to indulge it, but he does so purposely, and he can check it when he will with ease; but he rarely chooses to indulge it to the prejudice of his art, whatever that art may be. For the sake of his art, he wills to be temperate and he is; and while enjoying all things to the very top of enjoyment, he is always capable of staying his hand at the point where enjoyment threatens to pass into satiety.

Burns had neither of these qualities. "The great misfortune of my life," he says, "was to want an aim:" and bitterly he regrets it in hours when solemn thought was uppermost. The note he strikes at the end of his *Address to the Field Mouse* is still more plainly heard in the *Ode to Despondency*,—

> Happy, ye sons of busy life,
> Who, equal to the bustling strife,
>    No other view regard!
> E'en when the wished end's deny'd,
> Yet while the busy means are ply'd,
>    They bring their own reward:
> Whilst I, a hope-abandoned wight,
>    Unfitted with an aim,
> Meet every sad returning night
>    And joyless morn the same.

At other times—and how characteristic this is of such a nature—he accepts his aimlessness as a good thing, or at least, as something which cannot be helped, and is to be made the best of. He is in good spirits, his mood is happy, and he contrasts his thoughtless and wild enjoyment with the miserable state of those that live by rule, whose hearts are never touched by impulse:—

> For me, an aim I never fash;
>> I rhyme for fun.
>
> .     .     .
>
> I'll wander on, wi' tentless heed
> How never-halting moments speed,
> Till fate shall snap the brittle thread,
>> Then, all unknown,
> I'll lay me with th' inglorious dead,
>> Forgot and gone!
> But why o' death begin a tale?
> Just now we're living, sound an' hale;
> Then top and maintop crown the sail,
>> Heave Care o'er side!
> And large, before Enjoyment's gale,
>> Let's tak the tide.
>
> .     .     .
>
> An anxious e'e I never throws
> Behint my lug, or by my nose;
> I jouk beneath Misfortune's blows
>> As weel's I may:
> Sworn foe to Sorrow, Care, and Prose,
>> I rhyme away.

And then he turns upon those whose life he half despises, and at times half regrets:—

> O, ye douce folk, that live by rule,
> Grave, tideless-blooded, calm, and cool.
> Compared wi' you—O fool! fool! fool!
>> How much unlike;
> Your hearts are just a standing pool,
>> Your lives a dyke!

I have no special fondness for over-purpose in life, for living by rule. The common advice—find one aim, and pursue it to the exclusion of all others, is good worldly advice, but that is not always the best. He who allows

everything else to be absorbed in the pursuit of one aim
will probably succeed in his aim, and be called by the
world the most prudent and intelligent of men. He may
be prudent, but he will scarcely be intelligent. For he
will become a man of only one thought, and all those
parts of his nature which he cannot bring into activity
round his special thought will become dead for want of
use. He will not, and he cannot grow. It is better to
be like Burns than to be one of that type.

But if the aim you propose to yourself be one of those
which, because they are ideal, seek their food from every
quarter, and claim as helpers the powers of heart, spirit,
and brain; if it allow not only of enjoyment and growth
through variety of interests, but also of wise passiveness
and healthy idleness; and yet is itself so pure and high
as to prevent passiveness from producing sloth, and
activity from degenerating into a disease—then to have a
clear aim is absolutely right, and Man, in fact, cannot
achieve greatness in life, or worthiness within, unless he
have it. But if he has such an aim, its very essential
difference is, that it sets its possessor free from the slavery
of over-labour; that it takes him out of the class of the
" douce folk who live by rule." And the great artist
possesses it: Burns did not.

The other lesson of the life of Burns is that of the evil
of unrestrained passion. I do not use the word in the
sense of the passion of love, though that was the special
frailty of Burns; but of all deep emotion, whether arising
from appetite, or sense, or the vision of ideas. In this
large sense, it is not passion itself which is harmful; nay,
as I have often said, nothing can be done well without
emotion; nothing perfectly without intense emotion.
The cold-hearted folk, however practical, have no powerful
influence on the world. And in all art it is absolutely
necessary. " Put your passion into it," says Keats;
and he gives in that phrase the first principle of art. We
have already seen that because Burns possessed this
quality, he poured new life blood into English poetry.
And all that was best in the man and his poetry came
out of it—his spirit of universal kindness, his indigna-

tion at wrong, his inability to cringe, his insight into Nature, his love of animals, his vivid entrance into and his glorifying of common life, his deep religious feeling towards Him whose very self was Love—nay, we owe to it even the goodness in his badness, the touch of wild self-sacrifice, of a higher love than the sensuous love in his sins, which did not redeem them, but made them more capable of pardon, more open to repentance than those sins of self which do not shock Society. Nor was he unaware of this himself, and he has said it with his own special force:—

> I saw thy pulse's maddening play
> Wild send thee Pleasure's devious way,
> Misled by Fancy's meteor ray,
>       By Passion driven:
> But yet the light that led astray
>       Was light from Heaven.

You see he does not deceive himself, for Burns had one of the noblest qualities a man can possess—entire sincerity with himself; it never occurred to him to be untrue. Though the light of Heaven was in the affection, yet, through his own fault of will, it led him astray. There was no will towards right strong enough to check the rushing tide of enjoyment. Impulse and its gratification took the moment and became its master. Whether it was the pleasure of society, or the appetite for drink, or the passion of love, or the fire of indignation, it was all the same; he was swept away into their extreme: and of course became in turn the prey of dark despondency, of torturing remorse, of religious gloom, of the evils of over-indulged satire.

He ran the course so many run. Having no restraint of self, he sank into satiety, and the misery of satiety seeks a new excitement or new phases of the old—till excitement becomes the only food of life. But there is a limit to excitements. The time comes when either no more exist or we have exhausted all our powers of enjoyment. Then come the tyranny and the punishment.

We again seek the old excitement, driven by its lash,
but when we drain the cup which once was pleasure, it
is pain. The " crime of sense is avenged by sense that
wears with time." It is that very torture which the
mediæval poets invented for the avaricious—molten gold
poured down their throats; our enjoyments have become
red-hot and burn our life away; nor, worst of all, can
we get rid of them—we must drink them though we
abhor them.

Enjoyment is a necessity of life, and its morning air.
It is equally vain and wicked to lessen or decry it, for
we have not half enough of it. But it is a shameful
thing when men, not ruling it with temperance, degrade
it in the eyes of others by making it equivalent to satiety.
Enjoy then; but keep the beauty of enjoyment by self-
restraint in it; and then I venture to say—though there
are those so utterly base as to restrain themselves in
vicious enjoyment that they may keep the pleasures of
sin longer—that your enjoyments will on the whole keep
pure, that there will not be much in them which will
offend the eye of God, that they will serve your growth,
and give you power to do all your work in a stronger
and finer manner.

Again, wanting all will in passion, Burns wanted, when
under its dominion, the sense of right and wrong. In
the hour of excited feeling he was willing to let everything
go—Law, Honour, Conscience, and Religion. Nothing
remained but his passion; and it was right, and every-
thing that stood in its way, wrong. It made its own
wrong and right, and as usual the two became inextricably
mixed together—for apart from the moral question, it is
the oddest thing in all such states of feeling that there is
often really a touch of right in the wrongness, and a shade
of wrong in the rightness that we feel.

But it is not a good thing when the conscience gets
puzzled; and when it gets altogether confounded, as it
sometimes does, and goes, wearied out, to sleep, and
leaves passion to have its own way—not only is much sin
done, but this also happens—all the charm and good of
passionate feeling dies or begins to die.

> I wave the quantum of the sin,
> The hazard of concealing,
> But och! it hardens a' within,
> And petrifies the feeling.

There is no enduringness in passion of any kind when it deliberately drugs the conscience. For the conscience wakes out of its heavy sleep when the day of excitement has passed by, and wakes up so angry that it lets in remorse, and remorse is an ill companion. It does not heal, it so mauls the soul that the memory of the excitement becomes poisonous. And it finally ends by bringing on the reckless indulgence which is hated while it is going on, and which adds, when exhaustion comes, another bitter element to the curse of satiety. The glory and delight of true passion are destroyed, and the man ends as Burns ended, in a ruined and wasted life. "The wind bloweth over him and he is gone, and the place of him knoweth him no more." This is the lesson of the life of Burns. He knew it himself. He puts it at the close of the epitaph he wrote to himself.

> Reader, attend!—whether thy soul
> Soars fancy's flights beyond the pole,
> Or darkling grubs this earthly hole,
> In low pursuit:
> Know—prudent, cautious self-control
> Is wisdom's root.

Yes! and enjoyment's root also; though I should take exception to the words "prudent" and "cautious." For no life can be perfect which is overmastered by either prudence or caution.

Again, the special theological turn which some of his poems took, arose out of this unbridled passionateness. For their strong opposition to Calvinism was more the result of anger at the penance the kirk imposed on him for open sin than of any religious zeal. He seized on the patent objections to the doctrines of reprobation, effectual calling, and the rest, and used them as stalking horses for his avenging satire; and the bitter feud which existed on these doctrinal subjects between MacGill and Dalrymple, the two ministers of the town of Ayr, supplied him with all the opportunity he wanted. His first satirical poem, *The Holy Tulzie* (quarrel), ridiculed a quarrel between two ministers, Moodie and Russel, on " effectual calling," and delighted the opponents of Calvinism. It was followed by *Holy Willie's Prayer*, the most ferocious blow that was ever dealt at the ugly side of Calvinism—over-ferocious, as usual with Burns, to do any really good work against it; and so full of coarseness and wild irreverence that it only shows how high religious rancour ran among the clergy when these elements in it were condoned by one side for the sake of the occasion it gave them against their enemies.

It is true that Burns, in his wiser moments, would always have been a foe to the extreme Calvinistic doctrines, on the ground that he felt, being a lover of all things himself, that they made God into a demon of selfishness. His heart, like Shelley's, hated and denied that dreadful theology. But he never saw the good or the poetry which underlie its ideas, and his attack on it was just as much, if not more, caused by the natural reaction of the Bohemian nature against the ascetic type of Calvinism. Of that type he found two forms: one the stern, righteous asceticism, which condemned all gaiety as unworthy of an immortal soul; which secluded the religious man wholly from all worldly things as in themselves profane; which chastised with the utmost severity of word and deed all sin, and especially the sins of passion; and which lived up to this standard truthfully—the other the sham asceticism—a type Calvinism is sure to produce by its unnatural strictness—the crime of men who, wearing the mask of a stern religion, in secret indulged in all kinds of wickedness, and then fell back on their election by God to eternal life to free them from fear, and to enable them to sin at their ease.

Against the first Burns proclaimed the doctrine of a more liberal religion, and claimed the right of enjoyment; and so far he was right. But he could no more put limits to the statement of this than he could put limits to his own practice of it, and the statement went so far as to condone immorality of every kind. Conviviality was glorified, drunkenness was exalted into an excellence, illicit love was made poetical, and in the delight of the reaction from the over-strictness of Calvinism, which the poems of Burns encouraged, the whole tone of morality in Scotland was lowered; and in nothing more than in the frightful impulse given to a hospitality which insisted on the canonisation of drunkenness, and made the pleasures of the table the true impulse of art and song. We trace this even in the works of a man like Wilson, whose *Noctes* are deformed by it.

Whatever thanks then we may owe to Burns for his exposure of the ghastly side of Calvinism, must be largely modified by the evil he did in the way he exposed it. It is a bad thing to expel an evil opinion by an evil practice, and though it sounds like a paradox, it is not so uncommon.

Against the second, that is, the sham asceticism which was a cloak of sin, the indignation of Burns was righteous. We cannot but rejoice at the way in which he flayed alive William Fisher, the Holy Willie of the poem, a leading elder, " a great pretender to sanctity, austere of speech," and rigid in observance. He died drunk in a ditch, and his life was as immoral as his death was vile. But the besetting sin of want of self-restraint is as visible here as in the former case. Burns was overmastered by his impulse to satire as he was by his impulse to indulge appetite. In attacking hypocrisy he was swept away to impute hypocrisy to nearly all who lived a strict life or were severe in speech or manners. In condemning uncharitableness he became himself uncharitable.

A free life which loses love to the unloving is on the point of drifting into that temper in which liberty is made the servant of uncharitableness; and that freedom is not freedom which is bound to be abusive. Burns often had no mercy on unmercifulness, and it often wants it as much as frailty. Nothing can be better than his address to the unco guid or rigidly righteous; these lines that I read are steeped in the spirit of Christianity—

Then gently scan your brother Man,
　Still gentler sister Woman;
Though they may gang a kennin wrang,
　To step aside is human:
One point must still be greatly dark,
　The moving *Why* they do it;
And just as lamely can ye mark,
　How far perhaps they rue it.

Who made the heart, 'tis He alone
　Decidedly can try us,
He knows each chord its various tone,
　Each spring its various bias:
Then at the balance let's be mute,
　We never can adjust it;
What's *done* we partly may compute,
　But know not what's *resisted*.

But he forgot, and indeed it is the hardest thing Charity
has to remember, that the unco guid are often as much
the victims of circumstances as the weakly sinful. They
are born, many of them, with as much of the milk of
human kindness in them as others, but their education—
their sect and its restrictions, the severity of their parents,
the whole atmosphere of gloom and terror which their
religion gives them to breathe—have crushed all tender-
ness and mercy out of them, and when they come to be
men and women, they have stones for hearts. And they
are intensely disagreeable and often shamefully cruel.
But, if they are not hypocrites, they are worthy of infinite
pity: for their evil may partly be not their fault, and if
they wish to escape from it, nothing can be more difficult.
The anger they arouse in men, the way they are naturally
left alone, fixes them in their moroseness and seems to
excuse it. Their sin is bound upon them; if they strive
to break through it, they are met by a disbelief only
too well earned, and they are soured the more. It is
their punishment, but it is, if we think charitably, a
very pitiful thing. Our work on them should not be
that of abuse, but of effort to pierce through the rock
to where the springs of human kindness lie in them.
We should meet half-way any effort they may make,
forgive at once and say—" To-day I will abide at thine

house;" so shall we perhaps, with Christ, save a soul by love.

But Burns became still more wrong when he made the evil lives of persons who seemed to be religious into a kind of excuse for his own evil. "At least he made no boast," we may say, and we trace the spirit of this excuse in his poetry, "he did not conceal his wrong-doing, nor use religion as a garment to cover sin." But this is the worst of sophisms. That others are very bad, worse than we, does not make our badness one whit the less bad; and that we are sincere in the midst of our sin, while others are insincere in theirs, proves, it is true, that our character is higher, and that we have more chance of repentance, but it does not make our sinfulness less.

Nor, indeed, did Burns often make such an excuse for himself. It was only when he was irritated and in opposition. He was at root true, and he never flinched from self-blame. But he had no force to make self-blame into active repentance, and he went on sinning and being sorry, and sinning again, to the end of the chapter—

> To right or left, eternal swervin'
> He zigzagged on.—

Knowing the right, he could not consistently do it; and the misery of that was deep and was one of the things which killed him. You may remember his epistle to Andrew Aiken, a noble piece of good advice, the last two verses of which are worth quoting. The first shows how well he knew his own wrong and the right he wanted, while nothing can be more pathetic than the quiet despair of the last two lines, "Video meliora, deteriora sequor"—

> When ranting round in pleasure's ring,
>     Religion may be blinded;
> Or if she gie a random sting,
>     It may be little minded;
> But when in life we're tempest driven,
>     A conscience but a canker—

A correspondence fixed wi' Heaven
  Is sure a noble anchor!

Adieu, dear, amiable youth!
  Your heart can ne'er be wanting!
May prudence, fortitude, and truth
  Erect your brow undaunting!
In ploughman phrase, " God send you speed,"
  Still daily to grow wiser;
And may ye better reck the rede
  Than ever did th' Adviser.

His was not the temperament which drifts into irreligion. His sinfulness and his consciousness of it, which never became less bitter, kept him always from infidelity. He was always, like the Prodigal Son, coming to himself and saying—" I will arise and go to my Father " —but he never got more than half-way in this world. Even if he had been a philosopher as well as a poet, the need of his nature for sympathy and for some one to lean on would have always prevented him from Atheism. His fear and his love alike made him confess a God; but the God he confessed was never brought near enough to his heart and life to have over him the influence of a person whom he knew loved him well enough to die for him. I see no trace in Burns's poetry that Christ had any meaning to him; I see nothing but a fine Theism. God was the unknown, Almighty Cause of all his hope and fear, his judge, the author of his conscience; the giver to him of passions wild and strong, to whom he appealed for mercy since He was all-good; who could not act from cruelty or wrath, on whom with all his sins he threw himself for pity—

Where human weakness has come short,
    Or frailty stept aside,
Do thou, All Good! for such thou art,
    In shades of darkness hide.
Where with intention I have erred,
    No other plea I have,
But, thou art good, and Goodness still
    Delighteth to forgive.

It might have given Burns strength to conquer his errors

if he could have felt for Christ the same kind of personal love which he felt for Man and Nature. What he wanted is what most of us who have anything of his temperament want, a higher motive of love. The sins which arise from the weakness that passion engenders cannot be overcome by struggling with them; they are too strong for us. But when we have a higher love for a perfectly good and loving person who is our divine Friend than we have for any one on earth, then that love enables us to conquer. A heavenly passion only subdues the evil that is in earthly passion. But Burns could not get that. The Christ presented to him had, according to the teaching of that time and country, nothing in the world to do with him. He had not loved him, nor died for him, did not care about him: the Christian ministers of Ayrshire blotted out Christ for Burns, and threw him back unhelped upon himself. He had no refuge but Theism, and Theism was not enough for him, though it may be enough for some. So he died, still weak, still self-victimised, still longing for good, and still unable to realise it; and the tenderest and wisest thing we can say of his life in this world is in part of his own epitaph—

> Is there a man whose judgment clear
> Can others teach the course to steer,
> Yet runs, himself, life's mad career,
>     Wild as the wave:
> Here pause—and, through the starting tear,
>     Survey this grave.
>
> The poor Inhabitant below
> Was quick to learn and wise to know,
> And keenly felt the friendly glow,
>     And softer flame:
> But thoughtless follies laid him low,
>     And stained his name.

And the noblest thing we can say of him in the future we may say in the words of Wordsworth—words which concentrate much of what I have said as to the good and evil results of his life and work on mankind—words which finally leave the shattered life and wasted soul

in the arms where Burns would, at last, gladly nestle
and be at peace—

Enough of sorrow, wreck, and blight;
Think rather of those moments bright
When to the consciousness of right
    His course was true,
When Wisdom prospered in his sight
    And virtue grew.

Through busiest street and loneliest glen
Are felt the flashes of his pen;..
He rules mid winter snows, and when
    Bees fill their hives;
Deep in the general heart of men
    His power survives.

What need of fields in some far clime
Where Heroes, Sages, bards sublime,
And all that fetched the flowing rhyme
    From genuine springs,
Shall dwell together till old Time
    Folds up his wings?

Sweet Mercy! to the gates of Heaven
This Minstrel lead, his sins forgiven;
The rueful conflict, the heart riven
    With vain endeavour,
And memory of Earth's bitter leaven,
    Effaced for ever.

But why to Him confine the prayer,
When kindred thoughts and yearnings bear
On the frail heart the purest share
    With all that live?
The best of what we do and are,
    Just God, forgive!

THE TEMPLE PRESS, PRINTERS, LETCHWORTH